The Cambridge Introduction to
Edith Wharton

Born in New York into a world of wealth and privilege, and
writing with unique insight into the lives of the rich and
fashionable, Edith Wharton was a best-seller in her time, and
is now, again, one of the most widely read American authors.
This book provides an accessible and stimulating introduction
to Wharton's life and writings, to help map her work for new
readers, and to encourage more detailed exploration of her texts
and contexts. Suggesting a range of perspectives on her most
famous novels – *The House of Mirth* (1905), *Ethan Frome* (1911),
The Custom of the Country (1913) and *The Age of Innocence*
(1920) – it stimulates fresh lines of inquiry, examining these
alongside other writings that are now attracting lively critical
interest. With its clear structure, illustrations and guide to further
study, this book will form the ideal starting point for students and
for general readers.

Pamela Knights is Senior Lecturer in English at Durham
University, UK.

The Cambridge Introduction to
Edith Wharton

PAMELA KNIGHTS

CAMBRIDGE
UNIVERSITY PRESS

CAMBRIDGE UNIVERSITY PRESS

Cambridge, New York, Melbourne, Madrid, Cape Town, Singapore, São Paulo, Delhi

Cambridge University Press
The Edinburgh Building, Cambridge CB2 8RU, UK

Published in the United States of America by Cambridge University Press, New York

www.cambridge.org
Information on this title: www.cambridge.org/9780521687195

First published 2009

Printed in the United Kingdom at the University Press, Cambridge

A catalogue record for this publication is available from the British Library

ISBN 978-0-521-86765-8 hardback
ISBN 978-0-521-68719-5 paperback

Contents

Illustrations

Preface

In her publicity photographs, draped in furs and lace, festooned with small dogs, or posed at her writing desk, Edith Wharton became famous as the most sophisticated and cosmopolitan of American authors: brilliant, rich, snobbish, acerbic. Her biography and writings complicate this picture. Within the old and well-off New York clan into which she was born, only a couple of members, so she recalled, had ever 'stepped out of the strait path of the usual' (*ABG* 23). Although she sensed early that she was 'different', she never believed herself to be a particularly bright or confident child; and she felt an oddity in her family. But she grew up to forge for herself a remarkable life – as traveller, hostess, social observer, expatriate, divorcée, lover, conversationalist, arbiter on interior decoration, inspirational gardener, intellectual, wartime relief organiser and, above all, professional writer. Her fictions made her a best-seller in her own day and, in literary histories, a novelist of the highest rank. As the endless stream of new reprints attests, she still appeals to a wide general audience; and she was, and remains, a powerful influence on generations of younger writers. R. W. B. Lewis's revealing *Edith Wharton: A Biography* (1975) fired modern critical interest, stimulating a wealth of new approaches; Hermione Lee's 800-page life in 2007 has stirred a fresh wave of attention. *The Cambridge Introduction to Edith Wharton* aims to suggest to new readers some possible entry-points into her writings, and to encourage individuals to begin to map their own routes (and take diversions) into areas of particular interest.

Most readers first encounter the 'canonical Wharton': *The House of Mirth* (1905), *Ethan Frome* (1911), *The Custom of the Country* (1913), *Summer* (1917) and *The Age of Innocence* (1920); these remain central to this *Introduction*, where I consider them within various cultural and literary landscapes. Anyone wishing to venture further has a wealth of choices, which I also touch on here: Wharton's travelogues, ghost stories and other short fictions; her war writing; her narratives of 'new' America in the 1920s; her meditations upon the art of fiction, and her various 'backward glances' of the 1930s. Many first editions are now reproduced online; as are page-images of some of her most important manuscripts. We can read writings once unpublished or lost, such as her satirical/sentimental novelette, 'Fast and Loose' (finished shortly before her fifteenth birthday in 1877); or her journal of her early Mediterranean cruise, which came to light in the Municipal library at Hyères, on the Riviera, in 1991; her critical essays or literary reviews; her garden-plans or poetry. Readers acquainted only with the image of Mrs Wharton, the reserved upper-class lady, have been riveted by passages ignored in her published memoirs, but uncovered in her archives: her story of attempting on the eve of marriage to elicit the facts of life from her chilly mother; her tempestuous letters, verses and love diary from her mid-life affair with the journalist Morton Fullerton; her experimental erotic fragment, 'Beatrice Palmato', with its striking description of consensual father–daughter incest. Discussions of her notebooks, unfinished novels and unpublished plays and stories continue to intensify debate.

All these enrich readers' possibilities, but crowd a landscape already densely packed. Here, the opening chapters will map Wharton's life and writings onto the broader contours of her society and wider cultural and literary contexts. For completely new readers, I try to introduce her work in these chapters without disclosing too much about its turns of plot and narrative. The following chapter, 'Works', consolidates these contexts, beginning with some general perspectives and delineating some frameworks relevant to all her writing. As Wharton's details repay attention, I give a taste of reading in close-up, looking from various angles at an early short story, and at selected aspects of *The House of Mirth*. The rest of the chapter moves outwards, to give an outline of her career, highlighting a range of individual texts and groups of texts, and aligning significant events in her private and professional life. Within this dominantly linear model, I suggest other possible ways of thinking about Wharton – for example, through theme, place, genre, form or craft. The final chapter gives an overview of Wharton's changing critical reception, and points to the continuing life of her texts in the creative legacies she still inspires.

Engaging with Wharton the writer keeps us in touch with Wharton the lifelong reader: that 'interchange of thought' which overflowed in notebooks, memoirs, letters, essays, travel-writing and fictions, and, as biographers record, in her conversations and numerous literary friendships. Throughout her life, in private writings, as in her fiction, she presents encounters with books: descriptions of collaborative reading and writing, evocations of an ideal listener (her friend, Walter Berry) and the inadequate one (her husband, Teddy); her own literary enthusiasms and pilgrimages – all these hint at the kind of responses she may have wished for her own creative work. In her stories, she satirised popularisers and intellectual pretentiousness: the unstoppable parlour lecturer in 'The Pelican'; the explicators of a dead poet in 'The Muse's Tragedy'; and, most devastatingly, the ladies' reading circle in 'Xingu'. Duly cautioned, I attempt in this introduction simply to share my own enthusiasm, and to keep questions open: about the child, the woman, the writer and the author, 'Edith Wharton'; and, above all, the writings which come together under her name.

Acknowledgements

I wish to thank the many people, at Durham and elsewhere, who generously gave me time and support: Jennifer Terry, Michael O'Neill, Pat Waugh, Kay Sambell; Janet Beer and Liz Nolan; Ray Ryan and anonymous readers for Cambridge University Press and Monica Kendall, my copy-editor; staff at the Lit & Phil, Newcastle-upon-Tyne, The British Library Newspaper Library, Colindale, and the Beinecke Library, Yale University; Ben Knights for appearing keen to read drafts; and Richard Godden who introduced me to Wharton in 1978. My readings since have evolved in dialogue with many inspiring critics; particular thanks go to colleagues at the Edith Wharton Society. I have credited specific influences, and detailed further references as fully as possible within the space permitted. My chief debt is to Durham University English students, who, for over twenty years, have been ever-enthusiastic about discussing Wharton; and, especially, since 1997, all my special 'Wharton' groups, who flung themselves into the seminars which helped me to develop my own readings and to structure this book.

I gratefully acknowledge permission to reprint the following:

Extracts from Edith Wharton's manuscript/typescript collections held at the Beinecke Library, Yale University; photographs of The Mount, Edith Wharton's automobile permit and the manuscript page of *The Age of Innocence* (family tree) are reprinted by permission of the estate of Edith Wharton and the Watkins/Loomis Agency. 'American Beauties' is reproduced with permission of The Library of Congress.

Abbreviations

Unless noted otherwise: place, New York; publisher, Scribner's.

Works

ABG	*A Backward Glance* (Appleton-Century, 1934)
AI	*The Age of Innocence* (Appleton, 1920)
Beinecke	Edith Wharton Collection, Yale Collection of American Literature, Beinecke Rare Book and Manuscript Library, YCAL Mss 42 [with box and folder number]; now increasingly appearing online
C	*The Children* (Appleton, 1928)
CC	*The Custom of the Country* (1913)
CI	*Crucial Instances* (1901)
CR	James W. Tuttleton, Kristin O. Lauer and Margaret P. Murray (eds.), *Edith Wharton: The Contemporary Reviews* (Cambridge University Press, 1992)
DH	*The Decoration of Houses*, with Ogden Codman Jr (1897)
DM	*The Descent of Man and Other Stories* (1904)
EF	*Ethan Frome* (1911)
FF	*Fighting France: From Dunkerque to Belfort* (1915)
FT	*The Fruit of the Tree* (1907)
FWM	*French Ways and their Meaning* (Appleton, 1919)
GI	*The Greater Inclination* (1899)
GM	*The Glimpses of the Moon* (Appleton, 1922)
HM	*The House of Mirth* (1905)
HWW	*The Hermit and the Wild Woman* (1908)
IB	*Italian Backgrounds* (1905)
IM	*In Morocco* (1920)
IVG	*Italian Villas and their Gardens* (Century, 1904)

'L&I'	'Life and I' (in *Edith Wharton: Novellas and Other Writings*, ed. Cynthia Griffin Wolff. New York: Library of America, 1990)
Letters	*The Letters of Edith Wharton*, ed. R. W. B. Lewis and Nancy Lewis (London: Simon and Schuster, 1988)
'LGNY'	'A Little Girl's New York' (*Harper's Magazine*, 1938); in *UCW*
Lib	*Edith Wharton's Library: A Catalogue*, George Ramsden (compiler), foreword, Hermione Lee (Settrington, Yorkshire: Stone Trough Books, 1999)
M	*The Marne* (Appleton, 1918)
MFF	*A Motor-Flight through France* (1908)
MR	*The Mother's Recompense* (Appleton, 1925)
ONY	*Old New York* (1924; single-volume edition: Scribner's, 1952)
R	*The Reef* (Appleton, 1912)
S	*Summer* (Appleton, 1917)
SF	*A Son at the Front* (1923)
T	*The Touchstone* (1900)
TMG	*Tales of Men and Ghosts* (1910)
TS	*Twilight Sleep* (Appleton, 1927)
TVD	*The Valley of Decision* (1902)
UCW	*Edith Wharton: The Uncollected Critical Writings*, ed. Frederick Wegener (Princeton University Press, 1996)
WF	*The Writing of Fiction* (1925; Touchstone, 1997)
XS	*Xingu and Other Stories* (1916)

Other resources

BE	*Brooklyn Eagle* online: www.brooklynpubliclibrary.org/eagle/
Benstock	Shari Benstock, *No Gifts from Chance: A Biography of Edith Wharton* (London: Hamilton, 1994)
Lee	Hermione Lee, *Edith Wharton* (London: Chatto and Windus, 2007)
Lewis	R. W. B. Lewis, *Edith Wharton: A Biography* (London: Constable, 1975)
NYT	*New York Times*

Life

My childhood & youth were an intellectual desert.   ('L&I' 1089)

Edith Wharton always portrayed the New York of her origins as dull and provincial, 'a place in which external events were few and unexciting' ('LGNY' 287); but, somehow, she emerged to create her own world as a woman and as a writer. In this short outline, I can hope only to convey something of the sweep and energy of her life, from her birth in Manhattan during the Civil War, in January 1862, to her death in France, not long before another war, in August 1937.

Although many aspects of her experiences remain opaque, Wharton's life has been well documented; and my outline is indebted to the work of her modern biographer, R. W. B. Lewis, and of those who have followed (see 'Critical reception'). In trying to sketch the wider picture within the smaller compass of this *Introduction,* I also draw on original contemporary sources – many of them now available to general readers online. Even the briefest encounter with these gossip columns, travellers' tales or advertisements of Wharton's day can give snapshots of her period, and bring alive the voices of her culture, refracted and debated in writings throughout her career. Wharton's own autobiographical writings serve as another set of reference points: her dignified memoir, *A Backward Glance* (1934); her emotionally vivid fragment, 'Life and I'; and 'A Little Girl's New York' (1938), published the year after her death. While all her reminiscences must be read with caveats, the colouring of her memories helps to convey something of her impressions of the contours of her formative years; and biographers have generally taken at her word her sense of a disjunction between her inner and outer worlds, and her reflections on feeling a stranger in her culture. These are features which will appear, reshaped, throughout her work.

Edith Wharton (1862–1937): biographical overview

Though as an adult, Edith Wharton awed friends with her energy and authority, the young Edith Newbold Jones was 'a painfully shy self-conscious' child ('L&I' 1089). Arriving on 24 January 1862, some dozen years after her two brothers, Freddy and Harry, she was an only daughter, and she grew up regarding herself the least important, and certainly 'least attractive-looking', member of the family ('L&I' 1089). Nicknamed in her family 'Pussy', 'Lily' and 'John', she recalled her brothers teasing her about her red hair, and remembered, with most warmth, her Irish nurse, Hannah Doyle ('Doyley'), and George Frederic Jones (1821–82), her 'dear kind father' ('L&I' 1094); throughout her memoirs, her mother, Lucretia Stevens Rhinelander Jones (1825–1901), appears ever-critical and sarcastic. Like many girls of her class, she had no formal schooling, but, spending six years in Europe as a child, she acquired fluent French, German and Italian, and became formidably well read – 'saturated', as she put it ('L&I' 1095) – in European literature, culture and aesthetic values. Her return to the United States at the age of ten filled her with dismay at what she saw as its 'deadly uniformity of mean ugliness' (*ABG* 55), and impressed her with a lifelong sense that she was 'an exile in America' ('L&I' 1081). Thereafter, she was drawn to the idea of Europe, as a less philistine and conformist world. Many of her reflections, in letters and in memories, dwell on the differences:

> the contrast between the old & the new, between stored beauty & tradition & amenity over there, & the crassness here. My first few weeks in America are always miserable, because the tastes I am cursed with are all of a kind that cannot be gratified here.
>
> (5 June 1903: *Letters* 84)

These contrasts would be central to her writing.

The rest of her growing up took place in America – within the 'tiny fraction' of New York society which would inspire *The Age of Innocence* and many of her most memorable writings. Her perspectives, she said, were limited – those of a 'much governessed and guarded little girl – hardly less of a child when she "came out" (at seventeen) than when she first arrived on the scene, at ten' ('LGNY' 282, 283). At eighteen, however, her horizons expanded. After making her early social debut, she broke off her second season to return to Europe: 'I was going to see pictures & beautiful things again, & [. . .] I went without a backward glance' ('L&I' 1094). Although her father, for whose health this change was made, failed to recover, dying in

France, the tour confirmed her strength of feeling; and gave her the urge, in her writings, to capture 'things which the average Baedeker-led tourist' missed ('L&I' 1095). But having returned to the States with her mother, she resumed her life as a young lady in society. Following one broken engagement (with Harry Stevens), she met the future lawyer Walter Van Rensselaer Berry; the association seemed promising, but failed to blossom into romance. Renewed in later years, their friendship lasted lifelong; and Berry became 'the one comrade of my soul' as she hinted in her seventies (Diary (1934); Beinecke/51.1523). But at twenty-three, she accepted Edward (Teddy) Robbins Wharton, a socially suitable Boston gentleman, in his thirties, and married him in a quiet wedding in 1885.

The couple lived first in Lucretia's New York house, and at Pencraig cottage, in the grounds of the family house at Newport. But, with marriage, she seized the chance to extend her travels. She deepened her knowledge of Italy, England and France; and a chartered private steam-yacht (the *Vanadis*) took the pair, in 1888, as far as North Africa and the Ionian Islands. For many years, they divided their time across the Atlantic, in an annual routine: in Europe living in Paris, and touring, and in the States spending winters in Park Avenue, and summers in Land's End, their Newport home. In the 1890s, Wharton seems to have suffered some depression and illness (how seriously is still a matter of debate) – what she called in 1899, 'my almost continual ill health & mental lassitude' (*Letters* 39); and she would always, regularly, take spa treatments. But in these years she also began to shape the spaces where she could settle to work. At Land's End, with the advice of a fashionable architect, Ogden Codman Jr, she redesigned the interior, and created the first of several stunning gardens. In 1901, seeking tranquillity, she bought a 113-acre estate at Lenox in the Berkshire Hills; here she oversaw the building of The Mount (Figure 1), modelled on Belton House, a stately home in Lincolnshire; landscaped and replanted its elegant grounds; and settled into the discipline of writing.

An indefatigable correspondent and generous host, she drew together, in this summer home, a cosmopolitan circle of writers, intellectuals, artists and aristocrats – most significantly, Henry James and Walter Berry. Her friendship with her sister-in-law, Mary (Minnie) Cadwalader Jones, had outlasted Freddy and Minnie's divorce (1896); and she remained close to her niece, Beatrix (Trix), who helped her to draw up her plans for her estate. (Under her married name, Beatrix Farrand, Trix herself became known as a distinguished landscape gardener.) Wharton read aloud to guests her work in progress, and swept them off on motor expeditions into the Massachusetts hills. With Teddy, she shared a love of the outdoors, and a passion for animals (she was photographed, lifelong, with her decorative pet dogs, and

Figure 1 The Mount in winter.

she worked with Teddy on animal welfare); when in Europe, the couple enjoyed bicycling in Italy; but, as outsiders had long remarked, they had little else in common and the marriage deteriorated. In her forties, Wharton became involved (as had many others) with the American journalist Morton Fullerton, the Paris representative of the London *Times*. The affair dazzled and tormented her, as the elusive Fullerton drifted off, between his other complicated liaisons; and she poured her feelings into her letters and a secret love diary. Meanwhile, Teddy's increasing mental and emotional disturbances drained her energy and her resources, and, with his adultery and embezzlement of her finances, matters came to a crisis; The Mount was sold, and the marriage ended with a discreet divorce in 1913. Wharton retained her married name and title, and would be sharp with correspondents who were unfortunate enough to try addressing her as 'Miss'. She flirted with moving to England, but adopted France as her permanent home. On the onset of war, she remained in Paris, devoting her energies to relief-work with refugees and orphans, fundraising and rousing public feeling to bring the United States military into the Allied cause. Her efforts made her a Chevalier of the French Legion of Honour; and, in 1921, *The Age of Innocence* brought her the Pulitzer Prize for the novel (a female 'first'). At war's ending, she moved to the outskirts of Paris. Here, at Pavillon Colombe, and at Ste-Claire, Hyères, her Riviera home, she carried out her visions for yet more extraordinary gardens; she welcomed guests and planned new journeys (including chartering, with friends, a second Mediterranean cruise, in 1926).

Through all this time she wrote – preferably in bed, before launching into her day's activities, leaving her secretary to type up her manuscripts for revision. Feeling 'driven' to tell stories, she worked in a 'fever of authorship' (*ABG* 125); at the same time, she kept a sharp eye on her publishers, chivvying them at any sign of slackening. Self-deprecating letters to her editor, while preparing her first collection (1899), give place after publication to protests about the firm's low-key advertising – 'I do not think I have been fairly treated' (*Letters* 37). While she enjoyed an independent income, from family trust funds, supplemented by various inheritances, as a best-selling author she came to command substantial earnings. But disappointed with Scribner's advances and, as she saw it, failure to improve her publicity, she began to break off their long association; and her secret deal with Appleton's, over the advance for *The Reef* (1912), shocked her long-time company: 'Mr Scribner is mortally hurt by my infidelity', she wrote to Morton Fullerton (*Benstock* 250).

Disciplined, dedicated, Wharton was enormously productive. She had begun as a child, when her 'story-telling', to use one of her favourite terms, fired her energies, along with avid reading in her father's library. She was first published in her teens – with *Verses*, poems privately printed when she was sixteen – and, in 1879–80, achieved what many an established writer would have envied: having her poems accepted by William Dean Howells, novelist, and editor of *The Atlantic Monthly*, America's leading literary journal. After a gap in the 1880s (the years of her social debut and early married life), poetry took her back into print, and stories and books followed. By the time she published *The House of Mirth* (1905), an unprecedented best-seller for Scribner's, she had become a well-known author: with her first book, on domestic interiors, *The Decoration of Houses* (1897), co-authored with Ogden Codman; her first novel, *The Valley of Decision* (1902); and seven other volumes behind her. She regarded her work on *The House of Mirth*, however, as her professional debut, bringing her 'the kingdom of mastery' over her tools (*ABG* 209).

In some forty years, she would publish over forty books, including more than twenty novels and novellas, around a dozen collections of short stories, as well as plays, poetry, travel-writing, autobiography, criticism and reviews. She began to earn sums which stirred Henry James to envy; she garnered acclaim as America's most brilliant novelist and cultural commentator; and her non-fiction gained her high regard. She was passionate about automobiles, and her first 'Motor-Flight' through France, chauffeured in her open-topped Panhard, introduced readers in 1906–8 to this very new excitement, which had 'restored the romance of travel' (*MFF* 1); her forays into the Massachusetts hill country in the hinterland of The Mount inspired *Ethan Frome* and *Summer*; her tour of French military hospitals in 1915 brought Americans unique reports from the war-zone. Visiting Morocco in 1917 (and housed by the French Resident General in the rooms of the former harem favourite), she thrilled to the challenge of a '*country without a guide-book*' (*IM* 3, opening sentence).

After the war, she came to regard the New York of her youth as 'a Babylonian tomb' recording its 'fragments' in her writings ('LGNY' 274). Although she never renounced her American citizenship, she found the States increasingly alien; after 1913, she returned only once, in 1923, to collect an honorary degree from Yale (the first to be awarded to a woman) and to revive impressions for her novels. She tried to capture the impact of new forms of society she found monstrous; and her stories of restless, rootless individuals, broken families and multiple marriages, of fads and fashions, in a new makeover culture, increased her fame. Popular magazines printed her works, though they found some of her material too downbeat or explicit. Disturbed by the social (and socialist) climate of the New Deal, she began to feel that her generation had been swept away; outliving Walter Berry and many friends, and mourning their deaths, and those of Catherine Gross, her housekeeper, and other long-time servants, she nevertheless kept writing. Holding, as ever, different projects in play, at the end of 1933 she reminds Rutger Jewett, her Appleton's editor: 'As you know, I usually interrupt the writing of a long novel to do two or three short stories, or a novelette' (Beinecke/35.1073) – a casual glimpse into her habitual industry. Although not all her projects came to fruition, and magazines began to refuse some of her writing, she saw *A Backward Glance* published in 1934, to respectful reviews. After bouts of illness, heart trouble and a first stroke (in 1935), she went on to make new plans, for work and for travel. In her last year, she sent her final story, 'All Souls'', to her agent in February, and with her novel *The Buccaneers* still in process, and jottings for characters still in her notebooks, she died of a stroke, at Pavillon Colombe, on 11 August 1937. She was buried at Versailles, in the Cimetière des Gonards, alongside Walter Berry.

Questions of how reviewers and critics viewed Wharton's achievements will feature throughout this guide; but on first encounter, readers might prefer to keep in mind one of her own jottings (quoted *Lib* 153):

> My ruling passions:
>
> Justice – Order
> Dogs –
> Books –
> Flowers
> Architecture –
> Travel –
> a good joke – &
> perhaps that should have come first –.

Growing up in old New York: family and social contexts

Looking back on herself as a 'child of the well-to-do, hedged in by nurses and governesses' (*ABG* 57), Wharton admits to only vague recollections of her parents' routine and world. The claim is surprising, as time and again in all her writings, readers encounter sharply realised details of her ancestors, her family and of Manhattan leisure-class life, as she knew it when growing up after the Civil War, in the 1860s–1880s. These minutiae of its habits, arte-facts, geographies and rituals are underlying contexts throughout her work. This was the milieu she later memorialised, like the ruins of Troy, in her fiction. It is the world of *The Age of Innocence* – one, she said, with a 'blind dread of innovation' (*ABG* 22); and the interplay between ideas of constraint and of stability are central to her writing. In this section, then, I return to Wharton's early years, to her own accounts and, in passing, to other writings of the period, in order to draw out more details of this narrow social group and of the currents of change she calibrated in her narratives.

Edith Jones's upbringing was shaped by the expectations of her class, whose lives she described as, 'with few exceptions, as monotonous as their architecture' ('LGNY' 280). This group's geographies were narrow; it occupied an exclusive habitat extending only a few blocks north from Washington Square. This world, the enclave of the well-to-do, would itself soon be overwhelmed, as, from the 1880s, with the influx of new money, the city would stream uptown, with the building along Fifth Avenue of ever more grandiose and attention-seeking residences. As a commentator wrote in *Vogue* (7 March 1895), anticipating Wharton's own later 'backward glance':

> The change in New York manners has been so swift and radical from the quiet dignity and formality habitual to the late thirties, forties and early fifties, that present-day customs and usages, together with our advanced social point of view, seem to have cast off all past relation to the old order [. . .] this is merely a backward glance at strong contrasts existing between old and new [. . .] The new rich element was then unknown, and such large fortunes as we are now familiar with were simply impossible, had no existence [. . .] While the houses of wealthy New Yorkers were kept up with becoming dignity, and oftentimes with elegance, there was no such luxury dreamed of as has become quite general in these days. Drawing-rooms were severe and simple, and resembled each other like peas in a pod, in their mirrors, their mahogany and rose-wood carvings, their gaudy and large-flowered carpetings, crystal chandeliers, sconces, candelabras, girandoles.

So, in Wharton's childhood, the identical brownstone houses dominated; and, within her group, she said, everything was 'ordered according to convention' ('L&I' 1092). Her parents were both from long-established families, and, though Lucretia had grown up with a relatively reduced income, her marriage assured her prosperity. George Frederic lived on an allowance, coming into his independent fortune on his father's death. Drawing income largely from property and land rentals, the family suffered occasional dips in their revenues, as in the 'bad times' ('L&I' 1071) after the Civil War, when currency depreciated. The Joneses' response – to rent out their houses, and live more cheaply in Europe (1864–72) – gave their daughter the six years of travel which transformed her perspectives for life. Though Wharton later mused on her father's probable financial difficulties ('LGNY' 282), he and other men in the family, like her own husband later, existed as 'men of leisure'. Describing this species in *A Backward Glance*, published during the Great Depression, she anticipated her audience's responses: that it would 'probably seem unbelievable to present-day readers that only one of my own near relations, and not one of my husband's, was "in business"' (*ABG* 56).

Shades of difference, in breeding and in levels of income, were always central to Wharton's fictions; and in her late career, she took pains to emphasise that her family circle had not enjoyed vast fortunes. This group, she claimed, was content to remain merely comfortable, uninfected by the 'harsh desire for profit'[1] of the new speculators, entrepreneurs and industrialists in the post-Civil War 'Gilded Age'. (The inroads of new wealth – presented in *The House of Mirth* and *The Custom of the Country* – would eventually overturn Wharton's society.) The Joneses and their associates were neither New York aristocracy (those who could trace their lineage back to the aristocracy of their British or Dutch colonial origins), nor rising multi-millionaires still busy increasing their fortunes; but were descended from prosperous bankers, lawyers and ('mainly') merchant shipowners (*ABG* 10). Money-grubbing was despised as the sphere of trade. When her brother Freddy went briefly into business, the twelve-year-old Edith quipped:

> we have a great many jokes about buying candy & cabbages & standing behind the counter but he has not yet dropped the 'Esquire' from his name & is not absolutely a tradesman, so you need not be horrified at the announcement.   (*Letters* 30)

Even the most exclusive retail dealers were excluded from New York polite society until long after she was grown up (*ABG* 11). Her descriptions in *The Age of Innocence* struck a chord with her editor in 1920, who, too, remembered how his old grandmother, 'used to murmur incredulously at my descriptions of the growing city by saying, "Oh, no, my dear boy, do not tell me that trade has invaded Fifth Avenue!"' (letter, Rutger Jewett, 13 November 1920, Beinecke/33.1032).

In this world, Wharton said, 'one of the first rules of conversation was the one early instilled in me by my mother: "Never talk about money, and think about it as little as possible"' (*ABG* 57). The group prided itself on its uprightness, inflicting 'relentless social ostracism' (*ABG* 21) on the families of those believed to have lapsed from strict fair-dealing. To the outsider, defining oneself as of the rank just above 'plain people', rather than as 'the very apex of the pyramid' as *The Age of Innocence* expresses it (*AI* 46), might seem hair-splitting. Now, social historians sometimes play down the importance of such claims. As Eric Homberger emphasises, the Joneses belonged to leading New York clans, and Edith Wharton always moved in 'the highest social circles'.[2] Theodore Roosevelt was a distant cousin, and during his presidency Wharton dined at the White House and counted him as one of her intellectual kin. However, while Wharton's late-life chronicles of her family might seem tinged with over-defensiveness, such fine tuning is crucial to her fictional narratives. She teases out origins, places a detail of behaviour and registers the social status of rising or falling characters, in the precise cultural analysis which critics view as parallel to the anthropologists and new sociology of her day (more details will follow in context).

Wharton's memories of Lucretia's social pronouncements have counterparts in the many nineteenth-century commentaries which challenged myths of a classless America. Such discriminations (defining one's exact rank in the social scale) were essential to a group under threat: as the new rich advanced, old money appealed to lineage, to mark out its exclusiveness. As a visiting French woman, 'Madame Blanc' (Theresa Bentzon), observed:

> I have now the measure of the social divisions which exist in the land of equality. To cope with the insolence of newly-won wealth, one must be able to point to pre-Revolutionary ancestors, or at least to ancestors who distinguished themselves during the Revolution. Those who can boast of a Dutch or Swedish name established in the country before the English rule, feel all the pride of a Rohan or a Montmorency; and even those who do not possess these great advantages hasten, as soon as possible, on any pretext whatsoever, to draw the line as distinctly as possible between themselves and common mortals [...] Never, until I went to America, did I understand how humiliating it may be to bear the name of Smith or Jones.[3]

Lucretia Jones staved off possible confusion: it is said that, in response to inquiries about which Mrs Jones she was, she always asserted: 'I am *the* Mrs Jones' (*Lewis* 12). Like Mrs Archer in *The Age of Innocence*, she regretted the passing of the days when she knew 'everyone who kept a carriage' ('LGNY' 275).

In the 1870s, however, the excesses of new kinds of affluence were beginning to create another powerful class, which would amaze all spectators with demonstrations of undreamed-of heights of luxury – a social phenomenon which would permanently transform the Joneses' New York, and provide one of Wharton's richest fields of fiction. Her novels 'think about' money to an extent that would have appalled Lucretia. When we look at the *nouveaux riches*, in *The House of Mirth* or the novels of the 1920s, Wharton's demurrals about her clan's lifestyle come more clearly into perspective: 'How mild and leisurely it all seems in the glare of our new century!' (*ABG* 61). Though unostentatious in comparison, the household life she inventories was, however, one of privilege, resting on inherited wealth and taking for granted servants, town and country homes, horses and drives, and mild charitable interests. Lucretia perhaps had greater material aspirations – Wharton called her 'a born "shopper"' who could not resist a 'bargain' ('LGNY' 282). At what seems some cost to his health and finances, her husband managed to keep her in her annual trunk of gowns from Paris. Edith's excitement over 'seeing one resplendent dress after another shaken out of its tissue-paper' lived on in her texts, which itemised details of fabrics, colours and textures; and, in very different moods, Lily Bart's final review of her dresses (*HM* 512–13) and Undine Spragg's Parisian spree (*CC* 180–2) are key scenes in their narratives. Meals, too, figure significantly in Wharton's fictions, possibly drawing on memories of her father's special pleasure: a 'gastronomic enthusiasm', and dinner-giving, with fine wines and a cornucopia of dishes (prepared by Mary Johnson and Susan Minneman, the Joneses' 'famous' African American cooks (*ABG* 58)).

Their class occupied itself in a routine of hospitality and seasonal diversions. The Joneses spent winters in New York, in their house on West Twenty-third Street, and summers at Pencraig, their country place outside Newport, with its private bathing-beach and boat-landing. From the 1880s, Newport, on Rhode Island, would become known as 'the undisputed "Queen of American seaside-resorts"' famous for the summer homes of the Gilded Age multimillionaires. The so-called 'cottagers' competed with each other to commission ever more opulent retreats. These included such extravagances as The Breakers, a seventy-room Genoan palace, built for the railroad magnate Cornelius Vanderbilt II in 1893, or Alva Smith Vanderbilt's Marble House of 1892, a 'late Renaissance' mansion, modelled on the Petit Trianon at Versailles, with touches of the Temple of Apollo at Heliopolis. (Edith Wharton and her husband would receive invitations to Mrs Vanderbilt's dazzling inaugural ball there in August 1895.) Baedeker commented on the Marble House as 'a magnificent dwelling, but hardly in keeping with the *genius loci*'; and Wharton would share his general disapproval.[4] The old-fashioned moral tone diminished as the architecture became more overblown; Alva Vanderbilt's divorce and remarriage, and audacious lack of shame, put her in the vanguard; and as others followed, the *New York Times* remarked: 'Newport promises to be the headquarters for divorces of the swell set' (5 March 1899: 14).

Although the Whartons would set up their own first homes in Newport, Wharton found the fashionable resort agitating. In her youth, however, it was a beautiful spot, known for its balmy climate, where weary city-folk could find repose. The British writer Anthony Trollope, who spent a week in a dismal hotel, late-season in 1861, had anticipated 'the Brighton, and Tenby, and Scarborough, of New England', but found it less captivating. Even the swimming disappointed him: 'ladies and gentlemen bathe in decorous dresses and are very polite to each other' (he preferred 'to be hampered by no outward impediments'). But he appreciated the 'villa residences', their lawns stretching down to the rocks, and would have had 'no objection' to owning one had fate made him an American citizen.[5] At Pencraig, the Joneses and their set passed their time pleasantly: they supervised the laying-out of their lawns and gardens; the men went sea-fishing, raced boats and shot wildfowl. Ladies occupied themselves with the time-consuming business of 'calling' – the leaving and receiving of visitors' cards, in accordance with an elaborate protocol. This drew protests from many women, echoed in fiction by female characters from Jo March in Alcott's *Little Women* (1868) to Edna Pontellier in Kate Chopin's *The Awakening* (1899). But as far as etiquette was concerned, for a long time there seemed no alternative: 'No monkey, no "missing link," no Zulu, no savage, carries a card,' wrote one social arbiter; 'it cannot be dispensed with under our present environment'.[6] Wharton recalled Pencraig as a paradise for children, where she enjoyed freedom, friends, pets and contact with nature; but her Newport settings in fiction involve social manoeuvring in a rule-bound society (see *Lee* 50–1). The central characters in 'The Introducers' (1905) collude with and chafe against its rituals; Newland Archer in *The Age of Innocence* has a vision of freedom, in his glimpse of Ellen against the sunset of the bay, but is trapped and drawn back into the routines of the 'brightly peopled' lawns and 'square boxes on the cliffs' (*AI* 207).

Longer excursions – scenic and shopping tours in Europe – were another New York passion; and Wharton remembered, from earliest infancy, people around her 'just arriving from "abroad"' or on the verge of embarkation (*ABG* 61). This was the class whose movements were tracked in society columns; and passenger lists, names of ships and plans for Atlantic crossings feature significantly in many of Wharton's narratives. Although she shared this passion, she felt that it mattered to come to know a place, to extract meaning from what she saw. In her travel-writings she transmuted her circle's delight in natural landscapes ('water-falls – especially water-falls – were endlessly enjoyable'), and attraction to 'places about which some sentimental legend hung' (*ABG* 62, 61), into a sustained interest in art, history and locality. She did not venture as far as some of her contemporaries (the Kirklands, mother and daughter, for example, who in 1908 published *Some African Highways*, after journeys in Uganda and South Africa), but she travelled away from some of the usual tourist circuits: in Europe, and around the Mediterranean and northern Africa. An 'exotic' destination could, as she knew, become simply another Manhattan meeting-spot. *Vogue* magazine in the 1890s would host a regular Society column from Egypt; and Wharton had amusement with her fictional travellers – such as Mr Selfridge Merry who (like Teddy Wharton) has been 'round the world', and is 'anxious to have it understood that he was no frivolous globe-trotter' ('But you must have three weeks to do India properly' *AI* 340).

What was missing in her parents' world, at home or abroad, so Wharton insisted, was any intellectual or cultural engagement. Her fiction would satirise their circle's nervousness about new ideas, musicians, artists and 'people who wrote'. 'Mrs Trenor dreaded ideas as much as she dreaded contagious diseases,' she jotted in her early 'Donnée Book' (1900; Beinecke/21.699) – a character trait she gave to Mrs Peniston in *The House of Mirth*, and which sketches the fictional prototype for a line of fearsome social guardians. As in many scenes in her stories, music was cautiously welcomed, as drawing-room entertainment or social occasion. One went to the opera, Wharton commented, 'chiefly if not solely for the pleasure of conversing with one's friends' (*ABG* 57). Art was acceptable as décor, if genteel and sanitised. Etiquette books suggested, for example, that a young woman might even visit a studio unchaperoned, as art was sacred and ennobling. (In *The Mother's Recompense*, set in the 1920s, Wharton would portray a young woman of the new generation as a painter herself, with her own, wonderful, Manhattan studio.) Nevertheless, in her youth, writers and painters roused apprehension: 'In the eyes of our provincial society authorship was still regarded as something between a black art and a form of manual labour' (*ABG* 69). Wharton's generalisation has been questioned; Homberger lists a range of writers from the Joneses' class;[7] however, none of these came into Edith Jones's orbit.

Her own education was haphazard. She was enjoined by her mother to be elegant and polite, and by father to be kind; by both to be well-spoken ('L&I' 1073). Among her earliest ambitions, so she recorded, was to grow up to be 'The best-dressed woman in New York' (*ABG* 20). Looking back, she expressed resentment at her lack of systematic training or mental stimulus. Anxieties over her health (after an attack of typhoid, aged nine, during the family's travels in Germany), and belief in what Wharton later regarded as 'sentimental' theories of child-rearing (*ABG* 47), protected her from any forced learning. Fictions of the time have left images of the damaged child who was the supposed product of overtaxing. Alcott's *Little Men* (1871) – a book which the young Edith Jones scorned for its linguistic 'laxities' (*ABG* 51) – presents an example in thirteen-year-old Billy, his mind wiped clean after brain-fever, struggling with his alphabet like a six-year-old. Wharton's memoirs, perhaps surprisingly, would suggest that higher education for girls came at a cost to the arts of civilised living. But in her fiction, a recurring strand is the danger of lack of intellectual nurture, particularly for American girls: Lily in *The House of Mirth*, Mattie in *Ethan Frome*, Undine in *The Custom of the Country*, Charity in *Summer*, all, in different ways, reveal the price of ignorance.

In society, gentility and sweetness were preferred. As etiquette manuals reminded readers up to the end of the century, the drawing room demanded 'light, witty and quickly-changed subjects': 'Gentlemen are expected not to use classical quotations before ladies without a slight apology and a translation, unless they are aware that the lady's educational training has made it possible for her to appreciate them.'[8] Wharton, however, regretted being deprived of Greek and Latin; and lamented the limitations of her 'good little governess'. Her observations (over half a century later) mirror what she seemed to value most in reading and conversation: 'she never struck a spark from me, she never threw new light on any subject, or made me see the relation of things to each other' ('L&I' 1089). Later, however, she came to respect her parents' regard for the shades of English speech, and her mother's strictures on contemporary novels. Having had to ask permission to open works of fiction, lest they prove immoral, saved her, she claimed, from wasting her time 'on ephemeral rubbish' (*ABG* 65). Instead, she had turned to the shelves of classics, travels, histories, poets and philosophers in her father's 'gentleman's library'. Here she explored 'a sea of wonders' (*ABG* 66): 'I plunged with rapture into the great ocean of Goethe. At fifteen I had read every word of his plays and poems'; a volume on logic made her feel 'as if I had found the clue to life' ('L&I' 1086). Her discoveries remained with her, and her texts are rich in allusions. Commemorating her discoveries, with entranced exclamations over names and titles, in catalogues running to several pages, she asserts: 'By the time I was seventeen, though I had not read every book in my father's library, I had looked into them all' (*ABG* 71).

Her memories fuse writing and reading. She scribbled stories on old wrapping paper and, most notably, excited herself through 'making up' (as she puts it) – stimulated by densely printed books to tell her own story, as if it emanated from the page. As in one of her later fictions, where she endowed one of her most imaginative characters with this trait (see p. 34, below), her behaviour was watched by an anxious household. Although she comments that her mother later showed interest in her verse, the predominant image is of discouragement. In one of her most quoted anecdotes, she gives, in Lucretia's voice, the censorious note of the social arbiters in her later fictions – those who crush the creative or independent characters. Here, she recounts her first attempt at a story; it began:

> 'Oh, how do you do, Mrs Brown?' said Mrs Tompkins. 'If only
> I had known you were going to call I should have tidied up
> the drawing-room.'

'Timorously', Wharton adds, 'I submitted this to my mother, and never shall I forget the sudden drop of my creative frenzy when she returned it with the icy comment: "Drawing-rooms are always tidy." This was so crushing to a would-be novelist of manners that it shook me rudely out of my dream of writing fiction, and I took to poetry instead' (*ABG* 73). Nevertheless she persisted, completing at least one novella, at fifteen, under the name 'David Olivieri' – 'Fast and Loose' (first published 1977), a romantic comedy of the English upper classes; and a piece of satirical juvenilia that outshines Daisy Ashford's *The Young Visiters*. The narrative, with its well-caught epigrams, and its mimicry of critics' tones in the mock reviews she appended, are testimony to her reading.

For her parents, however, her studiousness was no matter for celebration. The conventional girl of her age and class was not expected to cultivate her mind, but to look forward to her social debut; if all went well, she would make an appropriate match, and settle into managing her own household and servants. Young women who remained unmarried within a few seasons from their 'coming out' at eighteen were described as 'elderly girls', probably destined for old-maidhood. In *The House of Mirth*, Lily Bart fears that, a decade on, she is on the verge of relegation: 'Younger and plainer girls had been married off by dozens, and she was nine-and-twenty, and still Miss Bart' (*HM* 60). In *The Age of Innocence*, Mrs Archer harbours hopes for her daughter, 'though poor Janey was reaching the age when [if at all] pearl grey poplin and no bridesmaids would be thought more "appropriate"' (*AI* 324). The Newport *Daily News* at the time of Edith Jones's broken engagement to Harry Stevens mentioned the lady's 'alleged preponderance of intellectuality' and her ambitions as 'an authoress' (quoted *Lewis* 45). Her wedding, later, at twenty-three, would have been viewed as timely. The column, 'Weddings Yesterday' (30 April 1885), in the *New York Times* reported it briefly, as a 'very quiet one', where 'the invitations were limited to the immediate relatives of the two families'. (Unlike the report in the same column of another ceremony, with 500 guests, it gave no details of the bride's dress, bouquet or any special decorations in the family house.)

She claimed later that she had entered marriage unprepared. In 'Life and I', she relates an attempt, on the eve of her wedding, to discover something about 'the whole dark mystery'; and records an icy response. In a passage which, incidentally, suggests another use for art, Lucretia dismissed her question as 'ridiculous', and forced out, as explanation: 'You've seen enough pictures & statues in your life. Haven't you noticed that men are – made differently from women?' On Edith's silence, she rebuked her for inquiring and terminated the exchange. Wharton's retrospective comment is blunt: 'I record this brief conversation, because the training of which it was the beautiful & logical conclusion did more than anything else to falsify & mis-direct my whole life...' ('L&I' 1088). The damage done to nineteenth-century American girls, through growing up in cultivated 'innocence', would later become an explicit theme in Wharton's writings, but, here, in her ellipsis, she allows readers freedom to guess at the inner history of her marriage.

Some women of Wharton's class succeeded in escaping the confined life of the lady: Mariana Griswold Schuyler Van Rensselaer (1851–1934), for example, who was (as *Lee* notes, 123–4) a distant relation of Walter Berry, and who anticipated Wharton's views on American taste. Educated at home and through European travel, she published her first poems when young (in *Harper's Magazine* in 1874), and was popular among *Century* readers; she later extended her sphere to gardening, landscape design, painting and anti-suffrage writing. The slightly younger Elsie Clews Parsons (1874–1941) was similarly known for her intellect. She featured in *Vogue*'s 'Society' columns as: 'an argumentative débutante who, though she has not inherited her mother's beauty, has a good mind and is a hard student. She is a tall, slight and attractive girl, who will always be popular with a certain set, although she says she does not care for society' (19 August 1893). Having struggled with her family, Parsons entered higher education, won her doctorate, and continued to write and lecture in sociology and anthropology at Barnard College throughout several pregnancies; fieldwork took her to Mexico, the Caribbean and Abyssinia. Others worked in settlement houses (sheltered, safe accommodation for poorer city workers) or similar charities; or, like Parsons, campaigned for women's suffrage, breaking away from convention.

Wharton's rebellion was less overt and she took longer to find her sphere. Like many of her female characters, she began with her own houses, shaping them to her taste – neither the monumental, dark, cluttered interiors of her ancestors; nor the gilded excrescences of the fashionable new rich. At Pencraig cottage, and at Land's End, in her consultations with Codman, Wharton developed the principles expressed in *The Decoration of Houses*. (There, her examples were on a grander scale, many drawn from European palaces.) Such activities, with her travels, took up some of her energy, but she and Teddy and their guests continued to participate in the customary routine of their circle, featuring in the society notes. Teddy is remarked, for instance, purchasing an expensive 'bathing room' in a fashionable new pavilion at Bailey's Beach in Newport (*NYT* 28 July 1895); Mrs Wharton's name appears as a 'patroness' for Mrs Langtry's concert benefit at Sherry's for wounded English and Boer soldiers (*BE* 11 February 1900); and Mr and Mrs Edward Wharton appear among the 300 or so invited to hear Mme Melba sing at the Reids' musicale at their Madison Avenue residence, 'one of the most notable entertainments of the season' (*NYT* 14 February 1901). But by 1901, she had resolved to seek a quiet retreat elsewhere. As 'Mrs Edith Wharton, the novelist' she is noted in Lenox, 'building a fine place on the shores of Laurel Lake', where she 'has leased the Struthers cottage for the season' (*BE* 29 June 1902). Although Lenox was itself another luxury resort, here she believed she could escape the 'flat frivolity' of Newport (*ABG* 143) to create the environment she wanted. In transforming herself into a professional writer, Wharton at last established her own rules of engagement: her society, its reluctant participants and its leaders, its prejudices, gossip and fashion notes – and the forces which threatened it – all became part of her material.

Chapter 2

Contexts

Stepping back from Wharton's individual experiences, this chapter looks at her writing within broader contexts, a process that will continue into discussion of specific works. However, contexts are not in themselves separable – a 'background' to be noted, then curtained off. The multi-stranded currents of change in the turbulent years Wharton lived through echo even in the 'secret garden', as she called it (*ABG* 197), of her creative endeavour. They inform her narratives, the nuance of dialogue, the shades of characters' behaviour. As Wharton observed, reading can spark the 'chase after a fleeting allusion suggested sometimes by the turn of a phrase or by the mere complexion of a word' ('The Vice of Reading' (1903), *UCW* 101–2). Readers will differ, as critics do, in their emphasis: which voices they hear, which strands they wish to follow.

Modernity

Wharton lived through an astonishing sweep of social change. Her writings move through cultural and historical transformations, involving both Europe and America, and presenting fictions of the self and the group, within society, from the 1840s through to the later 1930s. Her field encompasses, in the United States, the expanding economy (the 'Billion-Dollar' spree) of the late nineteenth and early twentieth centuries, as the nation emerged from the Civil War into the entrepreneurial and industrial developments of the Gilded Age (at a peak in the 1880s–90s); the attempts to regulate the excesses of capital in the 'Progressive Era' (*c.* 1897–1914); and later, after another war, in the boom of the 1920s. She witnessed, too, her nation's increasing colonialist interventions and expansion abroad, and its white population's growing racist anxieties over immigrant and African American groups at home. In Europe, from her home in Paris, she experienced the end of the Belle Époque and the devastation of World War I; she lived to see the rise of Mussolini and fascism in Italy and was horrified by Hitler's radio broadcasts (*Lewis* 510). All these reverberate in her writing.

With few exceptions, her texts fix their gaze on modernity, especially, to use Freud's 1901 title, on the psychopathology of everyday life – the mundane details, so important in all her narratives. But these details open up large concerns: about writing, form, genre and representation; about the transformations of the self within changing cultures; about gender, display and performance; the role of the leisure classes and 'manners'; alternatives to commodity and consumer culture; and questions of values (economic, aesthetic and moral) in the new society. Her war-writing attempts to face the worldwide political upheavals and catastrophes which devastated the social fabric. Her texts also register other currents, transmitted by developing technologies, modes of transport, communications and visual media. As she reminded her readers in 1934: 'I was born into a world in which telephones, motors, electric light, central heating (except by hot air furnaces), X-rays, cinemas, radium, aeroplanes and wireless telegraphy were not only unknown but still mostly unforeseen' (*ABG* 6–7). But when she comes to analyse her own creativity and writing, she draws on a sharply contemporary image, comparing her difficulties to 'the nightmare weight of a cinema "close-up"' (*ABG* 197).

Such elements shaped, even invaded, the self, altering ways of looking, ways of being. Electricity, the telephone, the motor, timetables and schedules, the press, the pace, noise and vibration of modern life – all, it was believed played directly on the nerves. As the pioneering German psychologist and Harvard professor Hugo Münsterberg (1863–1916) wrote of the condition of the United States in 1910:

> How often have we heard that our age is that of electricity. Every new invention and every discovery has hastened the whole rhythm of our life. The *adagio* of our forefathers has become a *prestissimo* which must keep us breathless. And with the haste has come the noise. The metropolitan who has to think while the telephone rings and the elevated roars and the typewriter hammers must be a wreck before he is through with his work. Yet, endlessly worse is the inner tension of the life, the multiplicity of our engagements, the pressure of the responsibilities, and above all the sharpness of the competition. It may be that the newspapers are especially responsible. They have enlarged our sphere, so that everyday heaps upon us a thousand exciting reports from all

over the globe [. . .] We are forced to automobile through life, and the
fugitive impressions of the world through which we are racing must
bewilder us and make us dizzy. There is no longer any repose or relief
[. . .] We instinctively feel that fresh air and sunshine may bring back
to us what we have lost among skyscrapers and smoky chimneys.[1]

Münsterberg proved unhappily accurate in his own case – he ignored doc-
tors' advice to relax, and died of a heart attack, at fifty-three, while giving a
lecture in New York City;[2] and his diagnosis is echoed in many a contemporary commentary, particularly by observers of the modern metropolis.

In both pre- and post-war fiction, Wharton captures the impression and
impact of this dizzying rush as it accelerates; and she pinpoints its mani-
festations. Throughout her work she would use references to electricity or
glare, as expressions of the abrasive, jarring elements of modernity,
destructive of civilised ways of living. *The Decoration of Houses* deplored the
replacement, by gas and electricity, of wax candles in the family living room:
'Nothing has done more to vulgarize interior decoration [. . .] Electric light
especially, with its harsh white glare, which no expedients have as yet over-
come, has taken from our drawing-rooms all air of privacy and distinction'
(*DH* 126). As markers of bad taste, the electric glare often intensifies scenes of
excessive gilding and extravagant ornamentation: the 'vast gilded void' of Mrs
Hatch's hotel (*HM* 445) offers a memorable example. In a corresponding set
of images, time becomes another signal of contrasting and conflicting world-
views (the demands of the railroads imposed standard time on the United
States in 1883). Readers become alert to clocks, regimes, routines, obligations,
and to sudden shifts in the tempo and timbre of a narrative: the slow leisure of
a Sunday at a house party (as in *The House of Mirth*), or, in an even older
world, the torpor of wet days on a French country estate (*The Reef*, or *The
Custom of the Country*); the brisk pace of the early 1900s (celebrated by Dallas
Archer in the coda of *The Age of Innocence*); a record-breaking high-speed
divorce and remarriage (*The Custom of the Country*); Pauline's micro-
management of each hour in the time-obsessed 1920s (*Twilight Sleep*).

Wharton's narratives trace this emergence of a modern self – or rather its
fragmentation. Consistency of 'self' dissipates, giving place to image, or to a
public 'personality'. Although this kind of energy can be destructive (as it is
when embodied in a ruthless Undine Spragg (*CC*)), it fascinates Wharton in
all her texts. As all biographers point out, she herself thrilled (and exhausted)
her friends with her own pace and intensities. For Henry James, she was a
'fire-bird [. . .] never more wound up and going'; she 'rode the whirlwind
[. . .] played with the storm' (quoted *Lewis* 322–3). More dangerous (at least

to art) than energy are images of counterfeit or mass reproduction – references to 'chromolithograph' pictures in the texts usually code vulgarity ('Souls Belated' (1899), *GI* 104; *R* 365; *CC* 54) or a woman who communicates with inflections 'like a voice reproduced by a gramophone' ('The Pelican' (1899), *GI* 59). In *The House of Mirth*, Wharton creates effects of rapidly changing scenes – the 'dissolve' – implemented in images of conventional stage-scenery, but also of the slides of a 'stereopticon', a precursor of early cinema (*HM* 259). Allied to these are the artistic illusions of the tableaux vivants in which Lily takes a starring role. The constructed portraits turn women into miraculous artworks through 'the happy disposal of lights and the delusive interposition of layers of gauze' (*HM* 214); but the press agent of the 'cinematograph syndicate' setting up his apparatus (an invention of 1896) at the church for a society wedding (*HM* 139) heralds twentieth-century celebrity culture, mediated through the camera lens.

The symptoms identified by Münsterberg persisted, intensified, in the years post-1919, hastening and altering 'the rhythm' to frenetic, even, monstrous pitch. In her extraordinary rush of novels in the 1920s (including *The Mother's Recompense, Twilight Sleep* and *The Children*), Wharton stared into the new commodity culture, a nightmare of consumer-capitalism and standardised lives, mediated by advertising, cults, fashion and publicity – for new readers in the twenty-first century, these may well seem her most contemporary visions.

Palimpsests

But Wharton is also interested in older structures, other cultures, visible beneath the new. In her memoirs, and reconstructions of old New York, she creates effects out of what, in autobiography, at least, seems a difficulty: 'to disentangle these [early visual impressions] from the palimpsest of later impressions received in the same scenes' ('L&I' 1072). Such layerings of memory lead back, in one route, to the socio-cultural strands of her writing: the glimpsing of elements which stay in place, within the different rates of assimilation in any cultural cross-section. In the 1930s, anthropologists were to become increasingly interested in the processes of change – through 'resistance, innovation, and acculturation – the fitting of a borrowed element into an existing organization in a way that often transforms it'.[3] This summary, drawn from an account of the work of a pioneering woman anthropologist, could also describe phenomena traceable in a number of Wharton's narratives. *The Custom of the Country* and *The Age of Innocence* offer excellent case-studies, with their inflections of the terminology of earlier anthropology: the structuring images of aboriginal inhabitants, invaders and 'survivals' – the resistant outcrops of earlier traditions and customs.

These narratives could be read, too, as a culture in transition, exemplifying the model proposed later in the twentieth century by the Marxist critic Raymond Williams (in *Marxism and Literature*, 1977): with dominant, residual and emergent forms in all these categories. Later, I shall take *The House of Mirth* as a fuller illustration. Such transactions, as cultures, old and new, cross and mingle, raise questions about any simple evolutionary models. In her hesitations and qualifications about change, Wharton could not seem more opposite from, for example, her contemporary Charlotte Perkins (Stetson) Gilman (1860–1935), a feminist activist and utopian thinker. Although Gilman is now better known for her study of an entrapped and encircling mind in 'The Yellow Wall-Paper' (1892), her pioneering designs to open up the home and family, her vision of a women's utopia in *Herland* (1915) and upbeat stories of individual transformation in the feminist magazine the *Forerunner* (1909–16), present a trajectory of socio-political improvement alien to Wharton's narratives.

Wharton's sense of the impermanence of any culture or civilisation manifests itself in innumerable ways throughout her work. Many of the most frequently quoted episodes include actual or metaphorical scenes in museums or graveyards. Robert Browning's poems, 'Love Among the Ruins', 'Two in the Campagna' and 'A Toccata of Galuppi's', from *Men and Women* (1855), repay rereading as among her favourites – all speaking of the transience of human love or beauty. Wharton included the first two in her anthology of love poems, *Eternal Passion in English Poetry*, co-edited with Robert Norton (published posthumously, 1939); the first poem was her working title for a planned sequel to *The Glimpses of the Moon*; and a line from 'A Toccata' features, satirically, as part of Undine Spragg's cultural repertoire: a book ' "When the Kissing Had to Stop" of which Mrs Fairford seemed not to have heard' (*CC* 37). These images of 'infinite passion and the pain / Of finite hearts that yearn' (from 'Two in the Campagna'), in the settings of long-gone Roman or Venetian civilisation, emerge again in the leisurely, concentrated unfolding of her late and, for many readers, most powerful short story: 'Roman Fever' (1934). Contemplating her own New York, in autobiography or fiction, Wharton associates it with other past, or 'lost', civilisations: it is the 'world of the Pharaohs';[4] one of its old ladies seems 'a Rosetta Stone to which the clue was lost' (*ONY* 69); it is 'as much a vanished city as Atlantis or the lowest layer of Schliemann's Troy' (*ABG* 55).

Such images again draw into the text forms of scientific inquiry of the period, which Wharton deploys for her own effects. The quest for the legendary Atlantis had been given new life in the late nineteenth century by the Pennsylvania enthusiast Ignatius Donnelly (1831–1901) in *Atlantis: The Antediluvian World* (1882); earlier, the adventurer Heinrich Schliemann (1822–90) had roused public imagination with his archaeological exploits in Turkey in 1871–3, and his sensational claims to have discovered Homeric Troy and the golden treasures of Priam. But deeper perhaps than such associations, and older than any historical, archaeological or even geological past, are layers in her writing, hinted at through metaphor, allusion and myth. The Greek gods are a pervasive presence in Wharton's work; they give their title, for example, to her second collection of poetry, *Artemis to Actaeon and Other Verse* (1909), and are reanimated throughout individual poems. Here, again, great cities 'rise and have their fall', in a world, like a manuscript, in a state of constant revision: 'And ever on the palimpsest of earth / Impatient Time rubs out the word he writ' ('A Torchbearer'). In her fiction, Wharton releases into modern experience forces from Greek tragedy – Lily Bart in *The House of Mirth* flees from the beating wings of the Furies from Aeschylus' *Eumenides* (in *The Oresteia*); and the dark energies of another mythology, 'The Mothers', from Wharton's reading in Goethe's *Faust*, fill her story of the artist Vance Weston (*The Gods Arrive*). It is in their mysterious powers that Vance seeks the creative sources of his writing.

Transatlantic crossings and the expatriate literary tradition

As well as layering time, Wharton's texts also engage the reader in a spatio-geographical axis: in dialogues between Europe and America, and the artistic expatriate tradition within which Wharton defined her own ways of being and writing. In *A Backward Glance*, after listing the extraordinary inventions she had seen in her lifetime, she suggested that, nevertheless, between her youth and the present day (the 1930s) the truly 'vital change' lay elsewhere: 'that the Americans of the original States, who in moments of crisis still shaped the national point of view, were heirs of an old tradition of European culture which the country has now totally rejected' (*ABG* 7). Her narratives set off the phenomena of modern America against the wealth of beauty and cultural tradition, 'the old-established order' (*ABG* 44), she found in Europe and in her reading.

In her texts, simple oppositions are rare, and Europe and America, as with other narratives of encounter and contact, fuse and intertwine, to generate newer, hybrid cultures. The 'shuttle' (to use a period image) of taken-for-granted Atlantic crossings keeps the contrasts and complications in view. Weaving variegated threads from one direction are her array of Europeans visiting the States: aristocrats, eccentrics, intellectuals, emissaries, fortune-seekers; and, glimpsed occasionally, the influx of poorer immigrants (of whom there were 14 million between 1900 and 1920).[5] In the other direction flow the stream of American tourists, shoppers, socialites – some bemused by Europe's differences (like *The Custom of the Country*'s Mr Spragg, dazed by foreign hotels), others, like his daughter, Undine, bored by ruins, but roused to animation by Parisian dressmakers. For the unsophisticated May Archer, on honeymoon in *The Age of Innocence*, European scenes in the mid-1870s – the Austrian lakes and mountains, the Normandy resort of Étretat (which would inspire Monet in the 1880s) – are 'merely an enlarged opportunity for walking, riding, swimming, and trying her hand at the fascinating new game of lawn tennis' (*AI* 196). For the Manhattan smart-set in *The House of Mirth*, Monte Carlo represents merely a change of scene, a temporary backdrop (one of many in a novel of stagy images) for social manoeuvring and gossip. Further afield, her fiction casts a wide net, dispatching or returning characters from across the globe, from Cuba to Japan; two newly weds take off to Asia Minor, to sleep in tents among the Arabs. These non-European journeys are reported, largely, off the page (though Rio is the setting for a crucial scene in *The Mother's Recompense*); but far-flung places loom large in many of her characters' histories and imaginations. (Readers now have become greatly interested in the implications of such global-imperialist themes.) As in the title of Paramount's 1929 film of *The Children* (1928), novel after novel shows monied Americans treating Europe, and beyond, as 'The Marriage Playground', transacting their flirtations, affairs, divorces across a global canvas. Such Americans simply regard any destination as the United States elsewhere. Another set, however, creates more complex interrelations. These are the characters who engage with European culture, but in often ambiguous or destructive ways.

In writing of these characters, Wharton, as often, keeps the readers' eye on the objects and artefacts which travel with them: not just dresses and jewellery, but furnishings, works of art, antiquities. The collector – tasteless or, like Elmer Moffatt (*CC*), discriminating, with an eye for a priceless original – is a central figure in many of her fictions. Her early stories (discussed in the next chapter), or 'The Daunt Diana' (1909; in *TMG*), or the novella *False Dawn* in *Old New York* (1924), offer a variety of perspectives. Wharton herself enjoyed bargain-hunting, and became a connoisseur of eighteenth-century Italian furniture; she was friends with Bernard Berenson (1865–1959), the distinguished expert on Italian painting whose verdict on a work's authenticity could make prices soar. She might not have been aware of Berenson's possible collusions with the market,[6] and his percentage on works which benefited (*Lee*, 404, believes she was not), but her fiction makes clear the ambiguities of 'appreciation' – that art and 'values' are at once aesthetic and commercial. The collecting motif opens up questions of origin, provenance, ownership and authorship, all *fin-de-siècle* literary preoccupations, but which anticipate wider debates, still very much alive. The passion of the collector to acquire and preserve is a tribute to art, but also a kind of destructive lust (often with an imperialist edge) – the looting or pillage of the 'spoils'. This term, now fixed in the imagination by Henry James's *The Spoils of Poynton* (1897), is used by Wharton of her own first experiments in furnishing. She found 'amusement' in adorning her 'sixteen-foot-wide house in New York with the modest spoils' of her Italian travels (*ABG* 143). But her fiction looks at such acts critically; and shows their (often devastating) impact. *The Custom of the Country* closes with, perhaps, the most shocking instance.

A related form of spoils, which Wharton also represents as a kind of piracy, is the transatlantic marriage market. These complex interchanges between European titled aristocracy and American money filled the newspapers in the Gilded Age – 'the American mother can forgive the failings of a lord, provided he be a prospective son-in-law', as a Society column expressed it (*NYT* 14 April 1895). Rich young women invading England to capture husbands are 'The Buccaneers' who give Wharton's final, unfinished, novel its title. An earlier wave of 'foreign' marriages, regarded with suspicion by old New Yorkers, lies in the background of *The Age of Innocence*. In French settings, they drive the narrative of 'The Last Asset' (1904), or the novella *Madame de Treymes* (1907). This two-way traffic of art or marriage partners, between Europe and the United States, is part of a larger system of exchanges in Wharton's novels and in her culture. They are integral to the transactions of those rising through the social ranks to remake themselves as ladies and gentlemen. These strands – with their related contexts of issues of gender and class – will come into focus with *The House of Mirth*, and be a repeated concern. Europe, then, exists both as past and future – a space of remaking and possibility, in a strange inversion of old and new.

The vision of opportunity intensifies for Wharton's many American characters who are long-term visitors, exiles and expatriates: those who, like herself, culturally alienated from America, attempt to find a home in Europe. A recurrent figure is the artist who recoils from the United States, viewing it as an aesthetic wasteland, indifferent to, or hostile towards, art. Publishers' demands for wholesome stories further constrained literary experiment. Usually, though not exclusively, male, the artist plays key roles in her narratives, from her early writings through to her late epic diptych: *Hudson River Bracketed* and *The Gods Arrive*. For Wharton as a writer, travel became her mode of creating for herself a life beyond her inherited culture; and the trope of landscape and place, as Beer Goodwyn emphasises, would be a unifying thread throughout her work: 'the American's place in the Western world, the woman's place in her own and European society, the author's place in the larger life of a culture'.[7]

In her long-term choice of a home, Wharton followed a line of earlier writers who had migrated to live for substantial periods in mainland Europe – among them (notably in Italy) Byron, Keats and Shelley, or, from the mid-nineteenth century, Robert and Elizabeth Barrett Browning; and her texts are filled with allusions to their work. In *The Age of Innocence*, set in the mid-1870s, she slips a list of the 'latest books' on Italian art (*AI* 68) into Newland Archer's reading. However, specifically American expatriation also had a substantial literary lineage. Wharton's writings come between two broad generations, represented above all, in the mid- and late nineteenth century, by Nathaniel Hawthorne and Henry James, whom she admired, and the 1920s generation of F. Scott Fitzgerald and Ernest Hemingway, with whom she was out of sympathy. Although she wrote to Fitzgerald, in June 1925, in somewhat qualified praise of *The Great Gatsby* (*Letters* 481–2), their meeting, over tea at Pavillon Colombe, on 5 July 1925, is one of literary history's famous failures: Wharton jotted in her diary: 'To tea, Teddy Chanler and Scott Fitzgerald, the novelist (horrible)' (*Benstock* 383).

For women writers, too, Europe proffered richer opportunities. One such was Julia Constance Fletcher (1853–1938), who settled in Rome and, later, Venice; and, as 'George Fleming', wrote fictions set in Italy, Egypt and the Middle East. *A Nile Novel* (1876) (with its adventurous Midwestern heroine) was adapted for stage as *Kismet* – Wharton saw it in London, in the company of Henry James, who was one of Fletcher's friends (*Benstock* 260). Fletcher, 'a very kind and very artistic person' according to James,[8] was also admired by Oscar Wilde. Like Italy, Paris appealed to many women writers and painters. Mary Cassatt (1844–1926), the daughter of a wealthy banker, first showed her art in the *Salon* in the 1860s, going on to exhibit with the Impressionists in the 1870s; and she continued to live and work in the city until her death. The modernist writer Gertrude Stein (1874–1946), born (like Cassatt) in Pittsburgh, to a rich railroad executive, became the luminary of a Parisian set of painters and writers, including Matisse and Picasso. Freer expressions of sexuality (in life and writing) were important to many of these artists; but biographers suggest that Wharton would not have looked warmly on what she might have termed the 'degeneracy' (lesbianism) ('L&I' 1085) of several of this group. She had many male friends we might now think of as gay or bisexual (labels of sexual orientation became more fixed as the twentieth century progressed), including the French writers André Gide and Jean Cocteau, and, though she might not have known it, her lover, Morton Fullerton. Biographers remark on her geniality towards what she called 'The Brotherhood' of male homosexuals, but comment that she possibly failed to notice, or was uninterested in, some of her women friends' sexual diversity – Lewis instances the writer Vernon Lee (Violet Paget), whom she knew in Italy, and the French poet Anna de Noailles in Paris (*Lewis* 443–4; *Benstock* 76–7).

Wharton did not mingle in flamboyantly avant-garde circles; and did not approve of the experimentation of much modernist art. But, as readers now observe, she shared her more unconventional compatriots' attraction to the aesthetic pleasures and cultural wealth of Paris, and its possibilities of escape from the constraints and hypocrisy of nineteenth-century polite society. The United States was additionally hampered by 'Comstockery' – the legacy of the Comstock Law of 1873. Brought in to prohibit trade in 'obscene literature' and 'immoral articles', it extended its disapproval to a range of productions, from contraceptives to sex-education leaflets; and explicit or morally questioning art was no exception. In contrast, Europe, at least as myth, promised artistic and sexual freedom. As Benstock reminds us, for some, such as the Harlem writer Jessie Fauset, Paris also offered hope of an orbit beyond racism.[9] A number of Wharton's writings present a counter-vision of Europe: dreary scenes on the Riviera, in *The Mother's Recompense* and *The Gods Arrive*, for example, depict a parochial dead-end, as conformist as any small-town American community. But other texts reveal affinities with modernist quests for new expression; and the next chapter will turn (with *The Reef*, in particular) to her own search for a new kind of literary landscape in Europe; one where she could explore aspects of sexuality unspeakable in mainstream American art.

Wharton's closer fellowship seemed, for many of her contemporary readers, to lie with earlier generations: the lineage of Hawthorne and James. Hawthorne's *The Marble Faun* (1860), set in an artists' colony in Rome, had been a landmark, influencing James's own first significant European encounters: 'A Passionate Pilgrim' (1871) and *Roderick Hudson* (1876), his story of the dilemmas of an American artist. James's critical work *Hawthorne* (1879) celebrated 'the denser, richer, warmer European spectacle' with its 'accumulation of history and custom'; and, with amusement, unrolled a (much-quoted) list of negations: 'the items of high civilization', which, to the expatriate artist's view, America might seem to lack. The contrast is with England:

> No State, in the European sense of the word, and indeed barely a specific national name. No sovereign, no court, no personal loyalty, no aristocracy, no church, no clergy, no army, no diplomatic service, no country gentlemen, no palaces, no castles, nor manors, nor old country-houses, nor parsonages, nor thatched cottages, nor ivied ruins; no cathedrals, nor abbeys, nor little Norman churches; no great Universities nor public schools – no Oxford, nor Eton, nor Harrow.[10]

Mark Twain would be riled into rejoinder, satirising European antiquity in such novels as *A Connecticut Yankee in King Arthur's Court* (1889). More importantly, he created his own American classic out of United States vernacular materials, in the voice of a slangy, illiterate, ignorant boy who had certainly been nowhere near Eton (*Adventures of Huckleberry Finn*, 1884). Twain's enterprise tapped into American oral 'frontier' humour, or its recreation in the hands of urban writers. James however turned, as Wharton would, to European realist literature: the line of Thackeray, Trollope or George Eliot in England, or Balzac and Flaubert in France.

Such nationalist divides were an issue for artists throughout the century: James Fenimore Cooper had written a feudal drama of Italy, *The Bravo* (1831), as well as his famous pioneer fictions; Francis Marion Crawford filled a European map with his variously located romances, and balanced his books with novels of the United States Gilded Age. Others joined in the debate – allured by European tradition, but excited by American energy. Numerous popular narratives, of a kind no doubt deplored by Wharton's mother, took characters to France, Germany and Italy, to make comparisons, and return them (or not) to home. Family fictions mediated the arguments for all ages. In *Little Women* (Part II, 1869), for example, Louisa May Alcott sent Amy March to Rome, where, overwhelmed in the presence of European masterpieces, she loses faith in her own artistic capacity. But Amy does not choose Europe: she refuses the British upper-class heir to a grand estate to return to the United States and democracy; and by the end of the series, in *Jo's Boys* (1886), she presides over 'Parnassus', a foundation to nurture American artists at home. In *What Katy Did Next* (1886), Susan Coolidge (Sarah Chauncey Woolsey, 1835–1905) took an opposite course. She showed Katy Carr, her heroine, dazzled by Rome in terms paralleling Wharton's youthful revelation: 'Nothing seemed of any particular consequence except the deep sense of enjoyment, and the newly discovered world of thought and sensation of which she had become suddenly conscious';[11] and, in the closing section, in Venice, secures Katy's European links, with her engagement to an English navy lieutenant.

Wharton's novels and her characters, then, draw on a wealth of association: 'the legendary castellated Europe of keepsakes, brigands and old masters, that compensated, by one such "experience" [. . .] for an after-life of aesthetic privation' ('The Rembrandt', *CI* 130). Sentimental romances along more elevated lines than Katy's colour Lily Bart's first aspirations: 'for an English nobleman with political ambitions and vast estates; or, for second choice, an Italian prince with a castle in the Apennines and an hereditary office in the Vatican' (*HM* 55). In *The Age of Innocence*, Countess Olenska, born Ellen Mingott, returns to New York with a disastrous liaison behind her, alarming society with her aura of strange foreignness. Her air of European knowledge – of 'Art and beauty', as well as 'Jewels – historic pearls: the Sobieski emeralds' (*AI* 161) – seems more dangerous to her family than even the rumours of her husband's unthinkable depravity.

When Wharton took up this tradition, Henry James was its most distinguished practitioner. Although few readers would regard James as a writer in the vernacular, traces of more democratic, or at least less Europeanised, voices persist in his own high art – bringing in different energies. They are heard, for example, in the title characters of *The American* (1877) and *Daisy Miller* (1879), in Isabel Archer's friends and allies in *The Portrait of a Lady* (1881) and, more faintly, in the United States visitors to Paris in *The Ambassadors* (1903). All these texts on 'the international theme' offer suggestive interconnections, even intertexts, with Wharton, as dramas of cultural collision, misreading and misconception. The obdurate French aristocrats who block Christopher Newman's romance in *The American* seem to rise again in Wharton's novella *Madame de Treymes* (1907). Isabel Archer, the title character of *The Portrait of a Lady*, is an intertextual presence in *The Age of Innocence*, recalled in small allusions; and memories of her history hint at what might lie in the 'remote dark distances' Newland sees in Ellen's gaze (*AI* 106). By the time Wharton became friends with James he was at the peak of his career. Yet, to the regret of many readers, his writing was by now entering its 'late' period, and story seemed subordinate to manner. 'After being one of the simplest and most luminous writers of English he has become one of the most dense and grotesque' (*CR* 13), as one of Wharton's reviewers lamented. James's prose had become ever more elaborated, spun out into ever finer threads of consciousness, and, so Wharton thought, his 'technical theories and experiments' led him to sacrifice 'that spontaneity which is the life of fiction' (*ABG* 190). Her own writing never lost touch with a material world, always remaining socially situated, sensitive to an outer environment. Her characters come to consciousness within the specific life of the body and emotion, as well as through the intelligent play of perception. Feelings and observations remain physical, often signalled in blushes, or sudden gestures, or caught in a darting simile: as in *The Age of Innocence*, eyes 'glitter with victory', or turn 'sharp as pen-knives'; even syllables have weight, tapping 'like a little hammer on his brain' (*AI* 343, 304, 345).

In *A Backward Glance*, she commemorated European literature in her reading, but she also celebrated more democratic American voices. She revelled in Walt Whitman's work, marking her text of *Leaves of Grass* (a gift from Walter Berry in 1898), and planning an article on his achievement.[12] She recalls her youthful relish for the new 'humorous and expressive side of American slang', and its 'racy innovations' (*ABG* 50) – a claim borne out in her texts, where slang and loud neologism, in counterpoint to gentility or inwardness, often generate considerable energy. Although Wharton would choose France for her home, in her texts languages, nations and cultures, old and new, always cross and mingle, to keep all possibilities in play.

Chapter 3

Works

> I felt like some homeless waif who, after trying for years to take out
> naturalization papers, and being rejected by every country, has finally
> acquired a nationality. The Land of Letters was henceforth to be my
> country, and I gloried in my new citizenship.   (*ABG* 119)

Although Wharton marked many different milestones in her career, her
emphasis stayed constant: writing was where she felt at home. This chapter
will move, broadly chronologically, through Wharton's journey from the
literal places and passages of her European travels in her earlier married
years, into the imaginative territory of her fiction. Before turning to individual works, however, I shall begin by looking at some features important to
many of her narratives: a historical consciousness, and strongly expressed
evocations of rootedness and tradition, which are embedded, often, within
sharply contemporary analytical frames and cultural reference points. Such
elements, in general, have been at the centre of many arguments about
whether Wharton might be labelled as a conservative or a progressive writer,
and (as Chapter 4 will outline) continue to rouse debate.

General perspectives

History and tradition

Wharton's first novel, *The Valley of Decision* (1902), was a chronicle of
eighteenth-century Italy, a heavily researched reconstruction of a distant time

and culture, an exercise she did not repeat. But her interest in historical investigation imbues other works which treat closer (though, in some ways, as remote) societies. *The Age of Innocence* (1920) and the novella sequence, *Old New York* (1924), look back across the gulf of World War I and the changes wrought by the rise of new and undreamed-of wealth to the Manhattan of her family. Such an impulse of inquiry prompts the narrator of *Ethan Frome*, and lies beneath the autobiographical 'I' of her memoirs and her later-life considerations of her own earlier writings. All these narratives reach into the past, to gather and examine evidence, question, reassemble and take it apart: 'I had the story, bit by bit, from various people, and, as generally happens in such cases, each time it was a different story' (*EF* 3). The investigative field may be small scale (one man's life in a failed hill-farm; or the exclusive Fifth Avenue habitat, between Washington Square and Central Park); but all dissolve certainties of the present by opening up the complexity of societies now gone.

This interest in the past surfaces, also, in narratives more directly concerned with the present moment, as characters (and readers) are drawn into efforts of interpretation, the drive to uncover a history. At one end of the spectrum, this is the purview of gossip, or, more benignly, of concern: 'But what *is* your story, Lily?' asks the anxious Gerty Farish of her socially tainted friend (*HM* 363). *The House of Mirth*'s buzz of speculation ranges from *Town Talk* to the activities of the reader; it 'could flay its victims without the shedding of blood' (*HM* 177). But in Wharton's writing asking about histories also comes to mark what is serious in civilisation, represented here in the memorable evocation towards the end of Lily's story:

> In whatever form a slowly-accumulated past lives in the blood – whether in the concrete image of the old house stored with visual memories, or in the conception of the house not built with hands, but made up of inherited passions and loyalties – it has the same power of broadening and deepening the individual existence, of attaching it by mysterious links of kinship to all the mighty sum of human striving.   (*HM* 516)

The 'old house' carrying histories will reappear, and remain central, as far as Wharton's late novels, *Hudson River Bracketed* (1929) and *The Gods Arrive* (1932), and 'All Souls'', her final ghost story. In her manuscript 'Disintegration', which she worked on in the early 1900s, the image is already 'concrete'; as a broken marriage rends a man away from his associations:

> Clephane had a special tenderness for the old house which held under its gabled roof and on its panelled walls that fine dust of family tradition so seldom left to gather undisturbed in American dwellings.

> He had always cherished the family pieties, had been conscious in himself of vibrations prolonged from an unbroken past. The portraits of his great-grand-parents, the chairs they had sat in, the floors their feet had worn, kept the imprint of their living personalities – the whole house was as warm to him as a glove just drawn from the hand [. . .] To continue the family tradition, while adding to it new qualities of fine living and feeling, had been a part of his conception of life, the larger purpose enclosing his personal happiness; to have failed in this continuance meant the rending of innumerable fibres with which his own were inwoven.   (Beinecke/4.109, 50)

Two decades later, in an article, 'In General' (*Scribner's Magazine*, December 1924), Wharton applied such a concept to writing. She deplored the facile search for originality by the modern artist, who believed that immersion in 'the past history of his art' would impair his creativity: 'the whole history of that past – in every domain of art – disproves this by what survives'. The writer needs 'an accumulated wealth of knowledge and experience' to bring the private insight, 'this secret germ [seed] to fruition' (in *WF* 17–18). Without such connections, she asserts, the artist remains immature, the work ephemeral; and cultural amnesia is dangerous to nations, and to individuals.

Such connections need deep roots. Representing children in her writing, Wharton often registers the landmarks of growing up through encounters with words. In her depictions of adult consciousness, she embeds assumptions, quoted words of the family elders, as part of the scaffolding of character: 'Newland Archer had been aware of these things ever since he could remember, and had accepted them as part of the structure of his universe' (*AI* 101). Her descriptions of first meetings with literary or poetic language (words not always fully understood) often disrupt the consciousness, and disturb, glow or stun with their impact. Her portraits of young readers, young artists, depict them almost physically, absorbing the heritage of Western tradition, and transmuting it in their own vision. Her unfinished novels, 'Disintegration' and 'Literature', open with extended studies of their central characters' early years, and biographers have drawn out parallels between her own experiences and autobiographical reminiscence, and her accounts of these young protagonists. In 'Disintegration':

> Val's domain was built of strangely-mingled shreds of association, gathered from the talk of her elders, and from an unchecked exploration of her father's library; the whole fused by an intense visual sensibility into something not unlike one of those imaginary scenes in which the old landscape painters sought to sum up their beatific vision of earth's loveliness.   (Beinecke/4.109, 41)

In the later 'Literature', the intensity of a boy's behaviour again chimes with Wharton's recollections of herself, captivated by the materiality of language and the physical allure of the volumes. Dicky is overwhelmed by the cataracts of Biblical verses – 'O my so nabsalan my son my so nabsalan, wood god' – as he hears the syllables. He too, in a passage which hints at Wharton's potential, had she wished, for writing fantasy, is enchanted by the wizardry of creating his own story from the printed page – in an ecstatic 'rhapsode':

> The experiment once made, every other diversion seemed tame. The act was so exciting that it could not be done sitting still: he had to pace up and down, up and down, at a rapid trot that grew almost to a run in the more dramatic moments of the narrative. The story, as he walked, grew out of the book, seemed to curl up from it in a sort of silvery mist; he had to turn the pages as he would have done if he had really been reading what was printed on them. And his own story, somehow, *was* printed on them while he read: it overlay the other like a palimpsest. This feverish improvisation went on for hours.
>
> (Beinecke/10.273, 22)[1]

With no source in a deeper tradition, aesthetic sensibility merely evaporates, and, without roots or shaping forms, character lacks centre, lives fail to find direction. So, in *The House of Mirth*, without ties, without cultural nourishment, Lily becomes 'mere spin-drift of the whirling circle of existence' (*HM* 515). Yet in that novel, as in other texts, tradition, with all its long accumulations, can weigh down and imprison: Lily's aunt, Mrs Peniston, is its grimmest incarnation, her house and her heavy, dark furniture, 'as dreary as a tomb' (*HM* 160). Such narratives have themselves become the site for debate among Wharton's critics, raising arguments over questions of her values. Are these conservative, even anti-democratic, visions, in flight from change or innovation? Or critical, even progressive, engaging with the problem of the static, the energy of the new?

The social sciences

The issues are complicated by the cross-cutting of her representations of the past with observations garnered through alternative intellectual frameworks: particularly the discourses of science and evolutionary studies. Wharton kept copies of the augmented, corrected editions of Charles Darwin's *The Origin of Species* (1859) and *The Descent of Man* (1871) in both her Riviera and Paris houses; and marked passages in Ernest Haeckel's *The History of Creation* (1868) and in her set of Thomas Huxley's *Collected Essays* (nine volumes, published 1894–1900; see *Lib* 32, 55, 60). She used titles from Darwin for her second and third story collections: *Crucial Instances* (1901)[2] and *The Descent of Man* (1904). On board ship in 1908, she was 'deep in' Vernon Kellogg's *Darwinism Today* (1906), with Robert Lock's *The Recent Progress in the Study of Variation, Heredity and Evolution* (1906) on hand, to follow (*Letters* 146). The language of adaptation, adjustments, variants and dominant 'types', with characters figured in terms of insects or micro-organisms, often, again, serves to prompt the reader to keep an emotional distance, to move away from empathy with individuals to analysis of broader social schemes. The socio-political thinker Herbert Spencer, whom Wharton also acknowledged as a founding influence (*Letters* 136), provides another linking set of concepts in his ideas of social Darwinism.

This evolutionary model, which seemed peculiarly apt for the competitive individualism of the late nineteenth-century United States, informed naturalist writings of the period. These depicted human subjects, struggling for agency, caught up in sweeping economic, social or biological forces, often in brutal urban environments. In such narratives, characters are often represented as on a level with other insignificant species, and their will, emotions or choices seem almost irrelevant. Naturalism has itself become a contested term, more complicated than such a summary can suggest; but novels such as Stephen Crane's *Maggie: A Girl of the Streets* (1893; published 1896, a tale of abuse, prostitution and violent death), Frank Norris's *McTeague* (1899; featuring an emotionally unstable dentist) and Theodore Dreiser's *Sister Carrie* (1900; a narrative of social rise and fall, sex, shopping, show-business and the city, in the new twentieth century) offer examples of a spectrum of naturalist interests. Naturalism remains a useful lens into elements of a number of Wharton's fictions; and, with *The House of Mirth*, I shall return to this model, on a large-scale canvas.

Sociology and, especially from *The Custom of the Country* onwards, cultural anthropology offer another set of reference points. (Nancy Bentley's *The Ethnography of Manners: Hawthorne, James, Wharton*, 1995, offers a stimulating reading in these terms.) Using such modes of analysis, Wharton turns the lens on her readers' own New York lineage, to defamiliarise deeply embedded assumptions and practices. She seems to have made her own way towards an area of intellectual speculation which was currently absorbing younger American anthropologists ('ethnologists' was a term also then in use). *The Age of Innocence*, in particular, reads, in some aspects, like a report from her empirical fieldwork, where she carefully documents the rituals, the ceremonies and the daily practices of a people or a tribe. We might see a parallel in the work of the rebellious debutante Elsie Clews Parsons who, like Wharton, emerged from the New York upper set to publish widely read, but controversial, books which posed a challenge to her own society. Parsons's study-guide, *The Family* (1907), which advocated explicit sex-education as an ethical imperative, was followed by a series of witty, radical, socio-ethnological works – including *The Old-Fashioned Woman: Primitive Fancies about the Sex* (1913), *Fear and Conventionality* (1914) and *Social Freedom: A Study of the Conflicts between Social Classifications and Personality* (1915). These looked at the family, social custom, attitudes to sex or the position of women in the United States, as on the same level of cultures or tribes then usually assumed 'savage'; and overturned ideas that twentieth-century white, Anglo-Dutch New Yorkers could claim any superiority of 'civilisation'. Conversely (and paralleling something of Wharton's enterprise in *Ethan Frome* or *In Morocco*), Parsons's studies of south-western and Mexican pueblo culture sought to respect their complexity and distinctiveness. These, she always emphasised to her white, metropolitan audiences, were cultures as sophisticated as their own. Parsons's work connected her with a wider group of thinkers – among them, the anthropologists Franz Boas (1858–1952), author of *The Mind of Primitive Man* (1911), Ruth Underhill (1883–1984) and her own one-time assistant Ruth Benedict (1887–1948), who published groundbreaking research from the 1930s. Wharton would always distance herself from the kind of public projects which occupied Parsons and many of her associates (women's suffrage, campaigns for sexual freedom and – during the war – anti-militarism); but her analyses of social groups parallel, in fiction, such innovative studies. (A related set of frameworks, those of economic analysis, in terms of class and gender, will be addressed in my discussion of *The House of Mirth*.)

In various passages in 'Literature', Wharton highlighted strands that she would fuse into the structuring of other texts. Here, Dick, the young artist in the making, finds new vistas in a book called *Primitive Culture*: a key work (published 1871) by the British anthropologist Sir Edward Burnett Tylor (1832–1917). Tylor was among those who propounded an evolutionary model for culture. He was viewed as a radical, in that he suggested that all humankind belonged to a single species (a significant argument against extreme racist theories which classified some non-white groups as distinct kinds). But he was more conservative in emphasising the milestones of cultural achievement, which, he believed, demonstrated that societies progressed from 'primitive' ('savage') to 'advanced' ('civilised') states. Wharton, like Clews Parsons and her group, would challenge this view. In 'Literature', Dick's curiosity is roused: 'here were new channels for his straining imagination, and it rushed into them with a roar of many waters'. His tutors are no help. The first shows only 'a languid interest': ' "I've never,"

Mr Silmore avowed, "been able to work myself up the question as to how savages managed without matches, or disposed of their mothers-in-law." ' The encounter leads to a debate about the meanings of culture, whether they are all 'links in a chain'; but Dick's interest is frustrated, as often in her own sphere had Wharton's:

> The tutor in whose rooms he had found the volume of Tylor was not much more enlightening. Tylor was part of a 'course', and the tutor was able to furnish Dick with the names of other volumes on the same subject; but he did not seem to see it as an element of the great world-picture which was gradually unrolling itself before the boy's enchanted eyes. (Beinecke/10.274, 49–59)

Wharton extended her own explorations of a 'great world-picture' into dialogues within her texts. In her analyses of her own culture, she threads the old and the new: the cruder descriptive classifications of 'exotic' and, by inference, inferior peoples with more modern approaches attuned to the working of social systems.

'Types'

The language of 'types' was central to the period, and is visible in all these diverse social languages. This lexicon – words such as 'types', 'kind', 'typical', which now in the twenty-first century read more neutrally – carried culturally loaded meanings. The terminology forms part of a wider, general nineteenth-century interest in classification, and embraces issues of race, ethnicity, moral tendencies, intelligence, attractiveness, health and inherited characteristics, temperament, or features specific to a gender. Like the related period sciences of physiognomy and phrenology, or of racial taxonomies based on 'blood', belief in 'typical' characteristics enabled an observer to read another as a text. Essential characteristics and identity seemed stamped into every physical feature. Visitors to the United States spent much energy in analysing American types, and in trying to assess whether new varieties of good looks and physique were emerging from the gradual mingling of different nations (see Figure 2, discussed on p. 66). The racist discriminations between what was regarded as the 'pure' type (Nordic, Mediterranean, Norman, 'Anglian' and so on) and the 'amorphous', lie beneath many a commentary. In *The Age of Innocence*, Newland Archer, waiting outside a Boston hotel, can distinguish a visiting French intellectual with a 'foreign' face full of 'things so different' amid a throng of American 'typical countenances' (*AI* 238). Kate Clephane wonders at 'the sameness of the

Figure 2 Harrison Fisher, 'American Beauties' (1907).

American Face' (*MR* 90). In *The House of Mirth*, part of Selden's strong attraction for Lily is his 'height which lifted his head above the crowd, and the keenly-modelled dark features which, in a land of amorphous types, gave him the air of belonging to a more specialized race, of carrying the impress of a concentrated past' (*HM* 104). At the novel's centenary conference (Poughkeepsie, NY, 2005) this sentence stirred lively debate, not least in the session, '*The House of Mirth* and Race'. Could the text be hinting at a Mediterranean or, possibly, African heritage, for Selden? Or is this 'air', rather, Lily's romantic projection? After all, so we are told, she 'always carried an Omar Khayyám in her travelling bag' (*HM* 104). Even this fashion note, however, holds notes of orientalist exoticism: the poem ('The Rubáiyát of Omar Khayyám') in its translation by Edward Fitzgerald (1859) was hugely popular, read in slim gift-editions, performed in recitations or 'Persian' tableaux; and rendered in dance by Isadora Duncan at fashionable musicales (*NYT* 19 March 1898).

For a select white social group, the labelling of 'pure', 'ideal' or 'specialised' versus 'adulterated', 'degenerate' or 'foreign' types, was a handy instrument for identifying the undesirable. In the United States, with a populace of recent immigrants, and of excluded native-born 'foreign' citizens, Jewish Americans, African Americans, Native Americans and other disempowered groups, it became entangled with larger political issues. All these centred on the health of the future nation. Decisions about the 'best type', from the dominant white class's viewpoint, informed, for example, debates about eugenics (an agenda for scientific, selective breeding, designed to eliminate the so-called criminal, constitutionally weak, diseased, disabled or mentally 'defective' types); the rhetoric of 'race suicide' (espoused by President Theodore Roosevelt, who urged educated, upper-middle-class white groups, as a patriotic duty, to breed large families); and, during the 1920s, the imposing of lower quotas for immigrants from what were deemed the less desirable countries (no more than 100 a year from any African country; 34,007 annually from England or Northern Ireland) – a WASP (White Anglo-Saxon Protestant) rationale summed up by President Coolidge : 'America must be kept American' (Message to Congress 1923).

In Wharton's fiction, observation of 'types' is often embedded in characters' ways of looking, and judging, and appears in many narrative, descriptive passages. It is often set in quotation marks, as a technical term, and coloured with a particular character's consciousness. As literary device it is also a way of skewering and defining a character for the reader: 'Type, general character,' Wharton stated, 'may be set forth in a few strokes' (*WF* 37). Phrases such as 'She was the kind of woman who [. . .]' or even 'The kind of house which [. . .]' fill her earliest notebooks. Wharton held on to her pithiest observations, carefully copying as yet unused items from her 'Donnée Book' (1900) into a fresh notebook some ten years later (1910–14: Beinecke/21.700), and these, along with her similes, would always concentrate some of her sharpest satire. However, as her career went on, such features were also adduced in illustration of her air of social authority (a short step to accusing her of snobbery). Reading in their specific narrative contexts qualifies easy judgement: even Wharton's most acerbic witticisms are often offset, or threaded into, other very different kinds of literary language (coloured by myth, or more poetic, metaphorical allusions), to become part of more subtly complex total effects.

At her texts' most self-reflexive moments, Wharton fuses such terminology with the language of art, indicating levels of artifice and representation. In *The House of Mirth*, the women in the tableaux vivants are 'cleverly fitted with characters suitable to their types': Carry Fisher, a Spanish type, 'a typical Goya'; a young Mrs Van Alstyne 'the frailer Dutch type' (*HM* 215). Paintings often form a focal point in her narratives, and portraiture becomes a mode, too, of framing many of her characters. An early story, 'The Portrait' (1899), turns on whether art should capture a subject's essence, or idealise it. Hoping to 'frame' a villainous businessman, a realistic painter exclaims: 'I could think of nothing but that man's head. What a type! [. . .] But how was I to get at him?' (*GI* 239–40). Lily Bart is introduced through the eye of a man appraising her beauty, and reappears throughout *The House of Mirth* in a series of actual or verbal tableaux, as observers seek to identify 'the real Lily' (*HM* 218). Darrow, meeting Sophy Viner, in *The Reef*, 'immediately classified her as a compatriot: her small nose, her clear tints, a kind of sketchy delicacy in her face, as though she had been brightly but lightly washed in water-colour [. . .] She was clearly an American'. But struggling to remember where he has met her, further identification fails him: 'the etched and angular American was becoming rarer than the fluid type' (*R* 12–13).

Capturing the 'typical' was also, for a realist novelist, part of a broader narrative project. Identifying an individual type offered readers, in one succinct, sharply focused example a representative of a larger group. Through this character (the Parvenu; the Nice Girl; the Gentleman), the writer could trace wider social currents. In Wharton, this is, perhaps, never so crudely done as to become stereotype. Some instances, however, are particularly ambiguous, and make attribution difficult. Which are the more deep-rooted assumptions of the narrative vision, and which of specific characters? *The House of Mirth*, for instance, introduces Mr Rosedale as 'a plump rosy man of the blond Jewish type' (*HM* 21), a phrase which has fuelled debates about Wharton's putative anti-Semitism (see 'Critical reception'). In Wharton's lifetime, discussion could more generally take such classifications for granted. Praising the novel's theatrical potential, the American essayist and arts critic James Huneker (*c.* 1860–1921) wrote to a friend:

> that Jew Rosedale – he would loom up magnificently. I am not sure but that he would be the central figure in the play. He is wonderful. Studied from life, and yet a summing up of racial traits and tribal ambitions. He is much more vital and convincing than Selden, who, at the close, is a pale prig.[3]

Today, for some critics, the labelling of Rosedale, his position as an unstoppable, but unwelcome, social force, and Lily's sense of revulsion, remain stereotypical: a reminder of the widespread anti-Semitism of Wharton's day. For others, however, Wharton's presentation of his kindness, emotional warmth and his understanding of Lily render judgements about stereotyping more complex. The question of Wharton's attitudes, as a member of the dominant elite, remains a matter of strong critical contention.

For Wharton, however, the surface is far from all. Always interested in the way the individual comes to identity within the group, Wharton also takes readers into ideas of the unconscious, often through figuration or through setting. She began her career in the decade in which Sigmund Freud (1856–1939), her very near contemporary, was working on his first case histories on women's hysteria. *The Interpretation of Dreams*, with roots in Freud's private practice with Viennese upper classes, appeared in 1899. Freud's work was directly to influence many modernist writers: for example, the British writer May Sinclair (1863–1946), who explored psychoanalysis in her life, her fiction and her critical writings; and in novels such as *Mary Olivier: A Life* (1919) and *Life and Death of Harriett Frean* (1922) experimented with image and non-realist techniques. (Wharton would scorn such efforts.) The Southern novelist Ellen Glasgow (1873–1945) began her memoirs in 1934, possibly inspired by *A Backward Glance*, and emphasised that 'the novel as a living force, if not as a work of art, owes an incalculable debt to what we call, mistakenly, the new psychology [. . .] For my part, though I was never a disciple, I was among the first, in the South, to perceive the invigorating effect of this fresh approach.'[4] Wharton, however, distanced herself from what she viewed as, with the occult, part of 'the boundless Land of Tosh'; in one letter (1922) she enjoins a friend 'not to befuddle' another 'with Freudianism & all its jargon [. . .] what she wants is to develop the conscious, & not grub after the sub-conscious. She wants to be taught first to see, to attend, to reflect' (*Letters* 451).

Turn-of-the-century writings

Seeing, attending, reflecting: from the beginning, Wharton's work demonstrates her prescriptions in practice. With these qualities, much of her fiction, in spite of her disdain, parallels psychoanalysis (a term first used in the 1890s) in its approaches, its observation of small signs and symptoms of what is hidden, and in its insights: 'She is indeed no mean psychologist'

(*CR* 37), exclaims a review of her novella *The Touchstone* (1900). Revising 'Disintegration', she crosses out the word 'subconscious':

> He was glad of the chance to take up old ties from a new stand-point of experience; but he had a subconscious [replaced in ink by: latent] sense of the instability of the renewed relation.   (Beinecke/4.109, 28–9)

But the concept finds metaphorical expression throughout her work. She would write about the importance of thresholds, doors, corridors, walls, windows, barriers, private corners, curtains, lights and shades in *The Decoration of Houses*; and in her texts, interior spaces are often doubled (looking outwards to catch the note of social realities, and inwards to the psyche). So, a woman's meditation upon a marriage, in one of her earliest stories, 'The Fulness of Life' (1893), has become a key passage for many critics:

> But I have sometimes thought that a woman's nature is like a great house full of rooms: there is the hall, through which everyone passes in going in and out; the drawing-room, where one receives formal visits; the sitting-room, where the members of the family come and go as they list; but beyond that, far beyond, are other rooms, the handles of whose doors perhaps are never turned; no one knows the way to them, no one knows whither they lead; and in the innermost room, the holy of holies, the soul sits alone and waits for a footstep that never comes.   (*Scribner's Magazine*, December 1893, 700)

This single sentence, an elaborated simile, leads the reader step by step towards a secret, isolated place; towards impulses (erotic, emotional or spiritual) which could not surface in the genteel literature of the drawing room, but would find expression in Wharton's own pioneering writing.

In 'The Fulness of Life', as throughout her work of the 1890s, she tested in shorter fictions the terrain she would explore in her novels. These are the years when her reputation became established, before she emerged as a phenomenal best-seller with *The House of Mirth* (1905) – a period when, as she put it, she made the leap over the chasm separating the nouvelle and the novel. As a point of entry, I am going to spend some time pursuing some of the contexts, introduced earlier, in the intricacies of a single text – 'Souls Belated', the longest story of Wharton's first collection, *The Greater Inclination* (1899). Looking at this short fiction in close-up will open up ways of thinking about details in longer works; and, in its presentation of some of Wharton's recurring 'voices', methods and concerns, this section will offer a set of reference points for later, briefer, discussions. Further, taking a variety of perspectives on the text, I shall sketch how the story might be read from some major critical viewpoints on Wharton (outlined in 'Critical reception'), to suggest some possible approaches to the works which follow.

'Souls Belated' (1899)

Publishing her first book of fiction on the verge of the new century, Wharton was working on the cusp of the old and the new. An early treatment of cultural dislocation, marriage, freedom and form, her subject, as in many of her works, looks both back to her own society, and forward, to speculate about possible alternative ways of being. In technique, too, while the story clearly draws on a strong tradition of European realist writing, it prompts readings in other terms. Wharton would label herself as an old-fashioned writer, but here, as often, she appears in many ways as a daring and radical proto-modernist. In a strong collection, 'Souls Belated' was singled out by several reviewers, not merely for its courageous topical 'issue' – a woman's adulterous flight with another man, divorce and the question of what would follow – but for its remarkable handling of a relationship at a point of crisis, and for the 'small compass' (*CR* 15) in which Wharton turns round her theme. Writers despaired at the prevalent literary climate, summed up here by W. J. Ghent in 1904:

> 'Make it light and bright', is the order which the literary contributor hears in the editorial office when he submits his wares; and though the terms may be variously interpreted, he understands what is meant: he must write down to the level of childish minds and complacent natures.[5]

Later, Wharton would say that, as she did not rely upon her writing for her entire living, she resolved from the start not to censor her art at the dictates of convention, and on behalf of 'less lucky colleagues to fight for the independence they might not always be in a position to assert' (*ABG* 140).

The story indicates Wharton already in command of a social territory and a range of character-types she would make her own; it is a study of individual struggles for identity, within larger cultural groups. Opening on a desultory train journey in northern Italy, the narrative, focused through the woman's consciousness as she thinks about her just-arrived divorce certificate, leads us back into the history of a stifled marriage. Lydia's memories of life in the Tillotson Fifth-Avenue mansion evoke the claustrophobia of Wharton's New York, and the regulated climate and morality of its tribal elders. Cushioned and carpeted by money, screened against change, dreading ideas ('as much as a draught in the back'), in a routine where 'one could make sure of doing exactly the same thing every day at the same hour' (*GI* 87), Mrs Tillotson senior and her 'model' son, and their kind, will suffocate and bore a succession of Wharton's most vigorous protagonists throughout her fictions. Wharton concentrates this entire history into a few paragraphs, in a gap between stations, in the story's opening section. In this story, as elsewhere, her interest goes beyond a simple satirical record of the dull and familiar, to ask about the unknown, about new forms of experience. A summary could make it seem as if the text offers a richer vision, in Lydia's exchange of the dreary New York husband for the novelist lover; the outlaws' flight into romantic isolation; their European wanderings, arrival at the edge of the Italian lakes (the tale's main setting), and quest for a life nourishing art, the intellect and creativity. But, as often, Wharton turns the narrative round, to block facile notions of fulfilment.

In presenting the dialectic of individual and group, Wharton would always be interested in what lay outside: whether individuals could achieve an existence independent of the society which had formed them. Some, like Lydia's former husband here, never challenge 'doctrines, reverentially imbibed with his mother's milk' (*GI* 87). Her central characters always question. Few, if any, find their way through to forms of freedom – unlike, for example, Wharton herself. In making herself into a writer, discovering her 'new citizenship' in the 'Land of Letters', she achieved a kind of autonomy she seldom allows her characters. Here, 'Souls Belated' anticipates the fears of *The House of Mirth* that, outside the constraining social structures, there might be no sphere '*Beyond!*' (*HM* 249); fears which we shall see emerge again at a key point in *The Age of Innocence*, published twenty years later.

In Lydia and Gannett's turn-of-century journey, their individual images of a 'different' life – Gannett's glimpse of an Italian villa, with its (slightly ominously) ruined gardens, or Lydia's hint that they might 'drift' forever – are countered abruptly in a sequence of encounters mirroring the world they have fled. In glaring, parodic form, the fashionable Anglo-American hotel reproduces the gossip, manipulation, routine, hierarchies, social demands, surveillance and tyranny of convention of all they have left behind – including a more flamboyant replica of themselves in another eloping Society couple. As Lydia's grotesque double recognises, they are 'both in the same box' (*GI* 112) – an image of entrapment reinforced in scene and setting. Wharton's sharp social observation of this enclosed expatriate community, and the viciously comedic blackmail plot which embroils the lovers, would have furnished material enough for a complete story – indeed, Gannett sees in the hotel a 'Queer little microcosm', a good 'study' for his next novel (*GI* 100–1). But for Wharton it is only one aspect of a wider narrative.

Detail and dialogue, as always in Wharton, are revealing. One of the story's first reviews ended with praise for her 'half-elusive but exquisitely effective strokes that reveal in an instant a whole mental attitude or the hidden meaning of a profound emotion' (*CR* 21). In *The Writing of Fiction* (1925), Wharton echoed this, claiming that the short story should open with a few strokes that were a clue to all the details the writer had already brooded upon, but had then eliminated (*WF* 40). (Ernest Hemingway's observation, in turn, that the full force of a story lay in the unseen mass of the iceberg, offers a, perhaps surprising, parallel.) Here, the banal details of the train journey in her opening paragraphs (the dusty crumb-strewn seats, the fossilised station sandwiches, Lydia's fidgeting with the window-blind) all set the scene for the journey of a new relationship that is already going stale. Before the narration drifts, in a free indirect mode, into Lydia's view of her stagnant past, the signs are all in place that her future will be little different. Dialogue emerges, at first, in fragments: Lydia and Gannett exchange only two comments in the first nine pages. Here, through Lydia, Wharton glosses the process for the reader: Lydia is already aware that the couple are running out of topics, afraid of what they might say if they speak; and the fear is of an even sparser time ahead – 'a famine-stricken period when there would be nothing left to talk about' (*GI* 85). Dialogue, when it arrives, works in the way Wharton would suggest later, in *The Writing of Fiction*, to emphasise a rising crisis, a sense of climax, in contrast with 'the smooth effaced gliding of the narrative intervals' (*WF* 55). The lovers' conversation jolts into action in a series of questions (the story will be full of them) and hastily emended recriminations. Words operate as weapon, defence, screen. The fuller action, however, as often in Wharton, takes place as much in the pauses, silences and gaps which open up beneath and between the smallest syllables of small talk.

Structure, also, would always be important. One of the strengths of Wharton's treatment is that, as in most of her work, she never lets the story, or its readers, settle into a single mode, or mood. As often, she uses each structural division of her narrative (here, in five parts) to play against the others, even as, within each section, she cuts across its predominant mode with surprising, or disturbing, notes. So, in 'Souls Belated', she pulls attention back from this first intense focus on the couple, and its long, unbroken passages of narrative, opening out to the broader, almost stagy social comedy of the hotel scenes in the central sections. After the first section's strained verbal exchanges and silences, in the next three parts Wharton allows the spoken word full spate, showing Lydia battered by others' outpourings, in ever more damaging encounters. The second part sweeps her into the skirmish, overwhelming her with the torrent of Miss Pinsent's self-righteous gossip – an uninterrupted dramatic monologue, which Wharton places almost exactly halfway through the story (*GI* 102–4). The third section plays a variant, in Lydia's engagement with the object of the scandal, who launches her own rapid-fire appeal, inquisition and attack. The final sections return us to the lovers, as the relationship hangs in the balance: the fourth section predominantly in dialogue, and the fifth, strikingly, solely in narrative.

With this ending, however, Wharton, as often, effects her most arresting turn. Here, she exploits another vital aspect of structure: that of focalisation. In *The Writing of Fiction*, she would emphasise the importance, to the short tale in particular, of James's care for unity of vision. The 'reflecting mind' should be chosen, she wrote (characteristically associating fiction with architecture): 'as one would choose a building-site, or decide upon the orientation of one's house'. The writer should then 'live inside the mind chosen, trying to feel, see and react' exclusively in its terms (*WF* 36). So, she opens 'Souls Belated' from Lydia's viewpoint, sustaining the limits of her vision faithfully for the first four parts. In the fifth, she breaks the unity. The shock of the shift, from Lydia's focus to Gannett's, excludes the reader (as often in her fiction) from the central character's mind at the crucial instant of decision, and leaves us as spectators, trying to read, from a distance, a scene enacted in silence. The tale ends with reports of Lydia's movements not her feelings; with gaps, ellipses, not conclusions: Lydia, having left the gang-plank of the boat, 'with slow steps, was walking toward the garden...'; 'mechanically, without knowing what he did, he [Gannett] began looking out the trains to Paris...' (*GI* 128). Writing of her novels, Wharton claimed, 'My last page is always latent in my first' (*ABG* 208); and here, without being in any way predictable, she ends, as she began, with the onward movement of a journey, but with a sense of endless repetition and defeat.

With Wharton's works, mode and genre often elude simple categorisation. What kind of story is this? Wharton's contemporary reviewers sensed they were reading something for which current terms were not quite adequate. For some, 'Realism', though itself a slippery term, served as an approximate label. One such attempt at definition opened with a bold statement: 'Two hundred years ago things happened.' Instancing Daniel Defoe as the artist 'of an age that found its play in event rather than in experience', the reviewer explained that now, in the time of Henry James, art could be made from material hitherto found inconceivable: 'a man's feelings – and a woman's', 'not in events, but in experience of events' (*CR* 23–40). Realism has continued to be a term much discussed (see Chapter 4), but this review avoids critical simplification, to suggest Realism's attention to inward action revealed in its details.

Related to this perspective, but with more scientific distance on the human action, is to view Wharton's work in terms of literary Naturalism. Looking at 'Souls Belated' from this angle brings into the foreground, for instance, Lydia's own strongly modern strands of discourse. Addressing Gannett, as they debate marriage, morality, hypocrisy and compromise, she realises that she sounds as if she is giving 'a lecture in sociology'; she uses the terminology and analysis through which Wharton herself would slice into Society – aware of a social creed 'that classifies people by arbitrary signs' (*GI* 97). She makes observations about the different armoury of a gendered culture (men smoked to get away from things, women resorted to 'darkened windows and a headache' *GI* 84). She punctures romantic delusions: lovers, like married people, might 'be saved from madness only by the things that come between them – children, duties, visits, bores, relations' (*GI* 121). In the voice of a woman writer, and woman central character, the perspective of gender is resonant with the wider literary and social energies which were upsetting conventional notions of order, and challenging prevalent demands (especially in magazine publication) for sweetness, niceness and purity in fiction. Henrik Ibsen's *A Doll's House* (1879) had shocked polite audiences when it left its heroine, notoriously, slamming the door on her marriage. Wharton takes Lydia further, following her into her undefined relations beyond the confines of the house. While more optimistic feminist writers would celebrate Nora's actions as heralding a new liberty, Wharton's vision is more ambiguous – and like Kate Chopin's *The Awakening* (1899) published in the same year, 'Souls Belated' resists an easy ending. However, though Wharton would never have identified herself with the New Woman movement of the 1890s (and though the story shows that Lydia has internalised the conventions she despises), here both the writer and her heroine seem New Women in their bravery, their resourcefulness and their attempt to see life clearly.

Looking at the story with hindsight, readers now might also be struck by elements of more oblique approaches: *fin-de-siècle* impression, symbolism, notes of early modernism. While these are features common to many artists of the 1890s, again, for some readers, they gain a particular colouring in the work of women writers. Approaching Wharton in this light takes an observer into layers beneath the layers of conscious feeling. Beyond Lydia's self-aware analysis, Wharton gestures at vaguer dimensions of experience which her heroine does not articulate. As in 'The Fulness of Life', the story, published in the same year as Freud's *Interpretation of Dreams*, seems to reach into the unconscious. Elaine Showalter, introducing her anthology *Daughters of Decadence: Women Writers of the Fin-de-Siècle* (London: Virago, 1998), draws analogies between these women's work and Freud's contemporary studies of 'hysterical' women. Showalter includes two of Wharton's stories from this period – 'The Muse's Tragedy', *The Greater Inclination*'s marvellous opening story, and the uncollected set of teasing riddles: 'The Valley of Childish Things, and Other Emblems'. As Showalter emphasises, mentioning Wharton's play on James's title, *The Tragic Muse* (1890), women were beginning to question the role of being the inspiration, or the object of men's investigation, to author their own stories. For many, this entailed deliberate experiment in new plots, new forms. Although in 'Souls Belated' it is the men who lock themselves away to write, it is nevertheless very much also the women's story. In her introduction (xiii), Showalter quotes the claim of 'George Egerton' (Mary Chavelita Dunne, 1859–1945): that women needed to write on the 'one small plot left for her tell: the *terra incognita* of herself, as she knew herself to be, not as man liked to imagine her'. Egerton sought her own modes of expression: 'If I did not know the technical jargon current today of Freud and his psycho-analysts, I did know something of complexes and inhibitions, repressions and the subconscious impulses that determine actions and reactions.' The kind of indirection, allusion and gaps explored by Egerton were also part of Wharton's repertoire, in her own distinctive variants. Wharton did not include 'The Fulness of Life' in her first collection, explaining to her editor that she felt it 'was one long shriek' (and perhaps too revealing about her own marriage). While she hoped that *The Greater Inclination* worked 'in a lower key' (*Letters* 36), 'Souls Belated' is as revealing, as critical and as uncertain. Outside the familiar structures, is there any self to be known?

Such questions, as asked by feminist scholars (see 'Critical reception'), did much to bring Wharton back to readers' attention. In the light of current interests in constructions of masculinity, her work also opens up explorations of male identity (here, as in the doubles of Gannett and Lord Trevenna), again, in ambiguous states of transition: the ineffectual man would be one of her repeated character-types. Gannett's weakness is paralleled in images of the emasculated Trevenna in the thrall of Mrs Cope – 'a blond stripling, trailing after her, head downward, like a reluctant child dragged by his nurse' (*GI* 105); and contrasts with glimpses of Italian men: the courtly man eating garlic, or the porter, patron, priest, secure in traditional roles. Such minor figures, seen almost at the edges of a story, are always important in Wharton. In these years, she was writing the travel essays she collected under the title *Italian Backgrounds* (1905). There she drew attention to the 'real picture' in early Renaissance Italian paintings – in the 'bustling secular life' in the background behind the central figures (*IB* 174, 175).

Although Wharton's first readers regarded her as a realist, more recent critics have become interested in non-realist aspects: interior spaces, myth, fairy tale, the Gothic, the sentimental. Influential studies by Kathy Fedorko and others (see 'Critical reception') have brought such features into prominence within Wharton's most famous 'novels of manners'. Here already, in this story, Wharton uses techniques we find throughout her writings: the sudden, disconcerting simile or allusion; the concentrated visual image; the trailing of sentences away into ellipses. Jean Frantz Blackall highlights Wharton's use of this latter element as a key practice in her punctuation throughout her work: part of her 'awareness of the value of an absence, a pause, a silence, a gap'.[6] Breaking the solid surface, Wharton's careful documentation of social or scenic detail coexists with more resonant, grotesque, or poetic, images. As always, there is a sense that buildings are alive, even 'the inquisitorial façade of the hotel' is staring and watching. The guidebook details of the décor suddenly become backdrops for pantomimic figures – Mrs Cope's looming shadow and her 'great black crescents' of eyebrows (*GI* 108) give her a monstrous witchiness.

As often, Wharton doubles physical spaces, overlaying a civilised scene and a wild one – as in Gannett's notions of Lydia, 'as being swept away by some implacable current' (*GI* 121), or 'walking bare-footed through a stony waste' (*GI* 127). Scattered images throughout the text – Lydia's view of a stone satyr or stagnant fountain, or the 'shimmering blackness' or 'the cloud-muffled hills' reflected in the 'tarnished mirror' of the lake (*GI* 118, 125) – give hints of dream-like landscapes, a *terra incognita*. Even the 'laurustinus' alleys where she walks alone (Wharton, a gardener, was usually botanically precise) lead to darker vistas. Literal travels blur into psychic flight: the couple never reach the suggestive 'Monte Rosa'; and listing the places her outlaws have been wandering (and two years after the publication of Bram Stoker's *Dracula*) Wharton includes Transylvania – in a hint of vampirism, mutual destruction. In this story Gannett's final vision of the lovers takes up the air of fatality; Wharton gives him an obscure but precise image –they are 'bound in a *noyade* of passion' (*GI* 126), execution by drowning.[7] All these techniques pass the effort of interpretation over to the reader; there is no authoritative voice to give us an overview of the narrative development, no definitive insight into character, or any sure conclusion.

Short fictions and beginnings

> She is to-day the most promising figure we have. To-morrow is hers.[8]

Wharton's short fiction gained her critical respect even before she published a novel. The novella was a form which attracted her (as it did many of the best

American writers) with its concentration and force. The four wonderful novellas in this period – the pioneering *Bunner Sisters* (1892; published 1916), *The Touchstone* (1900), *Sanctuary* (1903) and *Madame de Treymes* (1907; first published, *Scribner's Magazine*, 1906) – and her first three story collections alone would have preserved her name. Indeed most works of this first, long phase of Wharton's career would repay the kind of consideration I have given just one story. Readers might trace recurring strands of interest across very different texts and, wherever they look, see Wharton experimenting. Her forms range from the cluster of gnomic emblems in 'The Valley of Childish Things', to (in *The Greater Inclination* alone) the sketch, as in 'A Journey', the play-format ('The Twilight of the God'), to the long stories, almost novellas, of 'The Muse's Tragedy' and 'Souls Belated'. Short stories (she left nearly ninety of them, as well as many fragments) remained important throughout her career, and have attracted serious attention from modern critics. As a sample, in this section I offer a selective overview of her earlier work; other individual stories will feature, in passing, later.

As well as highlighting interests driving the more famous novels, her short fictions offer rich scope for further exploration – for example, on gender, aesthetics or the uncanny. Even a small selection offers a view of Wharton's diversity of subject matter and tonal range, from the surprisingly 'low-life' angle on the city from Mrs Manstey's window in her first published story, 'Mrs Manstey's View' (1891), to steely social comedy. Writers, and struggles over texts, feature in several stories, leading readers into questions about inspiration, artistic compromises, the relations between aesthetic and commercial forces, the private self and the author; or the ethics of appropriating 'real' life or letters for art, or of benefiting from tainted income. These stories range, in their central figures, through writers of sentimental fiction or cheap journalism, to refined and respected poets. 'That Good May Come' (*Scribner's*, 1894), 'April Showers' (*Youth's Companion*, 1900), 'Copy: A Dialogue' (1900; in *CI* 1901), 'The Descent of Man', 'The Quicksand' or 'Expiation' (in *DM* 1904) offer diverse perspectives. Wharton includes self-referential touches. 'Expiation' includes a would-be New Woman-ish writer, and her novel *Fast and Loose* (the title of the fifteen-year-old Wharton's spoof) described in reviewers' jargon: 'A writer who dares to show up the hollowness of social conventions' (*DM* 206). Many stories bring gender into the foreground, for instance in questions about the erasure of women's lives, as inspiration or models, or in the service of the male artist. 'The Muse's Tragedy' (*GI* 1899) and 'The Angel at the Grave' (*CI* 1901) offer particularly complex and thoughtful treatments.

Fictions with visual art forms ('ekphrasis') at the centre bring fresh dimensions to such inquiries; and the dangers of representation, authenticity, connoisseurship and possession (sexual and monetary) come especially into force in these narratives. A story such as 'The House of the Dead Hand' (1898; *Atlantic Monthly*, 1904) concentrates debates about the interpretation of art, its sacred mystery as a 'presence' (resistant to reproduction, even by a sketch) and the role of the collector. This and others, such as 'The Moving Finger' (*CI* 1901), work through elements of the ghost story; others such as 'The Portrait' (*GI* 1899), 'The Rembrandt' (1900; in *CI*), 'The Recovery' (*CI*), the novella *Sanctuary* (1903) or 'The Pot-Boiler' (1904; in *HWW* 1908) examine personal and social relations within a more realist register. However, even in these, there are touches of other modes, as in the hint of the 'speaking picture' trope in the first-person narrative of 'The Portrait'. In this story, as always throughout Wharton's writings, the issue of work, and the differences between the dilettante and the professional, or the fashionable and the uncompromising artist, is a matter for keen attention.

Emotional relations – in the family, with social groups, and between men and women – are a constant focus. We could read many of the stories as studies of masculine identities, from the unbending brute to the sensitive self in crisis. Wharton gives glimpses of the anxieties attending the perceived 'sissification' of men in the 1890s – the dandy, or the angel child of the *Little Lord Fauntleroy* craze, following Frances Hodgson Burnett's best-seller of 1886. The narrator of 'The Pelican' finds his palms itching at the sight of young 'Lancelot', a mother's boy, with 'his black velvet dress and the exasperating length of his yellow curls [. . .] I have since had reason to think that he would prefer to have been called Billy, and to hunt cats with other boys in the block' (*GI* 58). But her view goes further. A spectrum of adult male ways of being appears in the different ambitions of the artistic coterie in 'The Pot-Boiler'; in women's changing images of their lovers and husbands (as in 'The Lamp of Psyche' or *Sanctuary*); in the poses of her occasional first-person narrators (as in 'The Pelican' or 'The Portrait'); or in the fascination of one man for another, in stories where male hero-worship, or the male-to-male gaze, is the most significant: 'I saw myself only with Meriton's eyes [. . .] from that hour to this I've hankered day and night for a chance to set myself right with the man that I meant to be' ('A Coward', *GI* 154). In 'The Eyes' (*TMG*), an uncanny tale of a homoerotic clique, this gaze attains supernatural status. As in Lydia and Gannett's story, Wharton returns repeatedly to images of constraint and traps, of lives dragging out in dead or deadly entanglements. Parents and children form a major strand in narratives of self-effacement, disappointment or exploitation: the sacrificial mothers drawing their lives from their sons in 'The Pelican' (1898; in *GI*) or in *Sanctuary*; or the tirelessly protective daughters and granddaughters of the patriarchs in 'The

Angel at the Grave' or 'The Portrait'. The tone ranges from the humorously treated chronicle of wearied adoptive parents in 'The Mission of Jane' (1902; in *DM*) to the Gothic riddles of a father's hold over his daughter in 'The House of the Dead Hand'. Named 'Sybilla' (the title of the guardian of the ancient Oracle), this story's daughter is unreadable to the narrator, but her tale hints at the unspeakable. Such writings have been read with the shades of biography, against Wharton's relationships with her parents, or with her husband; but these readings must remain largely conjecture.

Wharton is not uniformly bleak – 'The Last Asset' (1904; in *HWW*), for instance, offers a view of a romance unaffected by its roots in social manipulation: it 'was one more testimony to life's indefatigable renewals' (*HWW* 93). For the most part in the fiction, nevertheless, marriage seems at best a socially expedient alliance, or a familiar association; at worst a form of living burial. Wharton's discretion in public comment about Teddy leaves details of her daily married life obscure. But like the woman writer she satirises in 'Expiation', Wharton challenges cosy images of 'the sanctity of the hearth' (*DM* 218). She would often suggest that, as with Kate Orme in the novella *Sanctuary*, marriage is imagined 'as it means to girls brought up in ignorance of life, simply the exquisite prolongation of wooing' (*Sanctuary* 64). Violence sometimes comes close to the surface, as in her Renaissance reconstruction, 'The Duchess at Prayer' (1900; in *CI*), for which Robert Browning's 'My Last Duchess' provides an obvious predecessor; or in the vignettes of the drunken upper-class abuser at the heart of her ghost story 'The Lady's Maid's Bell' (1902; in *DM*). In 'A Journey', the young schoolteacher has to live with the 'helpless tyrannies' (*GI* 28) of her husband's sickness; and, in a disturbingly literal twist, finds herself travelling on a train with his corpse.

More prevalent are the hints of horrors conveyed through figuration and almost casual allusion. Again, in many texts, as in 'The Fulness of Life' and 'Souls Belated', Wharton's similes offer a series of miniature narratives: 'We had seen him sinking under the leaden embrace of her affection like a swimmer in a drowning clutch' ('The Moving Finger', *CI* 153); 'each beat a track about the outskirts of the subject that lay between them like a haunted wood' (*T* 150). Even happy marriages conceal secrets: as Delia, in 'The Lamp of Psyche' (1895), awakens to her husband's past, dodging the Civil War. Shame is often sexual. Beautiful settings mask terrible stories: even the Mount-like estate and silver lake of *Sanctuary* is the scene of an actual drowning. Family secrets hide beneath polite evasions, but emerge in sudden insights:

> *Luckily the scandal was hushed up*: the phrase burned out against the dark background of Kate's misery. That was doubtless what most

people felt – the words represented the consensus of respectable
opinion. The best way of repairing a fault was to hide it: to tear up the
floor and bury the victim at night. Above all, no coroner and no
autopsy!   (*Sanctuary* 59)

Sometimes it is the banal that is terrifying: Mr Mindon's coming to terms
with his faithless wife in 'The Line of Least Resistance' (1900); or, in 'The
Other Two', the 'elastic' ease of the thrice-married Alice, ambiguously
compared by her third husband to ' "an old shoe" – a shoe that too many feet
had worn' (*DM* 98). Tennyson's Lady of Shalott is a pervasive presence in
Wharton's texts, for her narratives of over-protected women, subject to
abrupt enlightenments. In the story's title emblem, women are kept ignorant,
like the little girls of 'The Valley of Childish Things'. So Kate Orme enters her
marriage, 'like some captive brought up in a windowless palace whose painted
walls she takes for the actual world' (*Sanctuary* 22). Others see only too
clearly – as to how, for example, 'The Dilettante' of the title 'just took what he
wanted [. . .] Burnt out the gold and left a heap of cinders' (*DM* 153).

    In terms of setting, again, Wharton's other interests of these years infuse
her fictions. As in 'The Fulness of Life', her theme of household decoration
extends, metaphorically, into her images of domestic interiors, where the
room, the psyche and the house are coextensive. (For an influential study,
see Fryer, Guide to further reading.) Buildings have character ('faces',
frames, bodies) – some quiet and dull, like her evocations of old New York;
others, like the Italian houses of 'The Duchess at Prayer', more extreme –
'The tall windows are like blind eyes, the great door is a shut mouth' (*CI* 1).
Some are bare and empty: 'Some houses are companions in themselves: the
walls, the book-shelves, the very chairs and tables, have the qualities of a
sympathetic mind; but Mrs Vance's interior was as impersonal as the setting
of a classic drama' ('The Portrait', *GI* 144); others cluttered, dark or
ominous. In some, women themselves are the artwork, the drawing-room
ornament (a motif we shall take up shortly with *The House of Mirth*), or, in a
double remove, the subject of its paintings: 'the picture, he said, promised to
be delightfully "in keeping" with the decorations of the ball-room, and the
lady's gown harmonised exquisitely with the window-curtains' ('The Pot-
Boiler', *HWW* 222). At times, such motifs fuse: in 'The Moving Finger', 'the
portrait became like a beautiful mausoleum in which she had been buried
alive' (*CI* 316); in 'The Angel at the Grave', Paulina does not marry, pre-
vented by 'an emanation from the walls of the House, from the bare desk, the
faded portraits, the dozen yellowing tomes that no hand but hers ever lifted
from the shelf' (*CI* 44).

The broader settings of Italy play a major role in Wharton's vision in these years. A Venetian legend inspires her first published poem as an adult writer: 'The Last Giustiniani', where an Italian monk, relieved from his vow, to beget an heir, is transfigured by the sight of his bride: 'the monk's garb shrivelled from my heart, / And left me man to face your womanhood' (*Scribner's Magazine*, October 1889: 406). But as in 'Souls Belated', Italy is the location for failing romances in many later works – including *The Custom of the Country*, *The Glimpses of the Moon* and *The Children*. A failure to appreciate Italy becomes a signifier for other forms of cultural and emotional insensitivity. In 'The Fulness of Life', the wife dreams of a soul mate who would share her soaring rapture in the church of Or San Michele in Florence – where her husband had only sat, hoping not to miss the hotel dinner 'at half-past-six o'clock' (*Scribner's Magazine*, December 1893: 701–2). It is significant that, at the very start of his marriage, Newland Archer, in *The Age of Innocence*, cannot, after all, imagine taking his bride to that country. In Wharton's view, at its snobbish extreme, even locals did not always understand what they were seeing. One of her letters of 1903 exclaims about the 'stupid Italians' who, in their everyday bustle, miss the beauty and tradition of Rome which she absorbs at every pore; she was beginning to think, she related, that it was better to bring a fresh American eye to the country (*Letters* 77). But her effort remains to learn, to see, the essentials. Another American novelist, William Dean Howells, in his earlier travelogues *Venetian Life* (1866) and *Italian Journeys* (1867), had gloried in the 'motley company', gossip and such everyday details as a hotel breakfast in Bologna of 'murky coffee and furry beefsteaks, associated with sleek, greasy, lukewarm fried potatoes' (*Italian Journeys*, ch. 4). Such experiences were paralleled in his novels of the United States in his relish for the medley of democracy – civic ugliness, polyglot population and all. Wharton, however, travelled as an appreciator of the aesthetic and the exclusive.

In her essays for *Scribner's Magazine* (1895–1903, collected as *Italian Backgrounds*, 1905), and in *Italian Villas and their Gardens* (illustrated by Maxfield Parrish, 1904), Wharton sought the aesthetic principles which would underlie other aspects of her work: notions of harmony, appropriateness, the relation of detail to the whole, which expressed what, to one of her sensibility, American culture was missing. Such principles informed her views on gardens, decoration, and the structure and detail of her fiction. She celebrated the most glorious garden scenes in Europe: the 'spell of quiet and serenity which falls on one at the very gateway' of the Villa Medici; the harmony of 'logic and beauty' in the plan of the Gamberaia (*IVG* 89, 47). At Como, she grieved over the way 'the old garden-magic' had been driven out by 'a fury of modern horticulture', where 'pleached alleys', and laurel and myrtle groves had been replaced by 'lawns dotted with palms and banana trees . . . star-shaped beds of begonias and cinerarias'. But, even in this vulgar box of all-sorts, she noticed remnants, and tried to imagine lost wonders: 'a flight of steps wreathed in Banksian roses [. . .] a fern-lined grotto with a stucco Pan or Syrinx' (*IVG* 214). She deplored the disenchantments wrought by 'the knife of "modern improvement"'; and nothing could be less in keeping, in her view, than a mountain slope in north Italy, 'cleared of its natural growth and planted with moribund palms and camellias, to form the "pleasure" grounds of a huge stucco hotel with failure written over every inch of its pretentious façade'. Turning her back on the 'offending' building, Wharton was relieved to find the 'rarest vision of wood and water and happily-blended architecture': 'diviner loveliness' (*IB* 54–5).

Wharton's habits of observation are evident in her earliest surviving travelogue: the journal of her first Mediterranean cruise with Teddy (1888), rediscovered in France, and published over a hundred years later, in a glossy, illustrated edition, as *The Cruise of the Vanadis* (2004). A substantial chronicle, possibly edited some time after the journey,[9] it reveals Wharton, at twenty-six, as an accomplished writer, recording shades of impressions, colouring a scene with her reading. In her first novel, she extended such interest into an imaginative narrative, spinning out her tale from frescoes in a neglected Italian chapel seen through the eyes of a boy: 'The chapel of Pontedorso was indeed as wonderful a storybook as fate ever unrolled before the eyes of a neglected and solitary child' (*TVD* 4). Here scenery opened into historical chronicle; and Wharton supplemented her own impressions with a programme of extensive note-taking and research. Under her 'Plan of Italian XVIII Century Novel', her notebooks list historical characters to be intro-duced and numerous books to consult, from Goldini's *Memoirs and Plays* to *History of the Ducal House of Parma in the 18th Century* to Mrs Pizzi's travels in Italy and Sir Horace Mann's *Letters to Walpole*, edited by Dr Doran. The love-plot is less important to the narrative than Wharton's intensive detailing for the reader the scenes of Italian culture, and her exploration of individuals caught up in historical change (she structures the novel with broad movements: 'The Old Order'; 'The New Light'; 'The Choice'; 'The Reward'). Favourable reviews praised the atmosphere and detail; others suggested that it was more of an essay, with illustrations. But as Wharton herself explained, 'I meant the book to be a picture of a social phase, not of two people's individual history, & Fulvia and Oddo are just little bits of looking-glass in which fragments of the great panorama are reflected' (*Letters* 57).

Her striking phrasing here provides a clue to the methods she would use in her next novels: but, crucially, the 'great panorama' would change. From the Dukes, Marquises and palaces of eighteenth-century Italy, she would turn to the spectacle of the modern United States.

Mapping the modern

> Naturally, first on our lists, this year is The House of Mirth.
>
> (*Vogue*, 1905)

In 1905, *The House of Mirth* seemed to be first on everybody's list. If *The Valley of Decision* had pleased readers as a charming historical tapestry, Wharton's new novel sent society into a spin of discussion, as the mirror of the present moment. To its author's disdain, many readers took it as the equivalent of today's celebrity exclusives, fighting to identify who was who in the real-life Manhattan smart-set. Six weeks after publication, *Vogue* drew comparisons with 'the society page of the Sunday newspaper so eagerly read by nursery maids and servant girls and ladies and gentlemen in the hall-rooms of cheap boarding-houses, and in the provinces' (30 November 1905: 715). (The novel had supplied its own example in Nettie Struther, eagerly watching for Lily's name in the papers.) Others argued over whether the rich were really as vicious and unpleasant as the novel represented them: 'One is not introduced to one charming, pleasant, attractive person in over 400 pages [. . .] as to the title it should be changed to "The House of Lies"' (*NYT* 18 November 1905), declared a correspondent signed 'Newport' in a long-running spat in the *New York Times*. For some, its up-to-the-minuteness went deeper: its author had found a style and a fictional form to capture New York society of the new century. In riposte to 'Newport', 'Lenox' compared the novel with journalistic 'muck-raking' exposés of the financial world: Wharton, as a social insider, was carrying out an important (though 'painful') task: 'to show up things as they exist' (*NYT* 16 December 1905). As an English reviewer expressed it: 'Mrs Wharton knows through and through the extremely modern types which she chooses. She registers to the last degree of delicacy the jumble of crudity and overcivilisation which she finds in New York life today.'[10] In this text and in her distinctive 'problem novel', *The Fruit of the Tree* (1907), which followed it, as in *The Custom of the Country* later, we see Wharton experimenting – engaging, in fiction, with the rapidly changing social vistas of the contemporary USA, and gazing into versions of the 'abyss' which might confront it. These novels, each with a young woman at the centre, go beyond documentary into issues of representation: the reshaping of time, space and civilisation at the start of the twentieth century. *The House of Mirth* is the main focus of attention here; but *The Fruit of the Tree* is recommended to those wishing to read further.

New York and the new money

Taking New York society as her topic seemed an innovation. In a now famous letter to Wharton, after the publication of *The Valley of Decision*, Henry James had exhorted her to be warned by his example, not to fall into 'exile & ignorance', but to keep hold of what she knew – 'the *American Subject*'; above all, to 'DO NEW YORK!'[11] However, she had been trying out ideas for *The House of Mirth* for some time. Her 'Donnée Book' (1900) contains notes for the novel, and she later described her long struggles to bring her ideas into focus. She was aware that fashionable New York 'in all its flatness and futility' provided incomparable material, in which she had been 'steeped since infancy', and could bring to hand without recourse to 'note-books and encyclopaedias' (*ABG* 207). In a later preface, she recalled as one of her 'trumps': 'the fact that New York society in the nineties was a field as yet unexploited by any novelist who had grown up in that little hot-house of traditions and conventions'.[12] As with most best-sellers, her success was also a matter of timing: her novel took up issues already exciting interest, but which had not yet found an artist who could do them justice. At the centre, was the spectacle of the unprecedented fortunes which were transforming society. As Lily Bart tells Selden, in one of the text's key exchanges: 'Money stands for all kinds of things' (*HM* 113) – but the nature of those 'things', and the kind of the culture they were shaping, were urgent questions.

Critics draw attention to an explicatory passage in Wharton's unfinished 'Disintegration' (Beinecke/4.110, 64): a character describes his projected book, a 'blueprint' *Lee* suggests (179) for *The House of Mirth*:

> 'It's to be a study of the new privileged class – a study of the effects of wealth without responsibility. Talk of the socialist peril! That's not where the danger lies. The inherent vice of democracy is the creation of a powerful class of which it can make no use – a kind of Frankenstein monster, and engine of social disintegration. Taine saw it long ago – I'm only preaching from his text. But he merely pointed out the danger: he didn't study its results. The place to study them is here and now – here in this huge breeding-place of inequalities that we call a

republic, where class-distinctions, instead of growing out of the inherent needs of the social organism, are arbitrarily established by a force that works against it! Think of the mass of evidence our society supplies! No laborious researches – no years wasted on the trail of a connecting link. All the species are here, spread out under the immense lens of our social publicity. Why, I'm the finest kind of an example myself: I can take down my own symptoms and note the progress of the disease in my own case.'

He broke off suddenly, seeing his daughter's eyes fixed on him.

Kassanoff argues that, in its fears of social chaos, the rising of the monstrous, this represents 'the more extreme edges of Wharton's conservative critique'.[13] However, the presence of the daughter's eye adds a touch of irony, which suggests a possible distance between Wharton's voice and that of Clephane, the fictional author. Like the hotel in 'Souls Belated', the subject is perhaps broader in Wharton's treatment than in the imagined writer's.

The passage is useful, however, in its presentation of a topical debate. Wharton picks up precisely the note of social commentators, of all political persuasions, who were concerned about what those with fabulous new fortunes would do. The steel magnate Andrew Carnegie, in his famous essay 'Wealth' in the *North American Review* (June 1889), opened with the 'problem of our age': how to administer wealth while retaining the brotherhood of rich and poor. Advocating programmes of public cultural regeneration, he concluded with the 'gospel' that 'The man who dies thus rich dies disgraced.' But discussion continued unabated. While visitors' guides to New York and gossip columns regaled readers with details of ever more novel and luxurious houses, dinners, yachts, private railcars and the excitements of the billionaire lifestyle, conservative social critics (like Wharton's Clephane) drew contrasts with European aristocracy where tradition shaped their taste and social duties. As E. L. Godkin (a political economist and, in Wharton's words, 'masterly editor' (*ABG* 139)) viewed the problem: the newly rich American 'has to decide for himself, what is decided for the European by tradition, by custom, by descent, if not by responsibilities, how to spend his money. The old rich class of Europe may be said to inherit their obligations of every kind.'[14]

A chorus echoed Godkin, deploring the lack of inherited good taste: the kind of extravagance that seemed 'only fancifulness running riot, bringing forth lavish ornament for ornament's sake: making for mere ostentation'.[15] All deplored the growing class divisions of the republic, the gulf between riches and poverty, and the flaunting of wealth by a self-created aristocracy. For the socialist Henry George, these were 'princes of privilege' who rivalled the decadence of the Roman Empire in their indulgence and excess; and Godkin concurred: 'To erect "palatial abodes" is to flaunt in the faces of the poor and the unsuccessful and greedy the most conspicuous possible evidence that the owner not only has enormous amounts of money, but does not know what to do with it.'[16] Reviewed alongside *The House of Mirth*, was David Graham Phillips's *The Reign of Gilt* (New York: James Pott, 1905), which explored the lives of the plutocracy, illustrating its thesis with vignettes of Mr and Mrs Multi-Millionaire: 'On dress she spends about fifty-five thousand dollars a year [. . .] But it is her mode of keeping house and entertaining that makes the thousands and tens of dollars fly' (42–4). Phillips concluded that in a democracy such groups, and particularly the women's 'fashionable "sets"', 'inevitably become a menace as their influence extends over the men and women of superior education or natural endowments who should be the leading exemplars of the American ideal' (257).

We can find a clear description of such forces throughout Wharton's writings. Her personal statements often echo such sentiments: in a letter of 1905, for instance, while playing down her own achievement as a chronicler on the times, she notes: 'Social conditions as they are just now in our new world, where the sudden possession of money has come without inherited obligations, or any traditional sense of solidarity between the classes, is a vast & absorbing field for the novelist, & I wish a great master could arise to deal with it' (*Letters* 99). She would always emphasise retrospectively that her New York had been uninterested in business, in Wall Street or 'the dollar' – that its leisure rested on wealth long established. The impact of the 'robber barons' – those who were making millions out of post-Civil War industrialisation, steel, oil and transport systems (Wharton blamed the western railroads in particular) – brought 'gold-fever' (*ABG* 56) to the city. In Wharton's summary, her own society had been extinguished by the new profit-motive, the onslaught of vast riches and the hitherto alien presence in New York of active men of business. 'It is from that time that New York high society, while parading its uncommon extravagance, lowered itself little by little to the social and intellectual level of the newcomers' ('Memories of Bourget', *UCW* 216). *The House of Mirth* charts the invasion and assimilation in process, as fresh waves of the ' "new people"', as the traditionalist Mrs Peniston thinks of them – the Welly Brys, Gormers, Simon Rosedale, Mrs Hatch – 'rose to the surface with each recurring tide, and were either submerged beneath its rush or landed triumphantly beyond the reach of envious breakers' (*HM* 193).

How, across her range of fictions, Wharton presents that process is a matter of continuing debate. Do her narratives lament lost gentility, celebrate new energies or deplore United States monied society in all its forms? Few would wish to affix a simple label to her work ('conservative' or 'radical'); most now would argue, rather, that such tags are inappropriate. *The House of Mirth*, for example, seems to present a vision far more complex than the elite tones of some of her private comments might suggest. Unlike the political thinkers, she does not advocate particular solutions (for Godkin, building grand public amenities; for George, a tax on owning land). Lily appeals to Selden, 'isn't it possible that, if I had the opportunities of these people, I might make a better use of them?'; but she never has the chance to 'expiate [her] enjoyment' by founding a hospital (Selden's wry suggestion), nor to realise her vague dream of a position of cultural influence (*HM* 113, 54); her sporadic charitable impulses produce a brief glow of self-approval, but she regards Gerty's philanthropic work as dreary. Gerty enthuses about the glamour of the rich ('Do look at Mrs George Dorset's pearls'), but never quite forgets its cost: ' – I suppose the smallest of them would pay the rent of our Girls' Club for a year' (*HM* 213–14). Lily loses in an evening's bridge a sum equivalent to the annual income of many Lower East-side families;[17] and gazes, with an empathetic, and 'envious throb', at the Van Osburgh wedding jewels (a scene which makes her ambitions particularly explicit): 'More completely than any other expression of wealth they symbolized the life she longed to lead, the life of fastidious aloofness and refinement in which every detail should have the finish of a jewel, and the whole form a harmonious setting to her own jewel-like rareness' (*HM* 144).

The social ladder

The Fruit of the Tree would place programmes of social benevolence at the heart of the plot; but, in *The House of Mirth*, Wharton analyses the cross-currents of a society in flux. In a myriad turns of metaphor (from forces of nature to theatrical scene changes, miracle and magic), Wharton captures old New York's complicities and accommodations with new money: the welcome it gave, especially during times of financial panic, to 'any magician powerful enough to turn the shrunken pumpkin back again into the golden coach' (*HM* 194). She can place an entire career in a single sentence, giving us, in one, the origins of the Gryce fortune ('a patent device for excluding fresh air from hotels') and Percy Gryce's progress from provincial mother's boy to Madison Avenue millionaire (*HM* 34–5); and, in another, the less cautious Greiner's meteoric rise, triumph, crash, disgrace and exile (*HM* 194–5). She draws the excesses that seemed, to all visitors to New York, to outstrip the powers of satire – the lavishing of fortunes on the new Fifth

Avenue palaces (the Wellington Brys' marble copy of the Trianon), the Long Island estates (like Mattie Gormer's) or the festal entertainments (the Brys' tableaux vivants staged under their Veronese ceiling). Her writing catches the language of social acceptance or exclusion: the snide hints of the gossip columns (*'Town Talk* was full of her this morning'); the power of a mere ten syllables, delivered in the wealthy Bertha's 'voice of singular distinctness': 'Miss Bart is not going back to the yacht' (*HM* 254, 350). As the numerous etiquette books, aimed at social aspirants, cautioned their readers:

> there is a tyranny in large cities of what is known as the 'fashionable set', formed of people willing to spend money; who make a sort of alliance, offensive and defensive; who can give balls and parties and keep certain people out; who have the place which many covet; who are too much feared and dreaded. If those who desire an introduction to this set strive for it too much, they will be sure to be snubbed; for this circle lives by snubbing.[18]

Wharton marks every level of this social ladder. She notes the weaponry of the rich – the subtle patronage which keeps Lily, Jack Stepney or Ned Silverton clinging precariously to its upper rungs, or the devastating 'cut' in Sherry's, which predicts social extinction. She brings home the force of the warning in social guides: 'The "cut" is given by a continued stare at a person. This can only be justified at all by extraordinary and notoriously bad conduct on the part of the one "cut"', as Walter R. Houghton explained in *Rules of Etiquette & Home Culture; or, What to Do & How to Do it* (1893). Wharton intensifies the attack in the blow of disinheritance, the murky cover-ups and rehabilitations, the vengeances and blackmail that Lily will reject. The narrative traces the manoeuvres of the incomers: Rosedale's efforts to associate with the right people ('to be seen walking down the platform at the crowded afternoon hour in the company of Miss Lily Bart would have been money in his pocket'); Mrs Hatch's hiring her, to achieve 'the right "look" to her hats' (*HM* 23, 443). In a culture which, as outsiders remarked, was distinctive for the power of women as social leaders, Wharton gives prominence to their roles – from the established Judy Trenor to the rising Mrs Bry; and she maps how they demarcate their territory, from the Hudson Estate to the Mediterranean steam-yacht, and guard its thresholds. Above all, she captures the ruthlessness beneath the polite surfaces: sensed 'like the gleam of a knife in the dusk' (*HM* 334). Beyond this, in her brilliant narrative turn, using her two-part structure, she takes Lily into scenes of ever-cheaper imitations: to Mattie Gormer's world, 'a caricature approximating the real thing as the "society play" approaches the manners of the drawing-room'; and, then 'behind the social tapestry', into the untidy 'haze' where Mrs Hatch still floats in a social void (*HM* 376, 446). In a further twist, she seems to shatter the scene altogether. Taking Lily into the milliner's (like Alice through the looking-glass), she reveals the foundations on which the decorative surface depends. As often in this text, she creates a social panorama through a passage of gossip – here, bringing high society back in a 'fragmentary and distorted image [. . .] reflected in the mirror of the working-girls' minds' (*HM* 461).

Locating, and publishing, her novel at the start of the new century, Wharton had already answered her own appeal for 'a great master' to attempt this social scene. Similar demands had been pressing for at least two decades. Although some (now forgotten) authors had made sporadic attempts, their pictures seemed drawn, so one commentator remarked, 'not from life, but from a well-worn and conventional model'. H. C. Bunner (in 1883) challenged writers to make the experiment, 'with a full appreciation of its multiform richness': 'The novelist of New York will find no competition,' he promised ('New York as a Field for Fiction', *Century*, September 1883). Henry James had made an attempt with *Washington Square* (1881); but, although his novel pointed to the accelerated changes, as new financial and commercial forces threatened, its field is narrower than Wharton's. (James published his own modern impressions, *The American Scene* (1907), after Wharton's triumph.) Other still well-known novels of the city, such as William Dean Howells's *A Hazard of New Fortunes* (1890), focused on lower social levels, with central characters from the working middle ranks.

The bottom layer of poverty was the sphere of the Naturalist writer or the social investigator – such as the early photo-journalist, the Danish immigrant Jacob Riis, whose *How the Other Half Lives* (1890) had roused public concern. Viewed from beneath in fiction, the realm of the rich represented heights almost beyond representation – a version of the unassailable New York Thomas Bender has termed the 'City of Ambition', the 'walled city' of Dreiser's *Sister Carrie*. Such perspectives contrasted with the 'City of Making Do [. . .] focused on daily life, on neighborhoods, local streets, and families [. . .] Here the aim is more to prevail than to triumph.'[19] Wharton's extraordinary early fictions, the story 'Mrs Manstey's View' (1891) and her novella *Bunner Sisters* (written 1892, but published 1916), both follow, with care, the 'making do' (and what threatens it) of women living literally in the lower regions of the city: a room, overshadowed by an extension in the former, a shabby basement shop in the latter. The city's darker side is present in 'A Cup of Cold Water' (*GI* 1899), in images of failure and extinction, in a story which spanned the social zones. It is glimpsed, too, in *The House of*

Mirth, in the chatter of the working-girls at the milliner's, and, more benignly, in Nettie Struther's gleaming kitchen – in a brief, magical dream of renewal, before the narrative moves to its bleaker ending. Beyond this, in the novel's imagination, is the 'abyss' – the depths of the city which loom for Lily. Wharton leaves the reader to surmise the peril, but offers hints in Nettie's near extinction, as a 'fallen woman', or the German-American char-woman Mrs Haffen's story of unemployment, desperation and disease – her 'pock-marked face and reddish baldness visible through thin strands of straw-coloured hair' (*HM* 163).

In treating the higher echelons, the complex negotiations between the older upper classes and the rising new money, Wharton produced, in fiction, insights that had much in common with recent radical social theories. The social activist and feminist Charlotte Perkins (Stetson) Gilman had presented the leisure-class woman's angle in the widely read *Women and Economics* (1898); there, she debunked myths of romantic love, to uncover the market forces which drove women to compete for the richest husbands, and of men to fight for the trophy wife. Lily echoes Gilman's awareness both of the economic dimensions of her ambitions, and of the moral degradation of dependency (akin to that of the harem). In pursuing Percy Gryce, she 'must submit to more boredom, must be ready with fresh compliances and adaptabilities, and all on the bare chance that he might ultimately decide to do her the honour of boring her for life' (*HM* 39). Yet she can imagine no role for herself other than as decorating a drawing room, 'diffusing elegance as a flower sheds perfume' (*HM* 161).

The sociologist Thorstein Veblen's *The Theory of the Leisure Class: An Economic Study of Institutions* (1899) had similarly presented woman as the 'chief ornament' – the most important of the status symbols through which the wealthy elite validated their credentials in the eyes of spectators. Com-menting on Veblen's work, William Dean Howells had again pleaded for a novelist, with 'the seeing eye and the thinking mind, not to mention the feeling heart', who could maximise the fictional opportunities of the spectacle of the American leisure class in action ('An Opportunity for American Fiction', *Literature*, 28 April and 5 May 1899). Reviewing *The Greater Inclination* in the same month, a prescient critic observed: 'A writer like Mrs Wharton ought to be able to give us some of those studies of our leisure class which Mr Howells has lately been asking for in the pages of *Literature*. She surely could not have a more fruitful field' (*CR* 14). Wharton details the kind of nuances through which the older money detected and excluded outsiders; and the gradations of 'display': of spending power and 'conspicuous con-sumption', or of the subtler arts of 'conspicuous leisure', through which newcomers established themselves as the 'real thing'. So at Monte Carlo, Selden watches his fellow New Yorkers posing against a European scene, as if part of a tableau: 'a conspicuously conspicuous group' in a show 'staged regardless of expense' (*HM* 295). Percy Gryce's time-consuming collection of expensive and useless Americana is a variant manifestation of conspicuous leisure; Rosedale's quest to acquire, first the showy house, then the exquisite wife, another. His growing sense of taste marks his developing grasp of social niceties; as Van Alstyne observes to Selden, the architectural mish-mash of a house: 'attracts attention, and awes the Western sight-seer. By and bye he'll get out of that phase, and want something that the crowd will pass and the few pause before. Especially if he marries [Lily] my clever cousin – ' (*HM* 258).

Lily Bart

> 'My story? – I don't believe I know it myself.'   (*HM* 363)

As Wharton wrote in *A Backward Glance*, her early difficulties with her theme lay in its complexity, its numerous sub-themes, all crowding for attention. She explains that her moment of illumination was to understand that the artistic interest of a 'frivolous society' lay in what it destroyed: 'its power of debasing people and ideals', in short, 'my heroine, Lily Bart' (*ABG* 207). The focus upon Lily, as society figure and as victim, drew the threads together, adding the intensity of an individual psychological study to the broad cultural analysis of the group. Wharton described the narrative as a 'conversation-piece';[20] and from the first, within the text and among its readers, Lily set people speculating, wondering, talking. *Vogue* reminded its audience (of similarly fashionable pretensions): 'She is a modern product and the tragedy of her life may seem to be trivial to all those who cannot look at life from her point of view' (30 November 1905). But what kind of 'product' is she?

Lily herself indeed may not know. The many mirrors in the text give back different faces, self-images that frighten Lily. Wharton evokes, for instance, the vision of the cracking glaze of a porcelain vase – the 'faint flaws in the smooth curve of her cheek' (*HM* 43) which alarm Lily at Bellomont – or the hideous disfigurement which haunts her imagination after Trenor's attempted rape.[21] We are told that, in her mind, there are 'certain closed doors she did not open' (*HM* 131). Her final setting-straight of her accounts leaves a clean sheet, but no definitive reading. Such uncertainty is a major part of the novel's fascination. It drives the narrative forward, through direct questions, through the testing of different angles and through 'the whirl of metaphor' (*HM* 256) which tries to capture her. And the novel's entire address, in the scrutiny of other characters, and of the narrative eye itself, seems to seek the 'real Lily' whether she is natural or manufactured (is her hair 'ever so slightly brightened by art?'); all surface, or unfathomably deep; precious or dispensable; a rare piece of porcelain or a micro-organism ('the sea-anemone torn from the rock'); innocent or irredeemably smeared; cheap or beyond price (*HM* 218, 6, 486).

Rejecting the privilege of a realist narrative, to give an overview, or to penetrate motive, Wharton never offers any settled answers. The text ends in a silence – while evoking a 'word' which 'made all clear' (*HM* 532). The gap leaves room for interpretation. Even Lily's final actions are ambiguous; and Judy Trenor's exasperated 'All I can say is, Lily, that I can't make you out!' (*HM* 119) reverberates in similar exclamations throughout the text, in the reviews which followed, and in modern rereadings. The kind of experiences which, as in Wharton's life, enrich and develop character – Lily's travels in Europe, her father's sensibility, her contact with books – all fail her. But she has glimmers of apprehension. When she thrills to Theocritus read by moonlight on the Mediterranean cruise, although her love of beauty is untrained and unfocused, the reader would probably not dismiss her as Ned Silverton does: 'Dead as a stone to art and poetry – the light never *was* on sea or land for her' (*HM* 309). Parading his own skill with allusion – here, to William Wordsworth's well-known 'Elegiac Stanzas Suggested by a Picture of Peele Castle' – Silverton is oblivious to Lily's (untutored) aesthetic sensibilities. But, for some readers, Wharton keeps her too much at a distance. As an early reviewer objected: we are 'not allowed to know her with real intimacy, to get behind the scenes' (*CR* 122).

A different thread of Naturalist discourse, and recurrent references to insects, plants, small creatures, suggests that character might be understood as scientific specimen – 'so it is with your rich people – they may not be thinking of money, but they're breathing it all the while; take them into another element and see how they squirm and gasp!' (*HM* 110–11); Lily is sometimes figured as a denizen of a rock-pool, or a 'cog' in a great machine (*HM* 498); even, in a novel full of references to food and rubbish, as a waste product, expelled from the body of the city, like the '*disjecta membra* of bygone dinners', in her final, sinking, neighbourhood (*HM* 474). In a draft, Wharton links Lily herself with a scientific investigator, Georges Cuvier, the pioneer biologist (1769–1832) and student of extinct organisms: '[in studying Gryce] she had the skill of a Cuvier in reconstructing a whole organism from a single bone, & in Mr Gryce's case the feat was not a complicated one' (Beinecke/7.182, 44); and she later frightens Gerty, as 'like some cruel creature experimenting in a laboratory' (*HM* 262).

However, Wharton again prevents readers from adopting the objective stance which was, at an extreme, the project of literary Naturalism. Readers are never allowed to settle into any clinical investigation; but are drawn into empathy, feeling – the sense of pathos and admiration, as evoked, for Lily herself, in the vision of 'a bird's nest built on the edge of a cliff' (*HM* 517). All this confuses judgement. Cutting across this general Darwinian lexicon, too, are other currents: a web of allusiveness to fairy tale, classical myth, poetry (Sleeping Beauty, Beauty and the Beast, Andromeda, the Lady of Shalott); or dream-like landscapes (the white road, the waste land, the rough seas), which place her destiny in more nebulous, timeless realms. Images of darkness, locked rooms, monsters (as critics such as Fedorko or Waid have argued) take us into Gothic interiors and the world of literary doubles. (Can we perhaps understand what Lily might become through what the venomous Bertha Dorset *is*?) The language of art creates a further set of terms for discussion: Lily, with her creative yearnings, is both a failed artist and an artwork. (Her pose as Sir Joshua Reynolds's portrait of Mrs Lloyd in the tableau-vivant scene at the centre of the text brings such discussions into the foreground.) Tracing through any network of association opens up the subtleties and complications of the text.

'A Moment's Ornament'

> She was like some rare flower grown for exhibition, a flower from which every bud had been nipped except the crowning blossom of her beauty.   (*HM* 513)

As one example of how even a single set of images can bring numerous conflicting elements into focus, I shall tease out a few associations which jostle in the frequent references to Lily as a 'highly specialized product' (*HM* 486): a rose, cultivated in a hothouse. While the new season's débutantes were conventionally termed 'buds', and the notion of 'bloom' for a young unmarried woman was a widespread literary and cultural trope,[22] as often Wharton takes up a cliché to create fresh layers of meaning. Her cluster combines economic, biological, cultural, sociological and aesthetic sets of references, as well as the conventional associations of frailty (as conveyed in the ominous shadow and the falling petals of Harrison Fisher's version, Figure 2). All spring up around one of Wharton's similes (the epigraph above). Wharton preserved the idea from her 'Donnée Book': 'She was like one of those bushes that are trained for flower-shows: all the buds had been pinched off but the one specimen-flower – the flower of her beauty', and placed it at the novel's climax, as Lily reviews her past life, reviving the associations of her dresses. The image lingered in her working titles, 'The Year of the Rose' and 'A Moment's Ornament', and in overlapping sets of metaphor – glasshouse, gilded cage, decorative drawing-room centrepiece, the bloom of surfaces (the state of Lily's complexion is a matter of constant fascination), expensive floral displays ('a pyramid of American beauties') and references to what such a product must cost: lilies-of-the-valley at 'two dollars a dozen this season' (*HM* 48–9). Appraising her in the opening chapter, Selden senses 'that she must have cost a great deal to make, that a great many dull and ugly people must, in some mysterious way, have been sacrificed to produce her' (*HM* 7). He later explains to Lily the 'decorative side of life' in terms of what is used up: 'the fish that dyes a purple cloak' (*HM* 112) – a reference to another tiny gastropod, the *Murex* genus, but one which once produced the rich Tyrian purple.

Such images, again, here made most explicit by the novel's nearest approximation to an intellectual, concentrate some elements at the centre of discussions of American wealth and privilege – and of the American woman who was its icon. The 'American beauty' as a new type fascinated travellers, as one possible clue to the nation's character. If she was compounded, as one writer viewed it, 'of all the fairy christening gifts to other nations',[23] then perhaps her loveliness legitimated the society's more worrying tendencies – its money-grabbing and ruthless social Darwinism. Among the commentators was Wharton's friend the French novelist Paul Bourget (1852–1935), who had visited her at Land's End in Newport in 1893 (see *Benstock* 74–6; *Lee* 95–7), while gathering impressions for his own United States travelogue, *Outre-mer* (1895). For Bourget, the American Beauty rose was the 'prototype' of rich Americans' luxury, refinement and excess, which made him long for the wild eglantine: both natural and (as 'we Europeans understand the word') aristocratic. The 'American Beauty': 'has so long a stem, it is so intensely red, so wide open, and so strongly perfumed, that it does not seem like a natural flower. It requires the greenhouse, the exposition, a public display.'[24] Similar notes passed into his description of John Singer Sargent's famous portrait of the Boston collector Isabella Stewart Gardner, which Bourget dubbed 'The American Idol'. In a sweeping paragraph, he listed the national resources that had gone into her making: including land speculations, trains, bridges and cable-cars, elevators and wheat-fields, 'colossal slaughter-houses, – all the formidable traffic of this country of effort and struggle, all its labor, – these are what have made possible this woman, this living orchid, unexpected masterpiece of this civilisation'.[25]

The popular press took up such descriptive dynamics – as in the report that year (1895) of the great Vanderbilt ball at Newport (to which the Whartons were invited): 'In Paris a well-known house had a large force making favors for some time, and away off in China natives had been engaged manufacturing a special lot of Chinese lanterns, all of pure white, for the exterior display' *(NYT* 29 August 1895: 3). That night, 'to the great disappointment to the curious, and to the sensationalists', Consuelo Vanderbilt, in whose honour the ball was given, did not announce her expected engagement to the Duke of Marlborough. But when, later that year, she married him, police held back the crowds, as women and 'camera fiends' fought to glimpse the bride. This transatlantic alliance (in personal terms unhappy) seemed the triumph of American beauty, the summit of American excess. The press could only keep repeating how even the church floral decorations alone 'exhausted the market'. A short extract (from the *Boston Globe*, 7 November 1895) gives a flavour:

> All night long a force of 80 men were employed there. During the night 30,000 white and 47,000 pink roses were delivered at the church in boxes specially constructed for their transportation.
>
> In the immediate vicinity of New York the average daily output of roses is 50,000, but for this occasion the growers were called upon to force their plants and to contribute their whole market supply. This means that the rose market has been exhausted, practically, for several days.
>
> Fifty thousand chrysanthemums were delivered at the church during the night, and about 20,000 lilies of the valley.

The flowers, wrought into a 'symphony' of garlands, torches and ribbons, concealed the base fabric of the building (wood and stone) to create a giant bower; they were, it was said, afterwards distributed to hospitals and public institutions, but florists also exclaimed over their short-lived frailty. It is Consuelo's ascent into the British aristocracy that is often cited as the kind of alliance ('the career of other beauties') Mrs Bart had in mind for Lily, with her face 'as the last asset in their fortunes'; and possibly Lily pictures herself in such a scene – as 'the mystically veiled figure occupying the centre of attention' (*HM* 53, 140).

Was this sheer profligacy or the summit of civilisation? Could such excess be justified? Or – to draw on pictures from *The House of Mirth* – is 'fortunate womanhood', arrayed in 'ever-varied settings' (*HM* 455) worth the price of the sallow, tired women in Mme Regina's workroom: the birds of paradise killed for their creations? Two variants on the central image add to its complexity. One is a much-circulated parable by John D. Rockefeller, which justified the seeming ruthlessness of the new capitalist enterprise and the divisions between those who succeeded and those who fell by the way. His image suggested that the millionaire was the pinnacle of God's plan and of Darwinian evolution. It is quoted here, in 1902, in a general discussion of the divide between rich and poor:

> Mr Rockefeller appeals to both evolution and to divine sanction. 'The growth of a large business', he is reported as declaring in one of his Sunday-school addresses, 'is merely a survival of the fittest.... The American Beauty rose can be produced in the splendor and fragrance which bring cheer to its beholder only by sacrificing the early buds which grow up around it. This is not an evil tendency in business. It is merely the working out of a law of nature and a law of God.'[26]

In May 1905, during the serial run of *The House of Mirth* in *Scribner's Magazine*, a cartoon in the *Literary Digest* contested this image of meritorious sacrifice. Depicted holding his pruning shears, Rockefeller appears as a gardener tending his 'Standard Oil Co' prize rose; small skulls, the nipped buds of his competitors, lie in heaps around its stem.[27]

Rockefeller's parable is picked up again here, by a severe critic of the robber barons, but linked to a European source – the historian Hippolyte Taine:

> 'It is said,' remarks Taine, 'that a hundred thousand roses are required to make an ounce of the unique perfume used by Persian kings; such is this drawing-room, the frail vial of crystal and gold containing the substance of a human vegetation. To fill it a great aristocracy had to be transplanted to a hothouse and become sterile in fruit and flowers, and then in the royal alembic, its pure sap is concentrated into a few drops of aroma. The price is excessive, but only at this price can the most delicate perfumes be manufactured.'
>
> How much this sounds like young Mr Rockefeller's parable, that modern great fortunes are produced like the American Beauty rose – by nipping off most of the surrounding buds.[28]

Taine's theme – the court of Versailles – re-enters *The House of Mirth* in a key moment towards its ending: where Lily learns that she has been Nettie Struthers's salvation. Nettie has named her baby 'Marry Anto'nette', 'after the French queen in that play' – 'the actress reminded me of you' (*HM* 508). Even the most aristocratic and ignorant society lady, perhaps then, justifies her useless life by sending light into dark places.

However, in the wider scope of the text, such layering of images returns us to the question: what kind of product is Lily? One set of readings argues that she is the rare, destroyed by the vulgar. Carol Singley, in a subtle argument, points to her 'Christlike qualities', and the meaning of her suffering within the reader's journey to wisdom.[29] A more general moral approach might suggest that, in the light of the novel's final title (an allusion to Ecclesiastes vii. 4), she emblematises what is destroyed in the house of fools. Viewed from another angle, her story might be read as a critique of the system which created her. In the early 1900s, the problem of idle young ladies featured in editorials: '[we] cannot but be disquieted at the waste of life perpetrated by the leisure-class woman. Freed from the necessity of self-support, she is apparently incapable of substituting any other purposeful and useful labor; so she falls into the way of idly drifting on pleasure's stream' (*Vogue*, 20 September 1900: 178). Advice books, such as Helen Churchill Candee's *How Women May Earn a Living*, covered a whole spectrum of options, including employment using the decorative skills with which Lily credits herself:

> The woman who essays this work should have great taste and ingenuity. On being called in she surveys the drawing-room with a critic's eye, knowing at a glance exactly what changes to make in order to transform an ugly apartment. She hangs rugs, drapes, portières, screens the piano, places lights, and in many ways works magic.[30]

But such books urged readers to think seriously about proper training. Like an earlier penury-stricken gentlewoman, Helen Harkness in William Dean Howells's novel, *A Woman's Reason* (1883), Lily suffers in the marketplace: whether china-painting or trimming hats, even the most refined good taste is no substitute for a professional apprenticeship. Later, twentieth-century critics would analyse Lily in the light of modern feminist theories as, herself, a commodity, a luxury product created to satisfy male needs and fantasies. Again, questions proliferate: Is she the last of a dying species or a lone freak of nature? Even, viewed by Selden among the 'average section of womanhood' at Grand Central Station: 'Was it possible that she belonged to the same race?' (*HM* 6). What kind of grander narratives move through Lily? A Darwinian story about survival of the fittest; a plot about degeneracy (Lily's addictions, or the decline of the city); a parable of consumerism; a tragedy of sacrifice?

Out of the hothouse

> I once heard a charming girl say that she would rather be dead than to have to live in New York without money, and, as shocking as the sentiment may seem, I think, upon reflection, that the girl's views were not altogether reprehensible.   (Editorial, *Vogue*, 8 July 1893)

For some readers, Lily's moral enlightenment, her final honesty, will seem her making – admitting her at last to the 'republic of the spirit', the '*Beyond!*' she could not reach through money. For others, such a conclusion would be wishful thinking: for these, the novel leaves any consolation behind in Nettie's kitchen. However interpreted, the text makes a lasting impact in Wharton's representation of Lily's decline once she is expelled from the hothouse. Lily inherits from her mother a dread of the 'dingy', the 'promiscuous' (that is, the non-exclusive), the poor. Throughout, Wharton presents her recoil from the physical and the ugly. The novel's first part preserves her aloofness, as in the spacious amenities of Bellomont. But Wharton keeps the 'dingy' in view from the start: at the station, and in Lily's skirting around the mess of the cleaning-woman. Ugliness returns to confront her – most notably in the dirty letters retrieved from the waste. In terms anticipating those of modern theorists of the city, Wharton creates a sense of crowding, of unavoidable face-to-face encounters. As Georg Simmel wrote in 'Sociology of the Senses' (1907): 'The modern person is shocked by innumerable things, and innumerable things appear intolerable to their senses which less differentiated, more robust modes of feeling would tolerate without any such reaction.' In registering Lily's sensitivities, Wharton is already carrying out what Simmel sees as a vital sociological project: 'One will no longer be able to consider as unworthy of attention the delicate, invisible threads that are spun from one person to another if one wishes to understand the web of society according to its productive form.'[31] She delineates the material spaces as Lily declines, even, almost, depicting a 'smell-scape' of the metropolis: from the sheltered sphere where labour is invisible, and cooking never smelt in the drawing room, to Lily's boarding house where the odours of the kitchen penetrate everywhere. Seeing allows control (it is crucial to Selden, for example, that he remains one of life's spectators); the trope of contagion, so John Urry reminds us (in 'City Life and the Senses'),[32] was key to the way nineteenth-century upper classes kept the poor unseen and at a distance. But smell, noise and touch invade. Lily is not a jewel, hard and invulnerable, but something more fragile, organic and perishing.

As ever, Wharton's narrative is attuned to the mixed histories within any cultural moment. Lily tries to maintain her poise in a sweep of movement, expressed in the text's references (literal and metaphorical) to rush and hurry, and to modes of transport. Throughout the text, past, present and future jostle for dominance. Lily is a 'modern' woman in her smoking, gambling and desire for independence; she ruins her chances through deviating from nineteenth-century rules of conduct. But she is drawn to old-fashioned graces. Her environment, similarly, jolts her between old and new. It is lit by candle-flames, lamps and electric lights; she uses sealing-wax for her correspondence, but telephone calls and telegrams intervene at key stages of the plot; she envies those parading Fifth Avenue, in 'C-spring barouche', or 'electric victoria'; she flirts on a train, in a light horse-drawn trap and on a steam-yacht; her most dangerous predator owns a motor car (in 1905, a rare and luxury item); her social decline opens her to the noise and roar of city public transport – the constant rattle of the 'elevated'.[33]

For some, this was part of the city's buzz: like the more robust G. Selden, the typewriter salesman of Frances Hodgson Burnett's popular novel *The Shuttle* (1907): 'the roar and rumbling rattle of the trains dashing by on the elevated railroad [. . .] was regarded as a rather cheerful sort of thing'.[34] For the most refined, it was debilitating: their systems (or 'organisations') were, it was believed, too highly tuned to withstand such an assault. Rosedale, like a nineteenth-century 'nerve' doctor, understands instantly that Lily, pale and unwell, needs shelter: 'He glanced at the dirty and unpropitious corner on which they stood, with the shriek of the "elevated" and the tumult of trams and waggons contending hideously in their ears [. . .] A cup of tea in quiet, somewhere out of the noise and ugliness, seemed for the moment the one solace she could bear' (*HM* 466–7). In the closing stages, these currents overwhelm her consciousness, allowing no shelter; in her terrible insomnia, 'every nerve started once more into separate wakefulness. It was as though a great blaze of electric light had been turned on in her head, and her poor little anguished self shrank and cowered in it, without knowing where to take refuge' (*HM* 520). Out of the shelter of the glasshouse, frail, ill-adapted to any role, the ornamental is battered, unstrung, swept away in the rush of the new century.

Industrial designs: The Fruit of the Tree *(1907)*

In his illustrated gift-book *The American Girl* (1906), the popular 'American Beauty' illustrator Howard Chandler Christy (1873–1952) suggested that any serialisation should display a reassuring frontispiece of the final wedding scene. *The House of Mirth*, the most famous serial of the previous year, still, in 1906, topping the best-seller lists as a book, had offered no such comfort. During serialisation, after publication, on adaptation for the stage and with its filming, readers pleaded with its author to let Lily live to marry Lawrence Selden (see *Lewis* 152); but Wharton remained adamant that her heroine could have no such destiny. As William Dean Howells remarked, what the American public wanted was 'a tragedy with a happy ending' (*ABG* 147); a taste which Wharton consistently refused to satisfy.

Readers interested in how Wharton presses her investigations further often turn to *The Custom of the Country* (1913); but they might wish to look first at an earlier novel, which impressed reviewers with her versatility. Less than a month after *The House of Mirth* appeared as a book, Wharton noted in her diary that she had started her new work. Just as the second part of Lily's narrative examined the social scene from a different perspective, again Wharton gave her angle of vision a further turn. Here, she carried the problems of rich and poor, of social obligation and of women's roles into the practical arena of the industrial novel[35] – she took a quick tour round a cotton mill in preparation (*Lewis* 181). With its similarly thoughtful, well-born heroine fallen upon harder times, and her transplantation to a factory colony, Elizabeth Gaskell's *North and South* (1855) offers a helpful comparison. In the American tradition, Herman Melville's dual tale 'The Paradise of Bachelors and The Tartarus of Maids' (1855), the latter part based on his visit to a paper mill in Massachusetts, and Rebecca Harding Davis's *Life in the Iron-Mills* (1861) raise earlier debates about gender and class divisions, the shaping of urban spaces, wasted potential and social ill-treatment.

The text presents nineteenth-century exploitation in a modernising scene: the debilitating diet of the workers (cultural and material), the choking cotton-dust, overcrowded machinery, moribund landscape and housing, devoid of beauty or 'amenities'. In this narrative, Wharton moves out of the metropolis to a New England town, far drearier, if that is possible, than even the dingiest city scenes: 'There is a fortuitous ugliness that has life and hope in it: the ugliness and drive of packed activities: but this out-spread meanness of the suburban working colony [. . .] seemed to Amherst the very negation of life and hope [. . .] "it's dead – stone dead: there isn't a drop of wholesome blood left in it"' (*FT* 22–3). Negated, ill, broken or dying bodies remain at the centre of the text – injured, drugged, paralysed, in pain, and numbed by guilt, mistrust and dead emotions. The countryside provides no countering energies. Although the text contains one of Wharton's most idyllic scenes of pastoral, even that is ruined in memory; and the beautiful country estate fails to sustain any image of a purer form of living.

Wharton's double-stranded narrative of public abuses and reform proceeds through another twofold story of women's lives. She retains her interest in what happens to the idle, leisure-class woman, intensifying her inertia in Bessy Westmore's plot where both body and mind end in literal paralysis. At the same time, she follows an alternative possibility in the woman who turns her hand to practical tasks. She used the name of its heroine, Justine Brent, as her working title, again using the story of a young woman to draw together her interests. The frontispiece, by Alonzo Kimball (Figure 3), gave readers a variant of the final hoped-for pairing: the

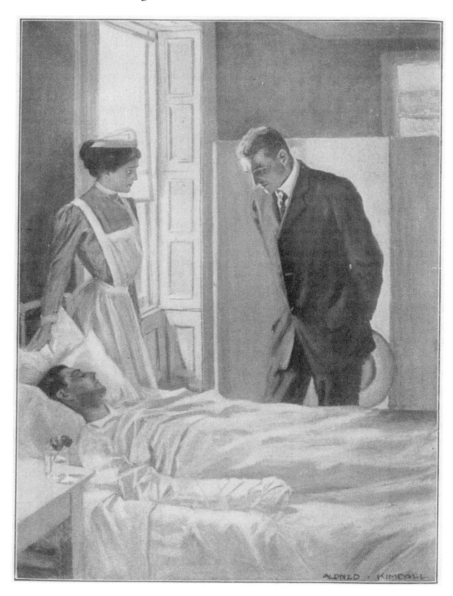

He stood by her in silence, his eyes on the injured man.

Figure 3 Alonzo Kimball, 'He stood by her in silence, his eyes on the injured man'; frontispiece, *The Fruit of the Tree* (1907).

woman is gazing at a tall handsome man, the idealist, Amherst (a romance which blossoms before the end of the novel); but they meet here over the injured body of a hospital patient. Whereas Lily, with her polished pink nails and bracelets, has not cultivated the 'other-regarding sentiments' (*HM* 179), Justine is practical, caring, a trained nurse. Fatally, so it turns out, she attempts to understand, to see into others: 'before I know it I've slipped into their skins' (*FT* 231). She is, as Joslin points out, also a writer, who rescued herself from an early love affair by writing the story of a suicidal heroine.[36] Wharton's own novel also hinges on questions of survival and extinction, of use and value. But here they are focused in dialogues about factory-management, urban design and private probity, and come most acutely into focus in Wharton's 'euthanasia' plot at the heart of the text.

Again, as each phase of the narrative darkens, the text raises the hope of miracle endings. In the concerns about the governance of the factory, torn between the leisure-class New York trustees and the needs of the workers, Amherst wants to denounce an abusive manager; 'to speak out, and yet escape the consequences; by some miraculous reversal of probability to retain his position and yet effect Truscomb's removal' (*FT* 54). The text invokes an alternative resolution of the story, through the sentimental mode, as if one injured man's case might 'prove a beautiful dispensation' (*FT* 19). The narrator's voice refers to hopes of redemption through benevolence, 'a Christmas-chrome vision of lovely woman dispensing coals and blankets' (*FT* 94). But this kind of closure, 'just like the end of a story-book with pretty morals' (*FT* 122), is alien to Wharton's twentieth-century vision. The emotional strands of the text fare no better; again, moral honesty encounters self-interest, doubt and constraint. Shadows and ghosts – of dead love, dead ambitions and dead ideals – seep into the realist text. Should any reader have assumed that Wharton would 'answer' the questions of *The House of Mirth* with a blueprint for more productive ways of living, the text would disappoint them.

Told in summary, at a distance, this might offer images of regeneration: the 'marsh' is drained; 'the dead city [. . .] had risen from its grave, and its blank face had taken on a meaning'; a young girl is 'being taught to follow in her mother's footsteps'; and there is 'the continuance of a beautiful, a sacred tradition. . .' (*FT* 622, 630). There is even a set of plans for new and wonderful social landscapes. But the optimism and pieties of the ending are delusions: a nineteenth-century fantasy of progress. In Wharton's map of the new America, the text ends on a twisted joke, a note of irony; a modern sense of the indefinite, the unfinished.

Culture and consciousness

The years covered in this section (1907–12), among the most turbulent of Wharton's life, produced an astonishing range of writings, which take readers on inward and outer journeys – in her private life, her travels and her fictions. These works experiment structurally and linguistically: in poetry, the novellas, novels and short fictions she intended for her public, and in the secret writings, uncovered in her archives. Writing as she embarked on her affair with Morton Fullerton, and resolving on divorce from Teddy, she pursued her explorations into how to give expression to nebulous emotions, repression, newfound sexual awakening, feelings of jealousy and betrayal. At the same time, she was contemplating a different kind of separation; The Mount, where she had found peace to write, was sold, and she parted from the United States, to settle finally in France. 'French Ways and their Meaning', to borrow one of her titles, become ever more significant in her works of these years, directly, or as a standard of comparison. She contemplated its architecture, literary associations and landscapes in *A Motor-Flight through France* (1908); its marriage conventions and family institutions in the American/French collisions in her novella *Madame de Treymes* (1907) and in her drafts for *The Custom of the Country* (1913); and used its poetics of place to convey sexual undercurrents in *The Reef* (1912). Paris and old country houses and estates are key settings in all these. Even *Ethan Frome* (1911), though drawing on Wharton's glimpses of isolated New England hill-farms during her motor excursions from The Mount, began as an exercise written in French for her Paris tutor, when polishing her grasp of the language.[37] Presenting these dramas of individuals, she reflected on and analysed the way different cultures and histories shape consciousness and feeling; she pressed further, in the locations of her fictions and in her travel-writings, into questions about perception, artistic sensibility, the scope for civilised forms of living.

'The Life Apart': letters and love diary

> 'A woman shouldn't write such letters if she doesn't mean them to be published . . .'   (*T* 71)

The novella *The Touchstone* (1900) turns on a kind of betrayal – the dilemmas raised by the legacy of a famous woman novelist's love letters; their success on publication; and the ensuing shadows over a marriage which their sale has funded. Edith Wharton's own life-writing, the extraordinary love diary ('L'âme close' – 'The Life Apart', 1907–8), and the stream of letters and poems she addressed to Morton Fullerton, face readers with the kind of dilemmas and textual uncertainties that confront many of her characters. The motif of private letters, widespread in turn-of-the-century fictions, raises problems about aesthetics and art: the identity of the writer; the relative authority of personal expression and the formal work. An intimate correspondence, particularly, can prompt feelings of voyeurism in the reader, and lead to uncomfortable issues of ethics: are the moral obligations of the critic due to the writer? Or to scholarship? Who 'owns' the letters? Fullerton himself was at the centre of various disputes about returning or keeping love letters, and he refused to return Wharton's (*Benstock* 198–201). Letters rouse new emotional entanglements in Henry James's *The Aspern Papers* (1888); drive a husband to suicide in Kate Chopin's 'Her Letters' (published in *Vogue* in 1895); and, revealing a dead writer's love affair in Alice Brown's 'The Discovery' (*Vanishing Points*, 1913), are burned by his literary biographers. Candace Waid in *Edith Wharton's Letters from the Underworld* (1991) traces the motif through Wharton's entire career; and even a small selection of her short fiction suggests the power Wharton found in this theme. A plot of a woman's private letters is also crucial to *The House of Mirth*. Letters exercise their sway from a distance, surviving their authors, outlasting relationships; in Wharton's late ghost story 'Pomegranate Seed' (1931) they seem to arrive, even, from beyond the grave. Ex-lovers spar over their own letters in the dialogue-story 'Copy' (1900); and epigrams give way to silence, as they 'burn the key to our garden' (*CI* 118). Worse, perhaps, than letters read by others, are those the recipient leaves unopened, as in 'The Letters' (*TMG* 1910); but even these can deliver unexpected messages.

In the writings addressed to Fullerton, or in those probably inspired by him, Wharton speaks in a voice that, not surprisingly, strikes most readers, first, with its rush of feeling, its vulnerability. Even in her most shaped and public utterances, the sonnet sequence 'The Mortal Lease' in *Artemis to Actaeon* (*Scribner's*, 1909: 37–43), she struggles to contain 'the primal flood' (I, line 2) and 'lovers' thirst' (III, line 2) within the formalities of the sonnet; and objectifies her experience in the personae of mythological and classical figures. The intimate 'Terminus', a poem she wrote for Fullerton after a passionate night in Suite 92 at the Charing Cross Station Hotel, sought a freer line, a sweeping form, celebrating their love within 'the human unceasing current' of other similar lovers. These currents flow through her private writings. In her forties, Wharton pours out the reproaches, hints, appeals and retractions of a first love affair, where the other partner controls the terms of the relationship. Even with no knowledge of her sensitivity and intelligence, or of Fullerton's evasiveness, her letters would be distressing, with their exclamations of joy, dashed down by disappointment. She tunes words to a high pitch, but jolts from questions back to accusation, frequently fearing that she has lost her command of language. 'Are you coming to dine tonight? And am I not wrong in asking you, when I know how stupid, disappointing, altogether "impossible" you found me yesterday? – Alas, the long isolation has made me inarticulate [. . .] And then yesterday morning I was *paralyzed* by not getting your note till 11' (*Letters* 176). While written at haste, however, even such letters display rhetorical craft – attempts, using her writer's tools, to make herself into someone whom the lover will continue to notice; and self-laceration, as she realises, at the same time, he loathes a woman who makes a 'scene'.

Her love diary, again, prompts questions about whether language can ever be entirely 'private'. Any diary posits an implied reader – perhaps some hypothetical witness, or possibly the writer, divided between the present self experiencing the crisis, and the unknown future self who will emerge to read it. The account helps to preserve identity in peril of erasure. Wharton's diary is full of images of a self in fragments, crumbling to ash; or, as in her fictions, seen as an imprisoned soul (the 'âme close' of the title), or as empty rooms full of cobwebs. As in her stories, fears and emotions seem to take on their own separate existence ('a veiled figure stole up & looked at me a moment. Was its name Happiness? I dare not lift the veil. . .'). Do her words celebrate the flow of passion and eroticism (the 'indescribable current of communication'); or does the diarist write to defend and enclose herself in a journey with no known destiny? In such contexts, chronology too falls to pieces. Wharton marks the details of time and place; but the lovers' time plays against the everyday calendar. Fullerton fills the 'dear half-hour', even the moment, more richly than she has ever known; but he spoils it: 'you broke the glass & spilled the drops'. She anticipates feeling 'as other women do'; but records happiness as it vanishes – as if the ending is already in view. There are silences between the entries, and the horror of 'the blankness, the intolerableness of the morrow'.[38]

In terms of audience, the diary presents further levels of complexity, through being addressed, in imagination, to Fullerton. Even in this space, he is dominant; quotations bring his voice into Wharton's pages. When she eventually showed it to him, he wrote in it (on a page which was then ripped out). The diary's material nature seems pertinent – the pressed flower in its pages, as its first editors observed, perhaps replaces words, as a code for 'the unspoken first consummation',[39] or for the life of touch, of the body. No single language or set of terms is adequate. Wharton uses allusion, snatches of French, passages of her own verse, along with specific associations –

evocations of the weather, their excursions around Paris and The Mount, French place names – to capture passion and suffering, to get beyond a commonplace register. The ecstasy of release, followed by recapture, reining in, seems the dynamic of torture – but in these writings, Wharton also represents it as her share in 'the wine of life', against the fear of the 'great blank behind'.

Similar emotional structures and phrases enter her fictions. In the painful story 'The Pretext' (1908), for instance, the middle-aged wife of a pompous professor believes, for a while, that an attractive young English aristocrat is in love with her. The text dwells upon the marks of time on her face and body, and on sequences where Mrs Ransom tries to see herself in a mirror, as if through another's eyes: 'It was a face which had grown middle-aged while it waited for the joys of youth' (*HWW* 130). There is the shock of breaking deep-held habits of thought – 'From childhood she had been taught to "collect herself" – ', and the shattering into new 'uncharted' sensations: 'little winged and scattered bits of self were dancing madly down the vagrant winds of fancy' (*HWW* 131–2). There is the self-constructed narrative of 'secret pilgrimages' to significant sites in their companionship; the fears of ending, in almost the words of the love diary ('She had the distinct sensations that her hour – her one hour – was over'); the sense of nullity, 'She wondered if any other woman had lived to whom *nothing had ever happened*' (*HWW* 152–7); and, the terror of the diary, the point where narrative seems to end: the 'aching vision of the length of the years that stretched before her' (*HWW* 172). Again, ellipses throughout the text invite the reader to imagine even deeper fears.

Great perspectives of feeling: Ethan Frome *(1911) and* The Reef *(1912)*

> She had forgotten how Darrow had widened her world and lengthened out all her perspectives, and with a pang of double destitution she saw herself alone among her shrunken thoughts.   (*R* 337)

This evocation of long vistas, or 'great perspectives of feeling' as *The Reef* expresses it (*R* 40), visions of the buried life and of lost chances, interest Wharton again in her next major works. Readers have found these, in different ways, among the most painful of her fictions, and *Ethan Frome*, in particular, unforgivably so. While *The Reef* delays its disclosures, readers often anticipate its next turns and surprises. Any reader of this *Introduction* who has not already read *Ethan Frome*, however, is urged to do so now, before continuing. It is a novella, of gathering intensity, and repays being read in a single sitting. Wharton regretted that Henry James encountered it first in serial form; he, nevertheless, admired its 'beautiful artful *kept-downness*, & yet effective cumulation'.[40] Writing these stories, Wharton was in command. Unlike the unfolding, minute-by-minute crises of a love affair in life, in fiction she had authority over form and language to express the chaos of passion, jealousy and despair. She later pinpointed the writing of *Ethan Frome* as the true end of her apprenticeship, when she 'felt the artisan's full control of his implements' (*ABG* 209).

Wharton sets her tales in contrasting geographical and social worlds. *Ethan Frome* moves into the remote rural Massachusetts hinterland Wharton saw, as a tourist, beyond the bounds of her own beautiful estate at The Mount (see Figure 1). Her imaginary Starkfield is a spot where cultivation seems to have exhausted its chances: worn-out land, a declined logging-industry, a farm bypassed by the railroad – 'That Frome farm was always 'bout as bare's as a milkpan when the cat's been round' (*EF* 14). Trying to look in close-up at poverty, she presented her riposte to what she saw as the 'rose-and-lavender' (*ABG* 294) fiction of her 'regionalist' contemporaries, Sarah Orne Jewett (1849–1909) and Mary E. Wilkins Freeman (1852–1930).[41] (Whatever Wharton thought, Jewett's story-cycle *The Country of the Pointed Firs* (1896) and Freeman's collection *A New England Nun and Other Stories* (1891) are now regarded as among the most poised and subtle of American turn-of-the-century writings, and reward reading alongside Wharton's texts.) *The Reef* is typically viewed as her most 'Jamesian' novel: not only for its stylistic manner, but in its settings – the sense of 'the unrolling of a vast tapestry' in Paris; the slow, densely layered atmosphere of the château at Givré. Here civilisation – the portraits, courtyards, statues, garden-borders, even peacocks – seems, visually, at its richest. Nevertheless, the texts have more in common than these descriptions would suggest, and so will be discussed together.

Ethan Frome and *The Reef* are two of Wharton's most elliptical fictions, teasing the reader, but encouraging interpretative participation. Structure is key to her effects. Writing later, in her 1922 preface to *Ethan Frome* (see *UCW* 259–61), Wharton attributed her method to 'La Grande Bretèche' (1832), a tale by Honoré de Balzac (1799–1850), and to Robert Browning's long poem 'The Ring and the Book': events relayed, she said, 'in fractions' (*WF* 92), from different observers' perspectives. In *The Reef*, she distributes the narrative between different characters' viewpoints, over five main divisions; in *Ethan Frome*, she plunges from the present (around the early 1900s) into the past (the late 1870s or 1880s), embedding young Ethan's story in the frame of the anonymous observer's first-person narrative. These fractures create spaces into which she invites the reader to speculate about the angle of vision, and to picture other possible versions. In planning *Ethan Frome*, she insisted on marking the transitions with a major visual break – the dramatically extended sets of ellipses at the thresholds of Ethan's section. Like a reader of one of her own fictions, its narrator tells us, 'I had the sense that the deeper meaning of the story was in the gaps' (*EF* 7).

As to what we look for in, or draw out of, the gaps in either text, there are potentially as many different stories as there are readers; and, to any single approach, many possible facets. One set of readings might concentrate on literary reworkings: many contemporary reviews viewed *Ethan Frome* as Greek tragedy; Henry James praised *The Reef* as a drama in the lineage of Racine; Keats features prominently in Killoran's reading of the latter and Lee's of the former.[42] Another might open up imperialist or post-colonial perspectives, looking at both global and regional contexts. *The Reef* is a novel full of American expatriates (some comically extreme), discussion of American 'types' and the preservation of national values, within French culture. With the States' annexation of Puerto Rico, Hawaii and the Philippines in the Spanish war of recent memory (1898), Wharton allows us to place the interpersonal power-struggles on a larger canvas by making Darrow a diplomat, shortly bound for South America. *Ethan Frome* taxed Wharton with problems about the angle of vision, about how (some readers might ask 'if at all'), as a privileged, educated, urban outsider, she might represent a regional culture. How could she avoid patronising or romanti-cising its inhabitants, as 'timeless' figures, or culturally exotic 'others'? (She remained defensive about her position in all her commentaries on her book.) Discussion will return to this general question with *Summer*. Here, I shall look at these texts simply through one topic, considering various aspects which might appear as a reader turns the lens.

Sexuality is at the forefront of many readings, sometimes with bio-graphical inflections. Lewis, for example, took the triangle of *Ethan Frome* as a transposed rendering of Wharton's own fears of being chained for life to Teddy (*Lewis* 309); Wolff points out Wharton's private reference in setting the scene of Darrow and Sophy's illicit passion in another 'Terminus Hotel'.[43] Here, more generally, Wharton seeks to represent in fiction experiences which, in her upbringing, and in the decorous literary estab-lishment, were unacknowledged and unexpressed. Musing on the prospects for art, in his essay 'The Future of the Novel' (1899), Henry James had wondered delicately whether it would be a woman who might bring to light the 'immense omission' ('the great relation between men and women, the constant world-renewal'): to see the woman's elbow, wielding the pen, to 'smash with final resonance the window all this time most superstitiously closed'.

Some readers might linger on Wharton's narrative methods, visual or temporal. Taking the former, we might consider the way she frames (even freezes) the action in tableaux, which emerge in many readers' accounts as among the most memorable scenes. Examples include the repeated pictures in *Ethan Frome* of women framed in the kitchen doorway – first Zeena, a grotesque, angular figure, viewed 'with the intense precision of the last dream before waking' (*EF* 58); then, Mattie 'just as Zeena had stood, a lifted lamp in her hand [. . .] striking upward, it threw a lustrous fleck on her lips' (*EF* 87–8). However, such scenes also direct the vision, through other characters' focus. Presenting dramas of desire from continually shifting angles, Wharton engages readers in the perspectives of the characters, watching each other, guessing and reappraising. A charming young working 'girl' draws the eyes of the central male characters away from his actual or intended partner. Wharton delineates each of these figures – Mattie Silver in *Ethan Frome*, Sophy Viner in *The Reef* – as fluid, mercurial, a creature of nature, or something sparkling, rendered in small touches of colour: Mattie's 'cherry-coloured "fascinator"' (*EF* 32), Sophy's pink cloak (*R* 114). All 'shimmer', Sophy confounds easy labelling: she might be 'any one of a dozen types' or 'a shifting and uncrystallized mixture' of them all (*R* 34, 60). Neither is given an individual narrative section or point of view, but, in the eyes of their male admirers, they emerge vividly against the drab or, in *The Reef*, paler tints of a sexually unfulfilled, largely housebound, older woman. (Though very different characters, in the French draft of *Ethan Frome* Zeena was called Anna: the name of her structural counterpart in the rivalries of *The Reef*.) Ammons plots the contrasts onto fairy tale, reading Mattie and her older cousin Zenobia (*EF*) as Snow-White and the witch.[44] In no less powerful form, Sophy and Anna (also a kind of stepmother) face each other in a younger/older-woman rivalry, within a series of complex erotic triangles. The agitation, self-devouring envy and venom of the older woman takes almost tangible form in each, represented in a figurative web of shadows and dark forms, with undercurrents of the Gothic or ghostly.[45] Searchable, electronic first editions now enable us to dip into Wharton's lexicon to demonstrate the small repetitions through which she creates her impressions: for example, in *The Reef*, 'blur', 'dim' or 'dark', or the more tangible 'dimness', 'darkness' or 'shadow(y)' (readers will find others equally revealing).

Some readers might emphasise setting. We could look at Wharton's construction of locale as erotic trope, expressed in recurring painterly images. In *Ethan Frome*, details of the cold have the nuances of American winter-genre painters: for example, John Henry Twachtman (1853–1902) or Ernest Lawson (1873–1939), of whose school Nat Fulmer in *The Glimpses of the Moon* is a follower. The snow, in *Ethan Frome*, is treated with naturalistic detail, but it also serves as blank canvas or stage-flat on which to project the utter deadness of the Fromes' marriage. In mythic or spiritual extensions, critics read their starved apple trees and withered cucumber vine (*EF* 21, 56) as the blight of all fertility.[46] In Mattie's vibrant presence, landscape radiates brilliant colours, scintillates with light, spinning off into simile: 'Her wonder and his laughter ran together like spring rills in a thaw' (*EF* 49). In her 1922 preface, Wharton described her figures as her '*granite outcroppings*' (*UCW* 259), a theme taken up by the narrator (a modern engineer) who views Ethan and his surroundings as one: 'a part of the mute melancholy land-scape, an incarnation of its frozen woe' (*EF* 15). *The Reef* shimmers with the effects of other, European, impressionists.[47] In the effects here, all its uncertainties, veiled hopes and half-truths seem to emanate into the atmosphere of Givré. Nothing is definite in this text, nobody can be sure of what they are seeing: 'The muffled sunlight gleamed like gold tissue through grey gauze, and the beech alleys tapered away to a blue haze blent of sky and forest. It was one of those elusive days when the familiar forms of things seem about to dissolve in a prismatic shimmer' (*R* 168).

Such narrative strategies capture the phenomenology of fascination, implicating the reader as admirer and voyeur. With the watching, come the inevitable 'little things . . . little signs' (*R* 271), written in the eyes, the face and body. When Ethan cranes at the church window to peep in at Mattie in the dance, Wharton brings out anticipation – the colour, movement and light – in a displaced eroticism, as Ethan's heart beats at the sight of Mattie's ecstasy, her lowered eyelids, her dancing partner's possessive gaze. In *The Reef* such moments are soon over – and, in any case, contain their opposite. There can be few scenes in her texts as sordid as Darrow's sight 'under his lowered eyelids' of 'the precise photographic picture' of the adjoining hotel room where he has spent ten days with Sophy; nor a stronger image of misogynistic distaste. Here, Wharton shows the end of fascination, as Darrow projects his revulsion at the young woman he has tired of onto the hotel room (its blotched marble chest of drawers, its cheap 'electrolier'); it (or she) now strikes him as the 'makeshift setting of innumerable transient collocations'; soaks into him 'like an ugly indelible blot' (*R* 73, 74). By extension, in such a vision, all women emerge as objects of male fantasy: whether sacred trust (Anna); wood-nymph (Sophy and Mattie); or demon (Zeena). Such fantasies are contaminating – by the end, even Anna demands to know everything, to be helped to see it.

As desire and disgust, admiration and voyeurism emerge as intertangled categories, so readers might wish to look further at Wharton's representations of sexual feeling. The narratives, together, present a spectrum of response from frigidity to the 'rage of possessorship' (*R* 88); or, as one critic views *Ethan Frome*, even sex-addiction.[48] As the image 'The Reef' suggests, landscapes are also seascapes, with hidden obstructions on which journeys founder. Beneath the emotions and sensitivities, Wharton hints at a level of sheer passion, of contesting sexual energies, which breaks down conscious intention: 'a startled sense of hidden powers, of a chaos of attractions and repulsions far beneath the ordered surfaces of intercourse' (*R* 353). As many critics note, in both texts, scenes and characters are repeated. Parallel scenes add to the effect that the rivals are competing for a single space – the role of the lover. At this submerged level, there lurks, perhaps, the appalling thought that lovers might be interchangeable. Darrow is a serial philanderer, who 'had had a fairly varied experience of feminine types' (*R* 25); but even in the novel's most intense and serious relationships, characters start to blur. At their most perfect moment, together in the farmhouse kitchen, Ethan sees Zeena's face in Mattie; Anna recognises that she is retreading Sophy's steps (and wondering how she compares); and, in another sudden 'spectral projection', she sees Darrow's 'figure [. . .] suddenly displaced by that of her husband' (*R* 107). These structures of compulsion, as Wharton understood, locked characters into repeated cycles of suffering. Her insights parallel those of Freud, who was interested in such structures' implications for therapy. As he would express it, in his own contemporary study of repetition, 'Remembering, Repeating, and Working Through' (1914): a subject does not recall anything of what he has forgotten, but 'acts it out'.

Such patterns shape the mind and body. In *Ethan Frome*, some critics have seen an extreme case-study of the 'hysteric' – a pathology of sexual thwarting – in Zeena's unnamed female ailments. As Showalter suggests, Wharton hints at an unconsummated marriage in the loaded symbol of the unused wedding gift – the red glass pickle dish hidden on the top-shelf of the china closet.[49] *The Reef* is explicit about Anna's distance from 'living', her 'ladylike repression' in youth, her disastrous marriage (to a refined man, with a kiss 'like a cold smooth pebble' (*R* 86, 91) and a kind of virginity that survives even the birth of her child. Wharton's angle on these locked-up characters varies. She keeps Zeena at a distance – the oppressor and the enemy; but she gives room for sharp reversals of sympathy. Even readers who view Ethan's wife as the embodiment of the monstrous might pause at her monosyllabic lament over the smashed pickle dish: 'now you've took from me the one I cared for most of all – ' (*EF* 138). *The Reef* places us within Anna's feelings for considerable stretches of the narrative, involving readers in her sufferings, past and present. In her desperation with Darrow, 'the vision of old miseries flocked like hungry ghosts about her fresh pain: she recalled her youthful disappointment, the failure of her marriage, the wasted years that followed; but those were negative sorrows, denials and postponements of life'; awakened, she suffers, instead, 'as a hurt animal must, blindly, furiously' (*R* 287). Within her viewpoint, we might almost be reading a description of Wharton's letters: 'Then, on the next wave of feeling, came the desire to confront him at once and wring from him she knew not what: avowal, denial, justification, anything that should open some channel of escape to the floor of her pent-up anguish' (*R* 287). But in both texts, once the treasured object is ruined, there seems no possible reparation: as Ethan searches for glue, so Darrow argues to Anna – 'Life's just a perpetual piecing together of broken bits' (*R* 315) – in futile, self-serving justification.

Some might wish to take such sympathy further, looking as Showalter does, in relation to *Ethan Frome*, at the social within the dimension of the sexual. Anna's history anticipates critiques in *The Age of Innocence* of the construction of the upper-class woman, the 'deadening process of forming a "lady"': 'The freshness he had marvelled at was like the unnatural whiteness of flowers forced in the dark' (*R* 28). As many of Anna's worries centre on her daughter Effie's future, so both Sophy and Mattie (like Charity, in *Summer*) continue Wharton's anxious examination of the meagreness of women's education and the narrowness of their lives. Between them, they encompass most of the options for ill-trained young women at the turn of the century. Sophy's 'career' of nursery-nurse, companion, social-secretary, governess, dreams of the stage, is precarious, improvised (she keeps a lesson ahead with Effie's Latin), and as random as 'a turn of the kaleidoscope' (*R* 24). Mattie's office-work and months in a department-store break down her health. Along with Zeena's nursing, their histories present a dreary catalogue, and the future seems still darker. Wharton leaves it to the reader to imagine the fate of younger women expelled from the domestic sphere; and, without a dowry, marriage promises no more security. One of Sophy's offers came from a drunk, another from an old widower, who, we assume, wants a cheap housekeeper (*R* 61). Within the home where Ethan has married Zeena for a similar reason, Wharton presents a vision of endemic suffering. Tied to uncommunicative men, women fall silent, begin 'turning "queer"', as Ethan expresses it. Within a region of 'lonely farm-houses [. . .] where stricken creatures pined' (*EF* 78), generalising Zeena's history alters the focus. So Fryer prompts us to envisage, in the novella, the wife's tragedy: 'imprisoned on an isolated farm, with only the taciturn and inarticulate Ethan for company';[50]

an invitation Elizabeth Cooke takes up in her reworking, *Zeena* (1996), as a novel.

However, as often, Wharton complicates the gender dynamics. In the force-fields of desire, as René Girard suggests, the bonds between rivals can be the most compelling. In the charged atmosphere of these texts, Wharton registers perhaps equally intense currents of fascination passing between male characters. As with her short fiction, readers interested in explorations of different models of masculinity, the recasting of conventional male/female plots in terms of male doubles, or queer studies, will find rich material here.[51] In *The Reef*, Darrow encounters Owen as both potential stepson and as sexual challenger. With barely concealed scorn, the older man of the world damns the young as asexual: 'Owen marry? Why, he always seems like a faun in flannels!' (*R* 118); but in the shifting geometries of alliances, the two men become powerful antagonists. Owen obsessively watches as Darrow tries to outwit him, reproducing and reading what he has seen, like a detective's climactic summary (*R* 245–8):

> 'How do you know? You could hardly hear them from the garden!'
>   'No; but I could see. *He* was sitting at my desk, with his face in his hands. *She* was standing in the window, looking away from him . . .'
>
> (*R* 247)

In *Ethan Frome*, the young engineer is intrigued by the damaged figure of the older farmer: 'thinking how gallantly his lean brown head, with its shock of light hair, must have sat on his strong shoulders before they were bent out of shape' (*EF* 6). As his narration proceeds, he sees in him a kind of archaic purity and power lacking in the softer modern age: 'his brown seamed profile, under the helmet-like peak of the cap, relieved against the banks of snow like the bronze image of a hero' (*EF* 15). In a challenging Freudian reading, Wolff extends the engineer's projection to the entire narrative, suggesting that the text is the narrator's story: that his 'vision' (*EF* 27) of *Ethan Frome* is a fantasy, generated out of his own chilling 'private nightmare'[52] of winter, impotence, defeat and death. Now, in the more general light of recent disability studies, and given the spectrum of bodily representations in the text, readers might wonder what such fascination implies. Why does Wharton return in her works to images of mangled hands, or spines, broken or diseased: Dillon and Bessy in *The Fruit of the Tree*, Ethan and Mattie, or the two tiny withered dwarfs, concealed for years, in her later short story 'The Young Gentlemen' (1926)? What does it mean that Zeena recovers strength out of the others' wreck? How significant are such images?

Returning at last to Wharton's temporal strategies, some readers will find the narratives' most powerful effects in the blockages and interruptions. Structurally, each text frustrates movement towards full understanding; a dynamic underlined in allusions to what might have been, but never came to fruition. *The Reef* turns on a motif of delay from its first page; it leads back to earlier losses: Darrow and Anna's early love affair seemed 'the fluttering apart of two seed-vessels on a wave of summer air' (*R* 29); Darrow feels that Effie might have been their child. In the narrative present, there is a kind of consummation, but no therapeutic release:

> The truth had come to light by the force of its irresistible pressure [. . .]
> She looked back with melancholy derision on her old conception of
> life, as a kind of well-lit and well-policed suburb to dark places one
> need never know about. Here they were, these dark places, in her own
> bosom, and henceforth she would always have to traverse them to
> reach the beings she loved best!   (*R* 353)

Characters are condemned, in an echo of Joseph Conrad's novella of 1902, to the 'heart of darkness', to sharing '*the horror*' (*R* 270).

Ethan Frome is full of potential happy-endings, roads not taken: Ethan's educational ambitions, his trip to Florida, flight west with Mattie, vision of a golden-haired child. These coexist with images of powerlessness, things not working. Electricity, for instance, supplies a network of signification, from the strike at the power-house which keeps the narrator in Starkfield for the winter, to Zeena's electric battery 'of which she had never been able to learn the use' (*EF* 68). (The 'Electropoise', Figure 4, suggests the galvanising energies 'Electrolibration' promised.) The 1993 film placed sexual contact, 'action', into the silences of the text, its director, John Madden, claiming that nowadays people expected: 'to say what they feel', as well as 'to screw who they like, to shoot who they like'.[53] But the text draws its most shocking effects from frustrated consummation: the fatal sledding ride offers images of fulfilment, love-in-death, release and catharsis – satisfactions which the final revelation refuses. (The fate of the lovers – 'young and charming and full of grace', lying dead together, with 'ineffable content' – in Willa Cather's *O Pioneers!* of 1913 might be read in contrast; even as a partial rewriting.)

Wharton offers no saving aesthetic tragedy. *Ethan Frome* brings the romanticised vistas of the past into the grimly enduring present. Mattie, cruelly, lives on as the image of Zeena; to bystanders, it seems, the Fromes at the farm might as well be the Fromes in the graveyard: 'all shut up there'n that one kitchen' (*EF* 194). *The Reef* opens out of its discretions and silences

Figure 4 The Electropoise, advertisement, *The Delineator* (March 1896).

into the vast pink display of decadence in the modern 'Hotel Chicago'. But this world without categories or repressions, conveyed in 'denationalized English' (*R* 364), presents no sense of liberation. Anna gropes for a 'formula of leave-taking' (*R* 366), but the text leaves the reader on a note of uncertainty and confusion – to be taken up again in Wharton's later novels.

Two American stories

> The first requisites for the enjoyment of a tour in the United States are an absence of prejudice and a willingness to accommodate oneself to the customs of the country. If the traveller exercise a little patience, he will often find that ways which strike him as unreasonable or even disagreeable are more suitable to the environment than those of his own home would be.[54]

Baedeker warned his (English) readers to be prepared for a lack of deference in those they might consider social inferiors; and for dirty city streets, rough country roads, overheated hotels and spitting on the floor. Wharton noted some of these. Florid 'American'-style hotels, in particular, loom large in *The Custom of the Country*: the 'Stentorian', 'the Olympian, the Incandescent, the Ormolu' in New York and the 'Nouveau Luxe' (the Ritz) in Paris (*CC* 27). As *The Reef* ends in a 'pink expanse' (*R* 365), so this novel begins in one. But she weaves such details into far-reaching meditations upon the nature of America. The texts here are among her most searching cultural investigations. Written and published during a time of extreme personal dislocation, during Wharton's move to France, through the onset and duration of the war, they raise difficult and complex questions.

The first, *The Custom of the Country* (1913), originally scheduled for serialisation at the start of 1909, occupied Wharton intermittently for several years, becoming ever more ambitious: she spoke of it 'piling up the words'; for her, it was 'the Big Novel' (*Letters* 240, 252). It is a sweeping, expansive chronicle, with immense geographical range, energy and movement, charting the devastating trajectory of the rapacious Undine Spragg – an intensely 'American' story, as Wharton referred to it. Wharton plots Undine's career and ambitions onto a narrative of the rise and fall of social groups, focused through the men she meets and marries. Ralph, the old New Yorker, is a study of a sensitive, would-be poet. (Wharton presents through him many of the concerns explored in her unpublished novel 'Literature', and later in *Hudson River Bracketed* and *The Gods Arrive*.) Elmer Moffatt is one of her strongest representations of the businessman, as robber and epic hero; he emerges from nowhere, traversing the passage Veblen described, from crudity to culture, West to East, Apex City to Paris, ascending to become a gentleman, collector and social power of the future. With all the ambiguities of the collector figure, he is both destroyer and cultural custodian. Raymond de Chelles, the French aristocrat, offers a counter-image of rootedness, European heritage and refinement; but is vulnerable to the force of newer energies. In its scale, the novel suggests an inspiration for next-generation American epics (William Faulkner's Flem Snopes descends, perhaps, from Elmer; Margaret Mitchell's Scarlett O'Hara, in *Gone with the Wind*, from Undine). Critics trace grander narratives. Taking up the resonances of Renaissance drama in the title (a play by Philip Massinger and John Fletcher), Orgel gestures at the dynamics of self-fashioning (the text itself compares Elmer with Othello; with Undine, a 'new Desdemona' hanging on his 'epic recital of plot and counterplot' (*CC* 537)). For Singley, the novel has the force of a 'jeremiad' – of a denunciatory Old Testament prophecy warning of 'gross materialism'; for Tichi, the plot dynamic is Darwinian, tracing the extinction of one species, and the tentative emergence of a new cycle.[55]

The other, *Summer* (1917), a novella written in France during the war ('in fits and starts because of the refugees', *Letters* 397), is a concentrated study in stasis. Another New England tale, this was Wharton's 'Hot Ethan' (*Letters* 385). She described its composition as a respite from reality, mentioning that she had never written with the 'inner scene' so clear in her mind (*ABG* 356). As well as provoking fierce critical debate, these novels also bring into vivid light Wharton's flexibility and scope. Undine Spragg, in the former, is one of her most brittle, denatured heroines; Charity Royall, in the latter, one of her most sensual, presented in some of Wharton's most passionate evocations of the natural world. Through their individual stories, Wharton opens up questions about cultural ideals, national character and aspirations, race, imperialism, the origins and destiny of the United States.

An intellectual desert?

A passing simile in Wharton's tale 'A Journey' (1899) echoes in both heroines' stories: 'her days had been as bare as the white-washed school-room where she forced innutritious facts upon reluctant children' (*GI* 28). Undine and Charity emerge from similarly bare habitats, and each text dwells on early cultural starvation. For some of Wharton's contemporaries, such environments were rich in possibility: these were the origins which guaranteed the future health of the nation. Scenes of rural white American schoolrooms, passionate teaching and of readings in Nature's book, were at the heart of many novels by Wharton's rival best-seller Gene (Geneva Grace) Stratton-Porter (1863–1924) – still remembered for *A Girl of the Limberlost* (1908); or, later, by Laura Ingalls Wilder (1867–1957), looking back to her prairie childhood in the 'Little House' series (1932–43). Here, strong American stock emerged from such beginnings. Others were more ambiguous. In *O Pioneers!* (1913) and *My Ántonia* (1918) Willa Cather represents the 'nothing' of the Midwest as both emptiness and plenitude; and reserves her strongest critiques for the blankness of the modern urban United States: 'Here, you are an individual, you have a background of your own [. . .] We are all alike [. . .] We have no house, no place, no people of our own. We live in the streets, in the parks, in the theatres.'[56] Cather hints at lost possibilities in the richer cultures and lives of marginalised or exiled minorities: Native Americans of the plains, or the inhabitants of the south-west pueblos.

In contrast, Wharton's attitude towards her native land seems negative. She parallels Cather's list – 'And you're all alike [. . .] every one of you [. . .] you come from hotels as big as towns, and from towns as flimsy as paper, where the streets haven't had time to be named, and the buildings are demolished before they're dry' (*CC* 545); but a Frenchman, Chelles, delivers the indictment. Though his own estate is called 'Saint Désert', France offers all that is rich, even 'sacred' (*CC* 545). Regarding her own New York youth as an 'intellectual desert', as we have seen, Wharton claimed similarly that her European experiences and her father's books were her salvation. As an adult, she joined efforts to spread such privileges more widely. When living at Newport, she volunteered her services to choose plaster busts and pictures of European mythological and classical figures to enhance schoolrooms, and made a speech advocating giving children 'this lesson of beauty';[57] at Lenox she was a member of the town Library Committee (*Lewis* 136; *Lee* 151). In creating Undine and Charity, she seems to picture what her mind might have been without inner resources; and to suggest, perhaps, that in the early 1900s the United States presents few redeeming features. While she might admire Undine's energy, she deplores as a cultural vacuum the West from which she emanates; she paints older New York as moribund, and the world of modern business and capital as barbaric. In *Summer*, the one-street country village (somnolent North Dormer) is atrophied, the beautiful architecture in the neighbourhood decrepit, and the Mountain, of dark, different folk (from whom Charity originates), is a place of 'savage misery' (*S* 259). This Mountain tribe, with its suggestions of racial 'otherness',[58] could not seem further from, say, Cather's representations of artistic pueblo peoples, let alone from the African American heritages explored by Alice Dunbar-Nelson (1875–1935) and Pauline Hopkins (1859–1930), among many other, then, 'minority' writers.

At a time when the United States was beginning to expand its global reach after the Spanish War (1898), the texts' constructions of national inadequacy stir up many questions. Was Wharton's writing effectively counter-cultural – in her refusal to present the United States as the pinnacle of nations? Or did it, in ways I shall note shortly, embody dominant myths of the superiority of white privileged groups? These are some of the questions asked by modern critics; reviewers of her day were more interested in Wharton's women, and her venture into squalid or 'repellent' territory (divorce, suicide, eroticism, the 'sex instinct', betrayal). However, even at the time, some observed broader themes. The reviewer in the English *Athenaeum* commented on her complex treatment, comparing the 'flower' of US soil, U(ndine) S(pragg), with nations viewed as exotic or inferior: 'we are introduced to a state of society as chaotic, crude, and purely imitative as that of Hayti or Liberia, but full of force, and held together by a curious patriotism. From this strange soil there rises like a flower Undine Spragg' (*CR* 209); and the *North American Review* praised *Summer* for its 'grave contempt for the clichés of sexual romance': Wharton was 'not projecting a social Utopia: she is denoting a social condition' (*CR* 259).

The Custom of the Country *(1913)*

This sense of nullity, a vision of life with no 'background' (shared, as Chapter 2 suggested, by many expatriate writers), fills Wharton's representations of the range of American social scenes in these texts. In *The Custom of the Country* (to take this first), narratorial comment suggests, time and again, that those who come close to Undine view her in terms of a 'school-girl' – from her bullying, toad-like, American lover, Van Degen, to the intelligent, poised, French aristocrat, the Princess Estradina (*CC* 369, 390). Wharton brings the image sharply into focus at key moments in Undine's story. More details of her early western years emerge late in the novel (in ch. 43, once readers have been immersed in scenes in France), taking Undine in memory back to the first church picnic with Moffatt. Here, for Undine, after the long days at Saint Désert, the prospect attracts her with its vividness; and complicates a reader's possible response. Wharton has, however, depicted the West earlier, in a vignette during Undine's drooping Italian honeymoon when her husband begins to intuit her cultural limitations: 'Her mind was as destitute of beauty and mystery as the prairie school-house in which she had been educated; and her ideals seemed to Ralph as pathetic as the ornaments made of corks and cigar-bands with which her infant hands had been taught to adorn it' (*CC* 147). Whether through references to homespun crafts or to Undine's half-remembered patriotic recitations and garbled versions of European history, Wharton's repeated images keep her in the schoolroom – 'The child-bride' of 'The *Apex Eagle*' (*CC* 111). (Even being a serial jilt and divorcée implies neither maturity nor sophistication.)

The contrast, throughout the text, is with the complexity of French culture, and with women's part in creating it. Wharton would make plain the differences in her article, 'Is There a New Frenchwoman?' addressed to the American readers of the *Ladies' Home Journal* (April 1917), reprinted as the penultimate chapter of *French Ways and their Meaning* (1919). (The piece was part of her war-effort, to represent to Americans the values at stake in the struggles in Europe.) Here, she delivered her now well-known tract about the immaturity of the 'average American woman', drawing an extended analogy with the world of the nursery. For all their bustle and activities, prosperous American women are still in the 'baby world': 'in comparison with women of the most highly civilised countries – such as France', they are only playing at living (*FWM* 101–2). Wharton's message was that deep-rooted traditions were essential. 'Real living' came from 'old and rich social experience' (*FWM* 102) which had to be acquired slowly – most of all, through mature, intellectual relations between men and women. French husbands and wives were partners in every sense – in business and in leisure. Devoting time to 'civilisation', to the 'intervals' of life, she (France and the Frenchwoman) led the world 'in art and taste and elegance', 'in ideas and in ideals' (*FWM* 113).

In the United States, in contrast, life was all hustle; husbands were obsessed with making money, so cutting themselves off from the family (Undine's father, the weary Mr Abner E. Spragg, is a sorry example); the women, left to each other's company – to shopping, self-adornment, gossip and self-indulgence, with no responsibilities or duties – remained infantilised. To the *Athenaeum*, they were exotic and pampered 'Circassian pets' (*CR* 210). The socially ascending female Spraggs present a devastating picture of the cost. With the manicurist/masseuse Mrs Heeny as mentor, from the opening page the narrative dwells on their bodies. Undine's lovely 'form' seems all decoration – with beauty as social weapon, she will be represented throughout the text being dressed, groomed, adorned, painted, bejewelled. Mrs Spragg seems useless, redundant. Without work, a home to run or purposeful activity, she has lost touch with materiality. She is sagging and aging: with 'a prematurely-wrinkled hand', 'soft-cheeked', 'puffy', 'drooping', suggesting 'a partially-melted waxed figure', girded together by corsets (*CC* 3–5). Cast loose from her origins, with no clear role or personal ambition, she 'seemed to have transferred her whole personality to her child' (*CC* 11); Mrs Heeny's 'manipulations' seem her last contact with the physical.

Wharton was not alone in her diagnosis. Reviews, such as the *Nation*'s, picked up on the phenomenon she depicts: what we might now call the de-skilling of hard-working pioneer women, translated by prosperity into a state of bewildering idleness (*CR* 201–2). Many social commentators were worrying over the long-term cultural dangers of segregating the social spheres of the sexes. E. L. Godkin, the *Nation*'s founding editor, emphasised the problem: that men were too exclusively concerned with 'business', leaving the arts to the women:

> How many of the men would wish to sit with the ladies in the evening and participate with them in conversation? [. . .] One fatal difficulty in the way of such modes of hospitality with us is the difference of social culture between our men and women. As a rule, in the European circle called 'society' the men and women are interested in the same topics, and these topics are entirely outside what is called 'business;' they are literary or artistic, or in some degree intellectual.[59]

In 'The American Woman', J. A. Hobson lamented, particularly, the silencing of men; he complained that, in company, an American husband with worthwhile things to say would permit 'the chatter of his commonplace wife and daughter' to dominate the entertainment: 'Woman in a word is the "show".'[60]

In *The Custom of the Country*, Charles Bowen, a man of the older leisure class (the 'Aborigines' as Ralph calls them), draws such views together in his long tirade to Mrs Fairford. He points out the irony of men's sacrifices: they work to make money, but neglect their women. He warns of women's vengeance: 'I fancy there's one who still sees through the humbug, and knows that money and motors and clothes are simply the big bribe she's paid for keeping out of some man's way!'; and nominates Undine as 'a monstrously perfect result of the system' (*CC* 208). Does the novel need such an explicit pronouncement? Undine's presence is a perpetual 'show'; she comes most alive before an audience, or a mirror, 'to twist and sparkle at her image'; a dinner brings the 'joy of dramatizing her beauty' (*CC* 22–3). Her narrative glitters with a trail of bribes: the new dress for the Fairford dinner, an opera box, a trip to St Moritz, the crowning 'pigeon-blood rubies' – the necklace and tiara once owned by Marie Antoinette (*CC* 586). She silences men with moods, 'nerves', wrath or (for her father) caresses: 'smothering his last word in little cries and kisses' (*CC* 31). But among the only other kisses mentioned in the text are Elmer's forfeits at the youthful picnic (*CC* 548), and little Paul's 'hot kisses' (*CC* 324), bestowed on Ralph his father. In the storms and chill that are Undine's speciality, Wharton's text takes soundings of yet deeper dangers within the new American male/female relations. After the passions of the 'Love Diary', *The Custom of the Country* reads as its antitype. Discussing American traits, Hobson also attributed to the dominant social patterns of marriage a reduction of 'sex emotion': 'Much vivacity on the surface, coldness below.'[61] As illustration, he cited *The House of Mirth*, but his hint seems appropriate for Undine.

Viewed from any angle, Undine seems all surface. One major strand of figuration renders her in glitter and dazzle. In contrast with coarser material – the freckled faces of Indiana Frusk, Undine's fellow Apex social-climber; Ralph's 'thick-set' cousins (*CC* 80); or Miss Hicks, the benevolent sick-nurse (*CC* 333) – Undine refracts and reflects light. Beneath the chandelier in the opera house, she is 'the core of that vast illumination' (*CC* 60), electricity (unusually in Wharton) is her medium. In the grey, rainy Saint Désert, she loses her lustre. She is to be looked at, rather than used. The image of Moffatt's rare pink crystals provides one analogy: for a collector's item, coarse handling seems desecration. For Ralph, at Moffatt's revelation of his past with Undine, the horror looms in the fact of his physical presence – 'his redness, his glossiness, his baldness' – visualised with the delicate 'crystal toy': 'Faugh! That such a hand should have touched it!' (*CC* 451, 460–1, 468). Other discourses, those of technology and business in particular, ally her with modernity. In the 'Reservation' as Ralph views it, time moves slowly; the model of self-identity seems stable. The superseded Harriet Ray is Undine's opposite, a thorough product of Wharton's own family background: 'She regarded Washington Square as the birthplace of Society, knew by heart all the cousinships of early New York, hated motor-cars, could not make herself understood on the telephone, and was determined, if she married, never to receive a divorced woman' (*CC* 78). Undine is an alarmingly contemporary heroine. The narratives she generates move rapidly; characters contact, miss and mislead each other, with telephone calls and telegrams, precipitate journeys and veering changes of plan. She seems a being without a centre – self-created, in a series of improvised personalities, made up of floating resources from the passing moment: she mimics the pose and the costume for looking at pictures in a gallery, constructs her lady's manners from the tips in *Boudoir Chat* (*CC* 48, 41). Different men bring out fresh prospects, as she toys with new imagined selves: the aesthetic, the religious. Like some twenty-first-century media celebrity, she is captured in a series of images – gazing out from formal portraits, pictures, press clippings; but, to readers and intimates, she remains elusive, whirling through the narrative, with each metamorphosis leaving family, child, husbands behind. In a strand parallel with the pre-varications and shades enacted in the sphere of business, she makes and unmakes contracts: she discounts flirtations and engagements, forgets her son's birthday party, dissolves her promise to return Van Degen's pearls. Even the weight of French Roman Catholicism fails to outface her, as she begins to reframe cancellation as 'annulment'. Where relationships are reduced to paper, Ralph learns of his own divorce through a newspaper and, inadvertently, signs away his rights to fatherhood; and, in one of the most desperate, and painful, scenes in the novel, he hopelessly attempts to strip his room of Undine's photographs: 'from book-shelves and mantel-piece and tables' (*CC* 330).

Another metaphorical network turns Undine's glitter into something colder, more lethal. Even in this most satirical of novels, Wharton draws on mythological, non-realist currents, in an extensive network of allusions. Undine's name, from the Spragg patent hair-waver, links her with the well-used late nineteenth-century myth of the water-sprite with no soul; elaborated by Wharton into the type of other dangerously sinuous creatures. As Killoran suggests, she is 'not simply a snake. She is Lamia, the reptile metamorphosed into a woman'; underwater scenes, caves and images of drowning stream into her association with Ralph.[62] As in 'Souls Belated', marriage is a '*noyade*': 'if they ceased to struggle perhaps the drowning would be easier for both' (*CC* 225). Does anything fill the place where a soul might be? For Undine's mother, unable to unlearn the dialect and outlook of her beginnings, luxury erases self; in the daughter's generation it intensifies it, to a terrifying extreme. If sexuality dissipates (and, the romantic Ralph aside, her lovers seem to lose interest once she has lost her mystery), so too does family. In the scenes in Washington Square, and in France, the Family remains the most significant entity, an overarching force for the individuals within it. For Undine, family is instrumental, emotions often a messy irrelevance. Her pregnancy provokes a tantrum – her new dress orders will be wasted. It affects Ralph, too, as something sordid, a 'hateful fact' (*CC* 185), a word which (as in her 'hateful' early memories (*CC* 68, 193)) serves Undine to blank out intimacy. Wharton cleverly leaves her actual affair with Van Degen as a narrative gap; she represents Raymond most vividly in his refusals of her initiatives.

Vibrant as she is, Undine seems to rip out, extinguish, life where it blocks her progress. She annuls marriages, breaks bonds between parent and child. Regarded in hindsight through *Summer*, even Mrs Heeny, in Undine's proximity, in her role of go-between, manipulator and facilitator, might seem to take on the air of an abortionist. Undine 'had avoided' her 'as she did everyone associated with her past'. The masseuse's 'extreme discretion', her 'fat flexible fingers' (*CC* 377, 378), her reserve and her warnings to 'go slow', the 'unclouded gaze' under which the 'whole episode took on a different aspect' (*CC* 378), seem to hint at unspoken stories. Such hints are unconfirmed; other acts of destruction all too explicit. Undine reduces Ralph (who is all taste and reflection) to the condition of 'some vivisected animal deprived of the power of discrimination' (*CC* 470); and drives him (literally) to blow his mind to pieces; she strikes at the very heart of Raymond's household, in the depredation of the tapestries; and she reduces the resolute Elmer to meekness, in a masculine alliance with his stepson – looking down at Paul 'with a queer smile: "If we two chaps stick together it won't be so bad – we can keep each other warm"' (*CC* 589). Youth and childhood prove no refuge. (Ralph's image of his enchanted cave, shared with his cousin, is inaccessible.) Wharton's extraordinary closing passages, following young Paul around the echoing house, again evoke, perhaps, the age's most famous literary child – the American Little Lord Fauntleroy (1886), inheritor of a grand house in Europe – who shaped images of boyhood into the twentieth century. Pastiched in Undine's brief Apex fame as a 'child-bride', or her wish (as Moffatt puts it) to be thought 'right out of Kindergarten' (*CC* 133), childhood, nevertheless, remains significant throughout the text. For Ralph, with his memories of his secret cave, seeking for glimpses of his youth in Clare, it codes lost possibilities, faint hopes of retrieval. The scene of the wistful Princess Estradina, gazing at her sleeping daughters as she worries about their future lovers, introduces uncertainties, but hints, also, at a richer kind of life, the 'European' fullness of experience that Undine never grasps. Paul's attempts to understand his heritage, to reach and read the books and paintings, might suggest a chance of renewal, even within the House of Undine – the traditional function played by a child at a narrative's ending. But Wharton's familiar ellipses ('it looks as if one of these days you'd be the richest boy in America . . .' (*CC* 589)) enable the more pessimistic to picture a darker future.

Summer *(1917)*

The Custom of the Country ends with Undine picturing herself in the role of an ambassador's wife; and leaves readers asking, perhaps, whether anything remains that is not for sale. In 1913, Wharton feared for the future of cultural values; writing *Summer* in France in 1917 after four years of war she was witnessing the prospect of an entire civilisation in jeopardy. While she claimed that her 'creative joy' in composition had been a refuge (*ABG* 356), it would be hard to read *Summer* as escapist. Wharton takes readers vividly

into various scenes that might seem 'beyond', in *The House of Mirth*'s terminology: into passion, into nature ('this bubbling of sap and slipping of
sheaths and bursting of calyxes' (*S* 54)); into wild topographies, into the area
outside the law on the Mountain; but she always brings us back, to ask
questions. (The motif of homecoming, as narrative pattern and as metaphor,
is central to this text.) Against *Summer*'s scaled-down 'jography' (*S* 21),
where a 'farm-waggon' excursion to a church lecture in Nettleton represents
an 'initiation' (*S* 10), Undine's mobility seems utopian. Charity briefly
glimpses life outside her 'prison-house' (*S* 14), but the narrative returns her
to a 'secure' life behind 'the door of the red house' (*S* 291). How readers
interpret that security is a matter for individual judgement. For some, it
represents protection, a mature accommodation with history, or, as one of
its first reviewers saw it: 'the power of simple human goodness [. . .] faithful,
unselfish devotion' (*CR* 262). For others it is an appalling, even unspeakable,
entrapment by a long-term sexual predator. That Lawyer Royall is Charity's
guardian, and (with his liaisons with prostitutes and the women of the
Mountain) possibly biological father, adds incest into the mix. (What might
seem to many readers an unambiguous horror is complicated by Wharton's
'Beatrice Palmato' fragment, which presents the daughter's abandonment to
her father as 'new abysses of bliss'.[63])

   Summer brings into the foreground much of what is missing in Undine's
story, and which (at least, in synopsis) might seem to suggest where renewal
could lie. Charity is Wharton's most passionate heroine; her love affair the
most sensuous in Wharton's fiction. Where Undine is all carapace, calcu-
lation and artifice, and chooses her settings carefully, Charity seems all body,
drawing her 'inarticulate well-being' (*S* 21) from nature. Here, for long
passages, Wharton sheds social epigram, and falls into rhapsodic lists,
evoking single sensations – 'to all that was light and air, perfume and colour,
every drop of blood in her responded' (*S* 21); 'melting of palm into palm and
mouth on mouth' (*S* 106). Even outside her most familiar fictional contexts,
she can still encompass a whole experience within a single sentence; as here,
where every sense seems gratified, in a description which turns nature into
Charity's lover: 'She loved the roughness of the dry mountain grass under
her palms, the smell of the thyme into which she crushed her face, the
fingering of the wind in her hair and through her cotton blouse, and the
creak of the larches as they swayed to it' (*S* 21). (Cather's *O Pioneers!*
embodies a similar fantasy, in the heroine's recurring dream of the Genius of
the Divide, a figure more powerful than any of the humans in her story.)

   Though the actual lover, when he materialises, is an architectural historian
from the city, such pastoral notes infuse the love affair – in its settings and its

soaring flights – 'Her soul was still winging through the forest' (*S* 186); and, after its ending, the pledge of the brooch preserves them. Lucius sets aside the 'trumpery' gold lily-of-the-valley, for the 'small round stone, blue as a mountain lake' (134). (Gifts in fictional, as in anthropological narratives, usually carry significance, and they are always worth pausing over in Wharton's fictions.) At the novella's close, Charity recaptures her jewel from the abortionist; and rejects her services. With her 'large and smooth and quick' hands, and her 'false murderous smile' (*S* 224, 225), Dr Merkle enacts what might be shadowed in Mrs Heeny; and Dale Bauer points to the even stronger description, in an earlier manuscript, of 'the unthinkable crime' as 'secret murder'.[64] Saved from her predations, the future child, like Nettie's baby in *The House of Mirth*, seems to unite opposites (nature/culture; rural/ urban; dark Charity/white Lucius) in a trope of regeneration.

But such a tidy reading smoothes out the novella's difficulties. In spite of the style and the narrative's movement forward (its brevity, as with *Ethan Frome*, makes for concentration), its lyricism is problematic. Reviewing the work in *The Egoist*, T. S. Eliot pronounced Wharton 'the satirist's satirist' (*CR* 263); and the book with all its complexities was Joseph Conrad's favourite of Wharton's novels.[65] Among the troublesome items are both Charity's father/ husband and her lover. Is Lawyer Royall a failure, drunk, and abuser; or the representative of order and authority? Lucius Harney the bearer of urban culture, or a colonialist exploiter? (The alternatives are not mutually exclusive.) Shades of commercial transactions (repeated allusions to prosti- tutes, gifts and money) pollute even Charity's most intensely passionate moments;[66] and her spontaneous physical raptures begin, like Undine's, in front of mirrors. The idea of literary and artistic heritage stirs further com- plications. As in 'The Angel at the Grave', with which *Summer* has been compared,[67] Wharton represents even intellectual tradition as stultifying. The Honorius Hatchard Memorial Library is a mausoleum, not the regionally invigorating force that one finds described in period documents. Wharton's first chapter, sketching the torpor of Charity's days among the mouldering volumes, could hardly seem further from her own rhapsodic memories of her father's bookshelves. It is remote too from the upbeat narratives of such articles as 'How a Library Woke up a Town' (Sarah B. Askew, *Suburban Life*, October 1909), enthusiastically reviewed in *City Journal* (November 1909): 'The library is in touch with every interest for miles around. It seems to stand by with a welcoming smile and beckoning finger, and everybody comes and lingers and learns.' Words (books, letters, arguments) stifle Charity; the excitement of the Nettleton lecture fades; she faints during Royall's central

'Old Home Week' address; and even Royall's exhortations, so readers might suspect, will fail to rouse North Dormer.

If words stupefy her, and passion awakes only to betray her, the Mountain presents another set of possibilities – the most disturbing in the text. Throughout the narrative, its inarticulate horde looms as antitype, 'otherness'. They are kin to the 'darkly pale' Charity (*S* 39–40), the furthest extreme from the refined, blue-eyed Annabel Balch. In a different kind of story, Charity's journey might be a rite of passage: to discovering herself in her origins, perhaps, in her union with her mother, or in a romanticised encounter with 'primitivism'. (The Mexican blanket in the deserted house provides an 'exotic' note, echoed in many a modernist quest for a purer way of being – Willa Cather or D. H. Lawrence offer examples.) But *Summer* resists sentimental or psychoanalytic closure. The outlaws are 'sodden', 'lolling', apathetic (*S* 245–7), not pagan beings full of the life-force. The vision of the body of Charity's mother, 'like a dead dog in a ditch' (*S* 250), matches the impact of the red door at the ending – a cul-de-sac not an opening. Along with Maggie Tulliver's venture to the gypsies in George Eliot's *The Mill on the Floss* (1860), the whole episode seems closer (possibly even as influence) to scenes which act as test-pieces for civilisation in other young women's stories. In L. M. Montgomery's *Rilla of Ingleside* (1921; written for a younger audience), the teenaged heroine, in wartime, is shocked by the sight of a dead poor-white woman in a tumbledown shack, and brings home her baby to raise; in Willa Cather's *Shadows on the Rock* (1932), a girl is disturbed by the slatternly ways and pale-eyed, 'furtive' children in a visit to a lower-class country family. In each, the encounter jolts the protagonist into appreciating traditional family values, and domestic (and national) order. Similarly Charity's first sight of the pale-eyed child and drunken, weak-minded adults in the desolate house, makes her long for the hitherto hated 'smell of yeast and coffee and soft-soap' at Mr Royall's as 'the very symbol of domestic order' (*S* 85).

The Mountain folk are 'gipsy-looking people' (*S* 63), rumoured to be early 'colonials', descendants of railroad workers (*S* 66). The possible identity of this group troubles critics: Ammons, for instance, asks whether these are racist fantasies about groups under the uneasy jurisdiction of Western authority – whether the sordid scenes justify imperialism. Bauer places them in the contexts of polemics about reproduction and eugenics, and alarmist case-studies (such as that of the Jukes family, 1877) about the breeding of degenerate 'white trash'.[68] (Folded back into Mr Royall's care, does Charity's baby escape such dangers, or exemplify the dangers of inbreeding?) With Wharton's circumstances of composition in mind, others see here, in the distances of

New England, scenes closer to wartime Europe. Olin-Ammentorp sums up such readings, making links with descriptions in Wharton's *Fighting France* (1915) and the short story 'Coming Home' (*XS* 1916), and of the refugees, in particular, with their 'look of concentrated horror': 'The "inner scene," so "intense," was not wholly separated from the outer scene of war.'[69] In some contemporary habits of thought, the two currents merged, to present war as a eugenic mechanism. As Sir James Barr, MD, argued, in a wartime fundraising volume, to which Wharton also contributed: the Great War ensured the raising of 'healthy, vigorous manhood and womanhood', 'imperial races whose influences will be felt for good throughout the world'.[70] Whether *Summer* represents an imaginative flight from a culture in ruins, or a conscious rendering of the cataclysm, the war severed Wharton's connections with her own past, in ways hitherto unimaginable.

The impact of World War I

> Every great architectural opening framed an emptiness   (*FF* 13)

At the start of the twenty-first century, Wharton's attempts to write war are attracting serious attention. New, highly visible global wars and atrocities, and concerns to acknowledge once buried experiences (as in the work of holocaust studies, or theories of trauma and survival), are returning readers to look afresh at these works, as literature and as resources for cultural memory. Wharton's texts are now again available and, along with fresh literary-biographical accounts of these years and Olin-Ammentorp's pioneering book-length critical exploration,[71] are opening up new horizons for readers. The texts are formally diverse: besides *French Ways and their Meaning* and *A Son at the Front*, they range from essays, a novella (*The Marne*, 1918) and short fictions, including the wry, self-mocking, 'Writing a War Story' (in the *Woman's Home Companion*, September 1919), to patriotic verse commissioned for fundraising tributes. Wharton marshalled a host of illustrious contributors for *The Book of the Homeless* (1915), which she edited, and donated her autograph and a poem, 'Belgium', to *King Albert's Book* (1914), a similar relief effort. (In Wharton's rallying lines, the nation's 'imperishable fires' survive 'her ruined silver spires' and the 'cities shamed and rent' (165), to become an inspiration.) Other poems appeared in newspapers, and some were gathered later in *Twelve Poems* (1926). Her account of her visit to French imperialist Morocco in 1917 (*In Morocco*, 1920) added further dimensions. On vacation from the war, she saw herself in 'a fairy world [. . .] Harun-al-Raschid land' (*Letters* 399); but, even here, the conventional orientalist exoticism of her travelogue, and her more individual reflections on women's lives in the harem, are underpinned with rationales for the order of French rule. Such wider contexts of mourning and commemoration colour *The Age of Innocence* (1920) and *Old New York* (1924), and shadow the dazzle of the new in Wharton's fictions of the post-war generation.

Writing war

The catastrophe of World War I created a chasm in which Wharton's confidence in the future of art nearly foundered; and it changed her vision permanently. She described her return to Paris in July 1914 after travels in Spain with Walter Berry. On the eve of the declaration of war: 'There were moments when I felt as if I had died, and waked up in an unknown world' (*ABG* 338); and images of gulfs, empty frames, hollowness and hauntings pervade her attempts at representation. As many artists have experienced in the face of world-scale disaster, her personal concerns diminished. Her plans for her great 'writer' novel, 'Literature', shaped in early 1914, never came to fruition; and after she completed her novel *A Son at the Front* (published 1923) she contemplated ceasing from writing altogether: 'the world I had grown up in and been formed by had been destroyed in 1914, and I felt myself incapable of transmuting the raw material of the after-war world into a work of art' (*ABG* 70). At the start of the conflict, in 1914, she arranged to rent an English country house, but found the seclusion intolerable: 'this loneliness in which I sit inactive seems to make things worse' (*Letters* 337, see also *Lee* 461–5). She chose, instead, to return to Paris, where she remained throughout the war, directing her despair into action. Biographies and photographs (for example, the range on the Beinecke Library website) make clear the impressive scope of her fundraising and of her involvement with refugee charities. She took on new identities, in her public life, in her work and in her travels. Documents such as her automobile permits for the front (Figure 5) can suggest only something of the contrast: she visited the war-zone with Walter Berry, and used her skill and professional status in polemical, as well as expressive, writings. Her effort, with regard to her American audience, was to raise attention, to gain commitment to the Allied cause – to France, especially: 'An Idea: that was what France [. . .] had always been in the story of civilisation: a luminous point about which striving visions and purposes could rally' (*SF* 366).

Figure 5 Edith Wharton's French automobile permit, World War I (May 1915).

Beyond this, her works raise questions about interpreting the cataclysmic disruptions of war; the role of the artist, the ethics of representation, the framing of unthinkable materials; and address issues of commemoration, cultural continuity and heritage. Wharton's essays from the front, *Fighting*

France: From Dunkerque to Belfort (1915), first published as articles in *Scribner's Magazine*, attempt to represent to far-distant readers in the United States exactly how war strikes an observer; photographs (ruins, a war-grave, a sandbag trench) and a sketch-map of the region around the Forest of Argonne supplement her accounts. Opening with 'The Look of Paris' in summer 1914, her series tries to acknowledge the seemingly inconsequential, as well as the apocalyptic; the oddities and corners missed by 'the huge tiger-scratches of the Beast' (*FF* 94). As Ouditt, writing of British women's war-writings, remarks of May Sinclair and Vera Brittain, there are tones of excitement, of the 'discourse of glamorous submission' to a mighty Power.[72] Wharton, too, as Olin-Ammentorp (*Writings from the Great War*: 28–42) and *Lee* (482) observe, expresses the thrill, the 'picturesqueness', as if in a specialised form of travel-writing.

But her texts struggle, also, with self-regard, a tension between what is, and the tendency of the observer to try to make it into art. Having presented her scene, she stands back to undercut the seeming precision of her methods: 'Looked back on [. . .] those early days [. . .] made the spectator feel as though he were reading a great poem on War rather than facing its realities' (*FF* 15). But seeking to face 'its realities' involves her in ethical and aesthetic problems. Throughout the essays, she refers to surfaces, musing on their normality. Literary and horticultural notes anchor what she is seeing: a little town seems 'sleepy as "Cranford"' (Elizabeth Gaskell's 1853 tale of the English provinces); its borders bloom in well-chosen harmonies; its air of 'placid and orderly bourgeois life' is intact (*FF* 107). The drama comes from heightened awareness of difference, rather than from eyewitness reportage of conflict: 'Nothing but the wreck of the bridge showed that we were on the edge of war' (*FF* 109). Wharton works through negations: it is 'the invisibility of the foe' which is 'oppressive and menacing'; the observers strive to make present what their guides know: ' "*There* they are – and *there* – and *there*." We strained our eyes obediently, but saw only calm hillsides, dozing farms' (*FF* 107–8). Again, a frame round an emptiness suddenly produces a horror: 'the whole place seemed to be sleeping the sleep of bucolic peace. "*They are there*," the officer said; and the innocent vignette framed by my field-glass suddenly glared back at me like a human mask of hate. The loudest cannonade had not made "them" seem as real as that' (*FF* 110–11).

Here, realising the impact of war, for one not engaged in the action, strains the perception and the imagination. Olin-Ammentorp (*Writings from the Great War*: 37–8) discusses such problems in terms of gender difference – Wharton would neither sentimentalise, nor attempt to relay (men's) action she has not seen. We might also read her efforts alongside writings by other American artists of the period, for example John Dos Passos, *Three Soldiers* (1921), E. E. Cummings, *The Enormous Room* (1922), Ernest Hemingway, 'Soldier's Home' (1925) and William Faulkner, *Soldiers' Pay* (1926). These, too, are preoccupied by problems of spectatorship: often allotted the role of ambulance driver, Americans could feel themselves, as Hemingway did, excluded from the heart of the conflict. Such writers address problems for combatants in conveying wartime experiences to outsiders; and such images as Donald Mahon's hideous facial scar in *Soldiers' Pay* become central, as visual emblems of impact. Women writers, similarly, described a communicative gap. The most involved were not exempt: for example Mary Borden (later Lady Spears) (1886–1968), the daughter of a Chicago millionaire, who had established a hospital unit on the Western Front. Recounting experiences in the operating room, Borden claimed that she could approach her subject only obliquely. Her book *The Forbidden Zone* (1929), like Wharton's work, used mixed genres (sketches, poems and stories), and her preface characterised it as both 'fragments of a great confusion', and as blurring 'the pale horror of facts [. . .] because I was incapable of a nearer approach to the truth'.

Wharton's fiction dramatises such problems. She puts William Dean Howells's words into 'Writing a War Story', where an editor urges Miss Ivy Spang, an American poet, to produce, for the general uplift of the wounded and disabled, a 'tragedy with a happy ending'. Her own narratives of war seem to hesitate before the problems of endings, as if backing off from finality. Dedicated to the memory of Ronald Simmons, a young American who had been a stalwart in her war-work, her novels are self-declared monuments to wider losses. In *The Marne*, she deflects tragedy into a miracle: Troy Belknap (taken on as an ambulance-driver) learns that, by a series of chances, 'he had really been in the action' – 'in it up to the hilt' (*M* 125). Wharton presents the reader with 'the small tap on the shoulders as if someone had touched him from behind' (*M* 122), but the last chapter transforms the anticipated shock of the bullet to the tale of a ghostly rescue: Troy has been saved in the arms of his dead tutor. Olin-Ammentorp (*Writings from the Great War*: 77–8) notes Wharton's original plan to end with Troy's death in battle; and she draws analogies with numinous legends, such as the Angel of Mons, as described in Paul Fussell's *The Great War and Modern Memory* (1975). Reading other cultural historians extends such contexts: Jay Winter, for example, points to the literal presence of the dead 'everywhere on the Western Front' and 'their invasion of the dreams and thoughts of the living'. Tales of the return of the fallen, penetrating the veil of Death, Winter suggests, 'produced a form of popular literature linking front and home front in a kind of spiritualist embrace'.[73] Reviewers were moved by *The Marne*'s simplicity, and its passion for France (*CR* 267–70), and Wharton's editor, Rutger Jewett, showered plaudits: 'No man with a drop of red blood in his veins can read your story of Troy without a lump in his throat. Thank you' (letter, 19 August 1918, Beinecke/33.1029).

Without the novella's concentration, *A Son at the Front* (composed 1918–22) presents readers with the problem of focus. Is it even a 'war story'? In the long delays before publication, facing the public's saturation with 'the Trench novel', Wharton described it as a psychological study of the Americans and French, and an atmospheric story of Paris (letter to Jewett, 25 July 1919, Beinecke/33.1030). Many reviewers lamented her theme, as dated; but some perceived other dimensions – that it was not about the conflict, but 'a study in sensibilities' (*CR* 341). As a narrative of action, it is frustrating; it is a repeated series of dissolving resolutions, false senses of closure and overturned revelations. Approached as decentred narrative, the text is far more compelling.[74] It could be read, for example, as an attempt to represent the shock of impact, or an exploration of mourning. Emerging out of the same structures of feeling (to use Raymond Williams's term) as Freud's 'Mourning and Melancholia' (1917), this seems to be Wharton's attempt to put a frame around an emptiness. Such a structure – a narrative swirling around an absence at the centre – would fascinate many modernist writers. George, the 'son' of the title, is a figure for speculation, represented indirectly, or on the other side of an 'unbridgeable abyss' (*SF* 403) – finally, of death. Again, linking the secular and the spiritual, a lexicon of transubstantiation, of changelings and crossings intensifies the mystery for the nonparticipants ('Transfigured, say; no, trans – what's the word in the theology books? A new substance...' (*SF* 390)); and hints of the rituals of *The Golden Bough* open up suggestions of deeper narratives of sacrifice.

It is also a study of the education of fathers; with his mother's divorce and remarriage, George has two – a painter and a banker. One narrative strand involves the change in feeling in the American fatherland as the United States is drawn into the war. However, with George's double parentage, the text offers further meditations on the future of art. Using her portrait-painter John Campton as the dominant viewpoint, Wharton, again, takes up the problems for perception, and for aesthetic values. Parisian scenes, vistas and 'silver-grey' hazes (*SF* 3) create contexts of familiarity and tradition. In the disruptions of war, once the frame goes from round his world, the painter can no longer compose the visual world, can even no longer see. (Wharton underlines her point in another painter's punning name: 'Beausite'.) Though Campton continues to mediate experience in terms of art (his son's face is a 'delicately pencilled white mask on the pillow' (*SF* 296)), here, sight and vision fail. The text is full of moments where portraits, identities, vanish, in images of 'featureless', 'obliterated' faces (*SF* 278); there are literal injuries to eyes and discomforts of the retina. As in the different crisis of Wharton's love diary, seeing extends to language. Meaning evaporates; Campton finds himself faltering 'like a child deciphering the words in a primer' (*SF* 266); he hears an injured patient give 'a nauseating scream in a bleached voice that might have been man, woman or monkey's' (*SF* 278). The ending moves towards reconnections, but also towards the process of separation from death, that, as Winter emphasises, is also part of mourning – a process sought through the making of a monument.[75] Paid for by one father, designed by the other, it also schematically reconciles business and art. The image of the father, creating new life out of clay, draws in the theologically charged strands of the narrative; but it also grounds it in the reality of grief – 'He pulled out all the sketches of his son from the old portfolio, spread them before him on the table, and began' (*SF* 426).

Memory and memorials: The Age of Innocence *(1920)*

Ideas of remembrance fill Wharton's commentaries on her work in the post-war years, reframing and repositioning the act of writing. She explained that since the war all fiction had to be 'historical', its time located on one side or other of the divide (Bernard Berenson's paraphrase, quoted *Lewis* 423–4). Now again, at the start of the twenty-first century, her terms seem all too familiar. In the words of Marita Sturken, a cultural analyst, September 11 2001 produced a similar sense of a radical break: 'on that date, the world changed forever into a "before" and an "after"'. Sturken warns of the nationalism inherent in such views of the 'shock of history', but acknowledges their force: that those who witness them face the problem of 'memorializing absence'.[76] Along with the losses of the immediate past, Wharton understood that the catastrophes of 1914 had torn down 'the old frame-work' of the society of her youth (*ABG* 6). Previously, she said, she had dismissed her life as too 'uneventful to be worth recording' (*ABG* 6); now, she turned to acts of reconstruction. Her commemoration of the pre-war world drew her espe-cially to the deeper past, the lost culture of New York of the sixties and seventies, as the city began to feel the first vibrations of change.

The Age of Innocence begins a process of recording, which Wharton would continue into her autobiographical writings of the 1930s. She would describe this both as an archaeological project, 'collecting and putting together' the 'smallest fragments' of the past, and as the task of a survivor, seeking to preserve the relics, 'before the last of those who knew the live structure are

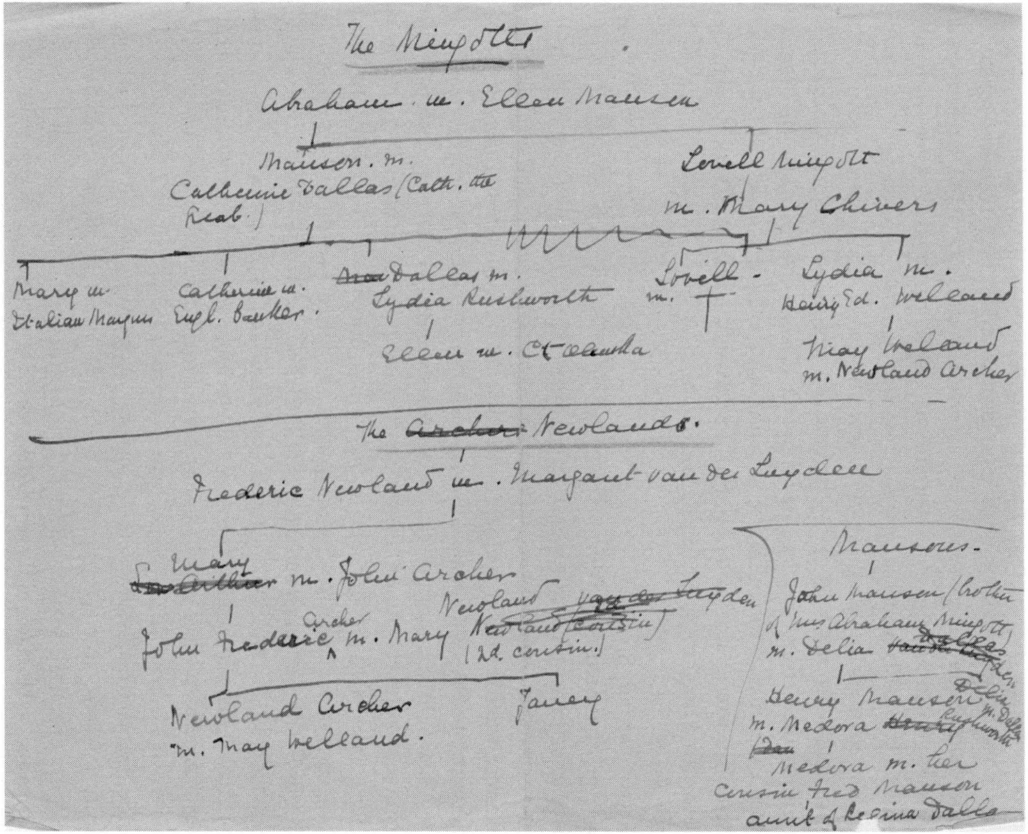

The Mingotts.

Abraham m. Ellen Manson

Manson m. Catherine Dallas (Cath. the Great.)

Lovell Mingott m. Mary Chivers

Mary m. Italian Marquis

Catherine m. Engl. Banker.

Dallas m. Lydia Rushworth

Ellen m. Ct Olenska

Lovell - m.

Lydia m. Henry Ed. Welland

May Welland m. Newland Archer

The Newlands.

Frederic Newland m. Margaret van der Luyden

Mary m. John Archer

John Archer m. Mary Newland (2d. cousin.)

Newland Archer m. May Welland.

Janey

Mansons.

John Manson (brother of Mrs Abraham Mingott) m. Delia

Henry Manson m. Medora

Medora m. her cousin Fred Manson aunt of Regina Dallas

Figure 6 Edith Wharton, genealogical sketch, *The Age of Innocence.*

swept away with it' (*ABG* 7). The genealogical sketch in Figure 6, a snapshot of her work in progress, offers an entry point. Here, with a great-grandfather Abraham adding the note of an Old Testament ur-lineage,[77] Wharton organises her narrative around two New York clans, linked in a dynastic union: 'May Welland m. Newland Archer' repeated (in mirror image) in each main branch. The name of Ellen, the exoticised cousin who will threaten this safe alliance, is visible at the centre of the page. The sketch is not Wharton's first vision of the story – in earlier manuscript outlines (now available online, Beinecke Library), Newland is 'Langdon' Archer, Ellen is 'Clementine' – but it presents, in miniature, many aspects of her novel's world.

Here defining society, 'Family' is the major reference point for Newland and all its individual members: 'New York, as far back as the mind of man could travel, had been divided into the two great fundamental groups of the Mingotts and Mansons and all their clan [. . .] and the Archer-Newland-van-der-Luyden tribe' (*AI* 30–1). To insiders this cosmology – 'the ramifications of New York's cousinships', elucidated fully for the reader through the tribal elder Sillerton Jackson (*AI* 7) – seems eternal and all-encompassing: it structures their habits of thought, regulates their behaviour and monitors their actions. Entering this universe through Newland's consciousness, readers encounter the constraints and securities of such a mindset: its certainties (perpetuated in the familiar names, repeated, with limited variations, through the generations), its rituals, totems and taboos. It is these very repetitions – the compulsion of Family to reproduce itself, the burdens of inheritance, the 'haunting horror of doing the same thing every day at the same hour' – that besiege Newland's brain, driving him to his, very limited, form of rebellion: ' "Sameness – sameness!" he muttered' (*AI* 82).

In its romance plot, the narrative marks the damage to individuals within this system. The family's efforts throughout the narrative are to tidy Ellen, out of her wayward paths in 'almost unmapped' quarters, back into a settled position, at whatever personal cost. The histories of her marriage (as bride of a Transylvanian count, with white eyelashes) are kept under lock and key at Mr Letterblair's, allowing us to imagine extreme horrors. With Newland, in contrast, Wharton admits us to every turn of consciousness. She treats his attempts to disentangle himself from the fabric of family ('What am I? A son-in-law' (*AI* 217)) as an almost physical rending, in a series of references to the whirling in his brain (*AI* 170), or the laughter of 'inner devils' (*AI* 343, 346). Like many other central characters in Wharton's writing, he yearns for a space 'beyond' the social. In her draft outline, Wharton played with a scenario of consummation, where the lovers:

> fly together (contrast between bridal night with May & *this* one)
> Archer is fascinated & yet terrified. They go to the South together –
> some little place in Florida. [Wharton first wrote: 'go to Egypt'.]
>
> Arrange somehow that all this is done *very secretly*. No one knows
> they are together. Both get tired – she of the idea of living in America,
> he of the idea of a scandal & a dislocation of his life.
>
> He cannot live without New York & respectability, nor she without
> Europe & emotions.   (Wharton's emphases; Beinecke/22.702, 39)

In the published text, however, Ellen, adept in the terminology of kinship, reminds Newland that a new form of identity (an '*us* in that sense!') is impossible: ' "You've never been beyond. And *I* have," she said in a strange voice, "and I know what it looks like there" ' (*AI* 294). A sexual relationship between 'the husband of Ellen Olenska's cousin' and 'the cousin of Newland Archer's wife' can only be sordid, injuring the lovers and those who trust them. There can be no world without 'categories' (familial labels such as 'wife' or 'mistress'), a reminder which returns readers to the territories of 'Souls Belated': that those who look for another country 'got out by mistake at wayside stations: at places like Boulogne, or Pisa, or Monte Carlo – and it wasn't at all different from the old world they'd left, but only rather smaller and dingier and more promiscuous' (*AI* 293).

Wharton's concerns, however, go beyond the individuals' story. Onto her design, she mapped the details of the New York described in the social and family contexts in Chapter 1 above. She wrote to her sister-in-law, listing facts she wanted checking, from the dates of Ash Wednesday in 1875 to the precise hour for dinner ('I *think* quiet people like the Archers still dined at seven'): 'There! that's what I call measuring-worm exactness, but we may as well be right' (Beinecke/1.15). She charted its topographies, its hierarchies (the 'small and slippery pyramid' of its social world (*AI* 46, 99)); its reverence for 'form' (*AI* 7); standards and habits; safeguards, fears and threats; its resistance to change, and its accommodations and means of social readjustment. The inventories of details, as Judith Fryer demonstrates (in *Felicitous Space*), act as a version of language, and readers might follow any one of its codes – among them, food, flowers, clothes, jewellery, table settings, furnishings, transportation – as a thread into the 'labyrinth' (*AI* 74) of the culture.

Wharton offers readers various analytical positions from which to examine this world. One such, as many critics have observed, is as ethnographer or sociologist: modes of interpretation Wharton reinforces through Newland's own amateur interest in 'the books on Primitive Man that people of advanced culture were beginning to read' (*AI* 42); and his impatient ordering of 'a new volume of Herbert Spencer' straight from London.

(Wharton's checklist confirmed that Spencer's *Principles of Sociology* came out in June 1874.) Another is as archaeologist. One of the most quoted passages in all Wharton's writings is Ellen and Newland's quiet meditation over a glass case in the Metropolitan Museum, as they gaze at 'the recovered fragments of Ilium' (Troy): 'little things that used to be necessary and important to forgotten people', now 'labelled: "Use unknown"' (*AI* 312). Such moments jolt Newland and readers into awareness of longer perspectives: what once seemed universal and permanent is local, relative and historically temporary. Returning home, after his Museum visit, Newland 'looked about at the familiar objects in the hall as if he viewed them from the other side of the grave' (*AI* 316).

From a different angle, we can read with the eyes of a family physician, noting the symptoms of social disturbance. Within the text as a whole, Wharton's repeated lexicon of 'clan' and 'tribe' creates the effect of a vast unified organism, a 'collective' (*AI* 110, 184) entity which reacts to shocks and rumours, and registers hazards to its wellbeing. Whether embodied in the regular rhythms of the social season or in Mr Welland's concern about his drops and his diet, the narrative keeps the greater health of the family in view. Given visible form in the dinner-table scenes of sniffing and chewing-over dubious elements, both culinary and human ('he would probably finish his meal on Ellen Olenska' (*AI* 36)),[78] what society finds palatable or indigestible presents itself in a myriad forms. Ellen and the banker Beaufort epitomise broader suspicions – of 'foreigners', artists and intellectuals, new money, trade, sexual and financial nonconformity – which seem to menace the body of old New York. The narrative depicts two major modes of response as society fights to preserve itself: violent rejection and gradual assimilation. As with Newland's pathological brain seizures, Wharton calibrates the former response in images of jarring impact; these come to crisis in the financial collapse and Mrs Manson Mingott's near-fatal stroke, the wound of family dishonour. At every stage of the struggle, she shows the group parrying the threat of the unknown, the outsider. Its weapons range from hints to coercion. From Sillerton Jackson's carefully modulated innuendoes, Mrs Archer's 'admonitory' glances (*AI* 89) or May's caresses, smiles and blushes, to the ceremonies of the climactic dinner party, the tribe rallies, wordlessly, to bring deviant individuals into line. As in *The House of Mirth*, Wharton presents her most conventional figures as the most unbending (for example, the corseted Mrs Welland in her purple satin drawing room). For an equally rigid social body, expulsion or elimination of unacceptable elements seems the only recourse.

In the wider narrative, however, assimilation and accommodation are more dominant. As the 'carnivorous' Mrs Manson Mingott asserts, the family needs 'new blood and new money' (*AI* 28–9) to perpetuate itself long term. Evident in Wharton's genealogical sketch are the seeds of change present within the family itself. In the Anglo-Dutch Newland lineage, Newland Archer exemplifies only a mild variation – a slightly more intellectual strain of his tribe's disdain for 'the grosser forms of pleasure' (*AI* 31). The Mingott pedigree is the more diverse. While it produces the most conservative types, Mrs Welland and her daughter, May, among them, the line also holds the most vibrant. Newland is drawn not only to Ellen, but to her audacious grandmother, and the energies she represents. Drawing on the character of her own indomitable aunt, Mary Mason Jones (see *Lewis* 13 and *Lee* 21–2), Wharton suggests a more flexible and pragmatic spirit of enterprise; the 'foreign' marriages (recorded on the genealogical chart, Figure 6) are swept up, in the text itself, into one of Wharton's single-sentence histories, beginning with Catherine (Dallas) Spicer's doubtful origins, and ending in her pioneering building of her 'large house of pale cream-coloured stone (when brown sandstone seemed as much the only wear as a frock-coat in the afternoon) in an inaccessible wilderness near the Central Park' (*AI* 10). Breaking away from Washington Square, Catherine ruptures the boundaries. In the 1880s, the newly rich would emulate her; by the end of the novel, such currents of change have 'swept away all the old landmarks' (*AI* 361).

The Age of Innocence keeps its central characters within the confines of family. The elite, settled corner Wharton depicts could not seem more remote from the teeming, multicultural, divided New York City that stunned outsiders, its extremes glossed here in the words of the Reverend David MacCrae, a visiting Scottish minister:

> Fling together Tyre and Sidon, the New Jerusalem, Sodom and Gomorrah, a little of heaven, and more of hell, and you have a faint picture of this mighty Babylon of the New World. City of colossal wealth and haggard poverty; city of virtue, with an abortionist occupying the most palatial residence in Fifth Avenue; city of churches and Bible houses, where one of the foremost citizens is a man who keeps his wife on one side of the street, and his mistress on the other.[79]

But Wharton allows readers to glimpse this world beyond the enclave. It is the more dubious presences outside the known securities of genealogy who now interest many critics: the sight of Fanny Ring in her 'canary-coloured brougham' (*AI* 83); the diverse ethnic and racial others – including Ellen's 'swarthy' maid, Nastasia, or Mrs Manson Mingott's 'mulatto maid-servant' in her 'bright turban' (*AI* 215); or hints of a Jewish ancestry for Beaufort; or, in a time of widespread depression, 'the spectre of the unemployed' which is evoked via a simile (*AI* 222).

If New York 'was beginning to dread and yet be drawn to' the 'new people' (*AI* 1), such figures complicate the dynamics of fear and desire in the narrative. Toni Morrison's account (in *Playing in the Dark: Whiteness and the Literary Imagination*, 1992) of the 'Africanist presence' in the European-American imagination seems pertinent here. These are the characters through whom white society validates itself and affirms its difference.[80] The draw of otherness is intensified by the markers within the family itself. Though Grandfather 'Abraham' does not feature in the published text, Wharton retains the strain of exciting and unsettling exoticism in the Mingott line – most notably in Ellen, with her 'dusky' blush (*AI* 56, 72), and air of 'a gipsy foundling' (*AI* 57). It is the alliance in the next generation (not included on this genealogy), between Dallas Archer and Fanny Beaufort, which at last fully accommodates the difference. Wharton's stunning use of her final section, her abrupt time-switch to the early 1900s, seems to reverse the movement of *Ethan Frome*, in bringing fresh air into the closed world of the main narrative. Her notebooks hold titles for a sequel, 'The Age of Experience' or:

> Homo Sapiens
> Continuation of "The Age of Innocence".
> History of Dallas Archer and Family.   (Beinecke/22.702, 48)

But for the readers, with after-knowledge, all changes are overshadowed by the divide of the war. As Wilfred Owen would write, the sons of Abraham (like the young Americans in *A Son at the Front*, and perhaps Dallas Archer) faced sacrifice, to be slain with 'half the seed of Europe, one by one'.[81]

The post-war welter

Delighted with *The Age of Innocence*, Wharton's editor exclaimed: 'How you would detest New York life to-day. If it seemed petty and narrow before, it would now seem blatant and chaotic, without rhyme or reason' (letter, Jewett, 16 August 1920, Beinecke/33.132). Its award of the Pulitzer Prize in 1921, for fiction best presenting 'the wholesome atmosphere of American life' (see *Lee* 586–7), might seem the seal of approval for a traditional realist novel, a museum piece, where Wharton simply 'honoured' the past and 'mourned' for 'the good in the old ways' (*AI* 350). However, riven by references to ghosts and other disturbing presences, the text is more radically unstable and critical than the formal assurance of its narrative voice, or its display of carefully itemised facts, might have suggested. Jay Cocks, the screenwriter for Martin Scorsese's film version (Columbia, 1993), found adaptation difficult: 'The book does have a tremendous problem dramatically, which is basically that the story stops dead in the middle and starts all over again.'[82] But for the narrative, the placing of the wedding almost exactly at the text's mid-point is crucial: it is, indeed, a kind of 'death' for Newland. Wharton even (inadvertently) used the words of the funeral service in the first magazine edition; and, after his marriage, Newland feels like a disembodied spirit. Such worries about fracture and continuity, about family secrets, hidden histories, loyalties and betrayals, sexual purity and deceit, and issues of paternal legitimacy – all unspoken and glossed over in *The Age of Innocence*'s social world – come to the surface in many of Wharton's other post-war writings. Here tidy genealogical tables, with their show of family stability, seem all but impossible as certainties collapse in multiple divorces, hints of incest, cross-generational or same-sex desire.

Depicting the early twentieth century as Newland Archer's story closed, 'the sign-posts and the danger-signal' (*AI* 361) swept away, Wharton hinted at the future: 'the huge kaleidoscope' of a society of 'fads and fetishes and frivolities' (*AI* 356) inherited by her audience in 1920. Her fictions of post-war America engage with what she viewed as almost unrepresentable, the crude, disturbing and monstrous, as evoked in this *Frankenstein* image in her essay 'The Great American Novel':

> It is useless, at least for the story-teller, to deplore what the new order of things has wiped out, vain to shudder at what it is creating; there it is, whether for better or worse, and the American novelist, whose compatriots have helped, above all others, to bring it into being, can best use his opportunity by plunging both hands into the motley welter.   (1927, *UCW* 157)

In *The Writing of Fiction* (essays published in 1924–5), she reflected on her craft, asserting her belief in order and selection, and, above all, form. However, in her fiction she confronted the formless and unspeakable, plunging into the 'welter'. *The Mother's Recompense* (1925), *Twilight Sleep* (1927), *The Children* (1928) and her epic *Hudson River Bracketed* (1929) and *The Gods Arrive* (1932) – her most sustained narrative of the would-be artist and those he sacrifices – all offer meditations on the depredations of a commodity culture, new versions of the self in a 'make-over' society and the nature of writing itself. *The Glimpses of the Moon* (1922), written 1916–21, was set pre-1914 (Wharton's plan for a sequel, 'Love Among the Ruins', mentions events during the war: Beinecke/22.284); however, as *Lee* notes (626), it, too, was generally received as a post-war story. Although Wharton herself concurred with those reviewers who began to find her modes old-fashioned (a view of these works perpetuated until relatively recently), the oblique and fragmented visions of these later fictions now suggest some experimentation. The books were popularly well received, and included some of Wharton's own favourites; and, while perhaps still not the place where a new reader would usually begin, they offer far more than the once dismissive label of 'magazine-fiction' would suggest. Despite editors' demands for upbeat endings, they are characterised by boundary-crossing, indeterminacy, blurring – in genre, theme, representations of marriage and the family, and, above all, sexuality. Here, society's very easiness undoes its fabric; as Wharton rendered it in her outline for *The Mother's Recompense*: 'Smoothness – shock-absorbers – the Taylorized life. When one husband bores you, you get another – "while you wait". Why go on marrying? It saves trouble – & besides, one is a "nice" woman' (Beinecke/22.702).

In these fictions, and in her further historical sequence *Old New York* (1924), all published as Wharton entered her sixties, the narrative eye dwells on signs of aging – dropped mouths, freckled hands, stiffening forms; on modes of growing old, and painful efforts to stay young, as sexual vitality or attractiveness dwindles. As Bauer (*Brave New Politics*) reminds us, the youth cult of the period sought scientific means – hormone treatments, 'monkey glands' – to arrest time. Pauline in *Twilight Sleep*, registering her husband's diminished interest, is a case-book of modish treatments. In *The Children*, Mrs Sellars, a more passive specimen, desperate to keep her prospective lover, appeals to traditional models of good behaviour, 'with lips that pined and withered for his kiss . . .' (*C* 236). Kate Clephane at 'forty-two or so (or was it really forty-four last week?)', even when recalling the perfection of 'her one week' with her younger lover, remembers touching up her face 'before he was awake, because the early light is so pitiless after thirty' (*MR* 4–5). Wharton does not go as far as Gertrude Atherton in *Black Oxen* (1923), where Madame Zattiany, a reworked Ellen Olenska, returns to Manhattan in her sixties, literarily rejuvenated, through X-rays on her ovaries, and restored to her former beauty. But she explores a theme which had long interested her: the question of what happens to those who try to reverse time, or step back into lives they have put behind them – Mrs Lidcote in the story 'Autre Temps. . .' (1911; in *XS* 1916) continues a narrative begun in 'Disintegration',[83] and anticipates Kate Clephane's painful journeys in *The Mother's Recompense*.

The body remains the site of memory, of the feeling self: disturbed, as in *The Age of Innocence*, central characters begin to experience themselves splitting or becoming spectral; possible and lost selves become visible at their vanishing point. Joslin suggests entering *The Mother's Recompense* through its ghosts, its silences and transgressions,[84] and this approach might extend to aspects of other characters' stories. Martin Boyne (*The Children*), or the younger Susy (*The Glimpses of the Moon*), try to reconstruct their lives, the phantom-forms of their relationships, in narratives full of images of mortality: 'To get used to being dead: that seemed to be her immediate business' (*GM* 281). Multiplying identities produce shadow selves: 'that other Nick [. . .] the other Susy': 'she had become an "other person" to him' (*GM* 255, 332). For Wharton's long-term readers, the fictions also evoke earlier stories, blurring and revising lines between past and present. Wharton reworks *The Reef* within *The Children*: at forty-six, Boyne, planning to renew a former relationship, finds himself ever more ambiguously fascinated by a younger woman – here, a fifteen-year-old girl. Susy and Nick are often read as revenants of Lily and Selden, taking their chances together, in a 'queer social whirligig' of 'moral parasites' (*GM* 145). In the post-war confusions of *The Mother's Recompense*, Anne, the daughter, unwittingly battles Kate, her mother, as sexual rival for Chris, Kate's one-time lover. (Wharton's very title, borrowed from the Victorian novelist Grace Aguilar, gives a dark twist to a sweet mid-century favourite, a sequel to *Home Influence*.)

Even in another historical reconstruction, the novella sequence *Old New York* (also a working title for *The Age of Innocence*), Wharton's form dissolves any air of certainty. Issued as a set in 1924, the series of novelettes (as she termed them) composed a linear chronicle: *False Dawn (The 'Forties)*, *The Old Maid (The 'Fifties)*, *The Spark (The 'Sixties)* and *New Year's Day (The 'Seventies)*. But the partial and provisional views, the gaps, missing connections and arbitrary revelations of the short-story-cycle genre, make reading an unsettling process. Here, there is no presiding narrative voice. Using some limited first-person narrators, dropping in hints of after-knowledge, using metaphors of evolutionary layering and darting to-and-fro chronologically, Wharton prevents any straightforward developmental reading. Intertextual allusions cut across the documentary detail; and the inclusion of historical figures (Poe, Whitman, Ruskin) along with familiar Wharton characters such as Sillerton Jackson or Mrs Struthers complicates the social vision.

The sequence returns readers to Wharton's familiar territory, to look again at what lies beneath the polished surfaces, the perfect manners: 'Mrs Mant's sympathy seemed more cruel than her cruelty. Every word that she used had a veiled taunt for its counterpart' (*New Year's Day*, *ONY* 276). She brings out the implications of her earlier texts, that the solid social scenes are hollow forms, riddled with secrets. *The Old Maid*, with its plot of concealed motherhood and illegitimacy, is outspoken about the disappointments of the 'placid bridal' bed; its 'dark revelations' present 'the grim drawing-room' in a new aspect, as 'the moonlit forest' of illicit passion (*ONY* 161, 169, 146). Misjudgements predominate. As in Willa Cather's *A Lost Lady* (1923) or Fitzgerald's *The Great Gatsby*, a charismatic central figure, Lizzie Hazeldean of *New Year's Day*, is rendered through the fascinated gaze of a younger character. As in *Ethan Frome*, Wharton uses a narrator who seeks meanings through hints and fragments; one 'boyish glimpse' of a 'bad' woman drives him thereafter to question the authority of the family guardians. Here, and in each novella, there are gulfs between different generations' ways of seeing, their imaginative 'topographies' (*ONY* 229). These are focused, in *False Dawn*, for example, through the story of a tragically unappreciated collection of Italian Primitive art, or in *The Spark*, through an encounter with Walt Whitman and his Civil War poetry. Goodwill cannot help those trained in traditional aesthetic forms to understand new modes of vision; even the youngest narrator ages during his chronicle, and comments that life has become 'too telegraphic' (*ONY* 229). This self-reflexive strand is intensified in numerous references to story-telling and to listening. Its larger effect in the narratives is to suggest the strain of change, and to articulate Wharton's own greater tensions in confronting the new.

Language, as ever, for Wharton is central. In *The Spark*, with the impositions of commerce, American society is 'already corrupting' words into 'hazy verbiage' (*ONY* 197); by the twenties and thirties, the sway of mass culture, the casualness of slang and the debasement of advertising imperil the very tools of art. Wharton's annotations of Margaret Ayers's draft stage-adaptation of *The Age of Innocence* are full of exclamations at her abuse of idiom: Ellen's 'right here at the Van der Luyden's' is marked 'Oh, oh, never'; 'I guess', from Newland, is crossed out with 'Oh, horror!' (Beinecke/1.18–20). Wharton gives similarly short shrift to an unsolicited manuscript (from a Mrs Robert Schauffler of Kansas City) dramatising *The Mother's Recompense*, and condemns its inept expression (letter 1929, Beinecke/39.1185). Distorted or distanced relationships to language compound many of her modern characters' crises and moral disorders: from the damage wrought by Susy's ethical fuzziness in *The Glimpses of the Moon* to Vance Weston's seductions and betrayals of his writing by modish movements, commercial contracts, patrons and prizes, in the mail-order civilisation of *The Gods Arrive*. In *Twilight Sleep*, Pauline delegates her syntax to her secretary, and presents herself, in a supreme act of cognitive dissonance, as spokeswoman for proponents of both Birth-Controllers and National Mothers. Her efforts to turn lying into truth through inauthentic letters and speeches only fuel the conflagration of the climax.

Issues of the differences in 'lingo' and the rise of a global Americanese within the peripatetic fast-set also feature in the multinational liaisons of *The Children*. Wharton represents verbal slippages as delightful in the children's mistakes (readers might not be as charmed), but, more usually, linguistic laxity is alarming: the sign of wider moral and cultural collapse. As Judith, the oldest, explains, her siblings 'talk about mother's old friend Sally Money. They've heard about her ever since they can remember. They think mother sends for her whenever anything goes wrong . . .' (*C* 109). One of the most threatening figures in these novels, endangering the coherence of the family, is the twenties vamp, whom Wharton depicts as the antitype of the expressive. Terrifyingly vacant, unreadable, with a history of nameless corruptions, she is also verbally null. Lilla Gates in *The Mother's Recompense* hates talking: 'I only like noises that don't mean anything' (*MR* 69). Lita Wyant, the epicentre for unspeakable horrors in *Twilight Sleep* (a quasi-incestuous affair with her father-in-law among them), neither receives nor writes letters, but functions iconically through surface. Anticipating the depthless 'spectacle' of post-modernity, she seems destined, to the dismay of the family, to become a screen-star, a publicity image on a Hollywood poster.

Much of Wharton's textual energy, however, is generated by play with words, with neologisms and slang. She gives readers Nick and Susy's celebration of 'togetherness' (*GM* 350) and Nona's 'new Bachelor Girls' Club ("The Singleton")' (*TS* 312), long before Helen Fielding's *Bridget Jones's Diary* (1996) and modern chick lit. Language retains the power to regenerate. This force can be delusive: Pauline (in a text buzzing with images of electricity) is galvanised into hopes of rejuvenation by the thrill of novelty, the cult-words of a new mental-hygiene guru. It can also be menacing: in *The Glimpses of the Moon*, for Susy, like many of Wharton's characters, letters represent presences holding potent futures; hoping for a transforming word, she cannot cross her hotel threshold without imagining the letter waiting in her room (*GM* 229). But, with these texts' pervasive interest in children, education and the future, literature and the arts remain key to rich, formative experience. Although early descriptions of their chaotic home-life read like a eugenicist nightmare, the intelligent Fulmer brood (*GM*) are nurtured by their musician mother and painter father; they exert their own redemptive force in the narrative through demands to visit the Louvre, and for Susy to read Shakespeare aloud. In *The Children*, in spite of the efforts of Boyne, another temporary parental surrogate, the multiple step-siblings never receive similar nourishment; their imaginations remain undirected, and the narrative closes after casual reference to the death of a child – one of Wharton's bleakest and most blighted images. At the close of *Twilight Sleep*, after the implosion of home and family, Pauline rebounds as 'more than ever resolutely two-dimensional' (*TS* 363); but her daughter, Nona, seeks negation. She can only stare 'with hard unwavering eyes' at the prospect of a 'happy' marriage or future (*TS* 372).

Retrospectives

> Everything that used to form the fabric of our daily life has been torn in shreds, trampled on, destroyed.   ('LGNY' 274)

In the years of the Depression, with the new social agendas of the 1930s, Wharton continued to feel the need to preserve her history. Her post-war writings are full of concerns about how to give meaning to a 'drifting, disorganised' existence (*GM* 143), and how to shape a story towards an ending. For these characters, with 'planless', 'inexplicable' lives, 'blown about' on 'winds of pleasure' (*GM* 143), what could make for a satisfying narrative? Nick, in *The Glimpses of the Moon*, recognising 'the Pyramid-instinct', seeks stability in writing history and archaeology; but, without Susy, loses the willpower to build a future (*GM* 243). Vance and Halo's story (in Wharton's epic *Hudson River Bracketed* and *The Gods Arrive*) is painfully episodic and peripatetic, and any sense of 'arrival' seems fragile. In an opposite dynamic, those who try to impose a rigid grid on experience risk the shattering of their inflexible structures: Pauline in *Twilight Sleep* and the Texan Princess Buondelmonte, in *The Children*, with her degree in Eugenics and Infant Psychology, are prime exemplars.

Wharton's autobiographical writings are interested in identifying deeper structures and significance. *A Backward Glance*, recalling a lost way of life, could be viewed as the last testimony of a last survivor. As she grew older, Wharton described herself as superseded – 'the literary equivalent of tufted furniture and gas chandeliers', as she wrote to Scott Fitzgerald in 1925 (*Letters* 481). As Hermione Lee suggests, we could look at all Wharton's memoirs as a novelist's textured version of her past; with herself as 'an alienated, solitary figure, a writer-in-the-making'; and at *A Backward Glance* as 'a series of key events' that precipitated her career (*Lee* 17, 41). Beyond social documentary, Wharton adopts the *fin-de-siècle* trope of the dreamy child. She uses Frances Hodgson Burnett's image of the 'secret garden' for her writings; and, particularly at the start of 'A Little Girl's New York', attempts the very young child's perspective (a device also found in Burnett's memoir, *The One I Knew Best of All*, 1893). Visible, too, however, is a Progressive-Era narrative of professional purpose, the opposite of the dangerous dilettantism of so many of Wharton's own characters. Such a narrative was in keeping with her management of her writing career, her continuing grip on the business aspects of her contracts: 'The editor with cold feet has come into line, & is paying the price agreed upon!', she exclaimed on securing $25,000 for the serialisation of *A Backward Glance*.[85] In her autobiographical highlighting of her writing as labour, Wharton, then, perhaps tacitly rebuts potential accusations that, like Susy in *Glimpses*, she was merely a creature of leisure ('Money, luxury, fashion, pleasure: those were the four cornerstones of her existence' *GM* 134); with her emphasis on discipline and the daily task, she remains true to Theodore Roosevelt's ideal of a 'strenuous life'.

Now in her seventies, she continued to follow, from France, her progress in the United States; she remained interested in the fate of her earlier works, and dealt vigorous advice on requests to adapt her fiction for stage and screen. She enjoyed the success of the play of *Ethan Frome*, though from a distance. She had lived to see it already a college classic, a distinction crowned, in 1935, by its winning the Pulitzer Prize for drama (in an adaptation by Zoë Akins). Crucially, she continued to write fiction. Her final novel, *The Buccaneers* (unfinished at her death), turns back to the transatlantic alliances of the Gilded Age, following young American women into the snares and labyrinths of their upper-class English marriages. (Frances Hodgson Burnett's *The Shuttle*, 1907, was an interesting precursor.) Read with Wharton's accompanying notes, rather than in a modern reconstruction, the novel's ambition survives. It opens out large-scale historical and cultural debates, and, in the resilient duo of Nan St George and her governess/mentor, Laura Testvalley, presents one of Wharton's most complex and constructive explorations of female subjectivity. 'Roman Fever' (1934; in *The World Over*, 1936), in its casually unravelling conversation, is for many readers Wharton's supreme expression of 'love among the ruins'; set at the heart of Europe, it leads into the tangles of the past, into the silences and sicknesses of a civilisation, and into the lasting force of emotion.

In all these texts, as always, Wharton's writings reverberate at levels beyond realism. She dedicated *A Backward Glance* to departed friends, who on All Souls' Night would share her fireside meditations. Ghosts rise, benign or menacing, throughout these years. Tales of the supernatural and uncanny, throughout her career, made visible many of the darker presences haunting her everyday spaces. Gathering eleven of these, along with a preface, into a collection, *Ghosts* (published posthumously, 1937), she left an assembly of some of her strongest lifelong themes. Looking back with these fictions sensitises the reader again to many undercurrents in her social dramas. From the 'The Lady's Maid's Bell' (1902), through 'The Triumph of Night' (1914) or 'Bewitched' (1926), to her final story, 'All Souls'' (1937), a white land-scape of snow creates a blank canvas to sketch chilling, almost unwritable, stories. In others – 'Afterward' (1910), 'Kerfol' (1916) or 'Mr Jones' (1928) – 'continuity and silence', as Wharton wrote in her preface, supply the requisite medium.

Critics have seen in these, and her other ghostly tales, sexual abuse, illegitimate desire, the horrors of solitude, the rising of repressed fears of dependency (as in the reliance of old age, or privilege, on servants); social or private guilt, vengeance and retribution; or the spectres of unfulfilled lives, for the individual (as for so many in her fictions) or the culture. At micro- and macro-level, their symbolic geographies, and confined short-story structure, return readers to Wharton's long-term literary territories: perilous thresholds, curtained rooms, houses with lives of their own. Here are the locked doors, watching eyes, buried brutality and half-glimpsed secrets which flicker in her similes from her earliest fictions. The stories seem to give narrative substance, too, to the nebulous feeling she frequently expressed, that all her characters were in some sense ghosts who haunted her: spectral forms, arriving mysteriously, often as merely a name, and demanding attention (see, for example, *ABG* 202). So, in 1937, her final year, she notes in her diary (Beinecke/22.703) a visit in January from a 'Lady Silverthread', and, in February, from a 'rather too lovely' Angelica Medway:

> Where from? What for? Short story? Novel? – First visit of the kind since my illness two years ago –
> I must try to meet them again –

Chapter 4

Critical reception

> Reading most reviews of my books – the kindest as well as the most
> disapproving – is like watching somebody in boxing gloves trying
> to dissect a flower.   (Diary, 1925, Beinecke/51.1523)

Although Wharton's judgement might be enough to deter anyone from
commentary, Wharton studies are flourishing, and biographies, fresh editions, theoretical and cultural reconfigurations, continue to generate dialogues, and to suggest new ways of mapping her work. In this final chapter,
I highlight some main critical themes mentioned throughout this *Introduction*, and indicate some shifts and turns in readers' approaches.

Wharton's readers

'Fashions in criticism change almost as rapidly as fashions in dress', Wharton
observed in 'Fiction and Criticism' (*UCW* 293) – a caution to be borne in
mind when surveying over a century of her critical reception. Readers wishing
to trace this history may take various routes. A wealth of material is reprinted
in *Edith Wharton: The Contemporary Reviews* (1992), edited by James W.
Tuttleton, Kristin O. Lauer and Margaret P. Murray. Helen Killoran, *The
Critical Reception of Edith Wharton* (2001), presents a bibliography and surveys
the reception of central texts. Wharton's publishing career is described in
Clare Colquitt, 'Bibliographic Essay: Visions and Revisions of Wharton'
(in Singley (ed.), *A Historical Guide to Edith Wharton*, see 'Guide to further
reading'); Kristin O. Lauer and Margaret P. Murray itemise a century of
criticism in *Edith Wharton: An Annotated Secondary Bibliography* (1990);
Stephen Garrison, *Edith Wharton: A Descriptive Bibliography* (1990),
focuses on the material history of Wharton's own writings. The

'Guide to further reading' below offers more suggestions. As will be evident, documenting Wharton scholarship has itself become a major task, and here I can hope only to draw out a few main strands.

As previous chapters have made clear, Wharton's fiction attracted respect from her earliest reviews; and even her non-fiction alone would have gained her a lasting reputation. Her first book, *The Decoration of Houses* (1897), and her guides to Italian landscapes, villas and gardens became standard texts; her commentaries on France were viewed as models of sensitive cultural mediation. Aspects of her work which later slipped out of view – her ventures into drama, for instance – brought her some initial success. The short story 'The Twilight of the God' (*GI*), an experiment in play-form, now generally taken as a paper exercise, roused approbation, even in amateur performance. Wharton herself objected to Mrs Gould's unauthorised production, in a lavish end-of-the-century house party where the hostess starred in the leading role of Isabel Warland; but Society columns took note. The part 'seemed to have been written expressly for her'; 'into Mrs Warland's mouth the author has put a string of epigrams which gave Mrs Gould an admirable opportunity [. . .] She was enthusiastically encored, and received a splendid bouquet of American Beauty roses at the end' (*NYT* 22 December 1899). Another performance, by students of the Empire Theatre Dramatic School, New York, again impressed its audiences, but here the plaudits went directly to Wharton:

> the lines rose to the heights of 'The Importance of Being Earnest.'
> They flashed with almost superhuman brilliancy, and in each of them
> lurked a bitter of impish malignity like the angostura that makes the
> cocktail. Such are the bibulous metaphors to which Mrs Wharton
> inspires one, even in the afternoon.   (*NYT* 19 December 1902)

Although the same school's production of another short play, 'Copy', the following year seemed sober in contrast (*NYT* 6 November 1903), Wharton proved herself versatile. Her translation of a German play, *The Joy of Living* (1902) by Hermann Sudermann, was praised as 'perfect', and compared with Ibsen (*BE* 12 November 1902). She worked, albeit reluctantly, on adapting *The House of Mirth* for the stage, collaborating with Clyde Fitch, then America's most popular playwright; and, although the New York production (October 1906) was a much publicised flop, its premiere in Detroit (September 1906), which Wharton attended, seemed promising. The play drew thoughtful commentary, which blamed not Wharton's dialogue (which Fitch described as brilliant), but the sombre themes and distaste of the American public for literary theatre. (Had Wharton allowed Lily to live, and marry Selden, matters might have been different.)

These theatrical reviews contain notes which reverberate in many assessments of her writing; and though fashions might change, such critical motifs recur, recycled with different emphases, through several generations. Wharton's brilliance, subtle observation and sharp style marked her, from the first, as a serious writer; and her nature and manner as a social commentator commanded attention. Critics noted her grasp of 'type' (discussed in Chapter 3), and praised her satirical cleverness. *Literary World*'s review of *The Greater Inclination* (1899) cited an aperçu from 'A Coward' – 'Mrs Carstyle was one of those women who make refinement vulgar' – and exclaimed: 'Could a certain well-known American type be more cleverly hit off than that?' (*CR* 14). In 'Mrs Wharton and Her Use of the Epigram', *The Book Buyer* glimpsed 'a coming dramatist', and explained:

> the successful phrase, the happy aphorism, gives a clew to character, an aid to your knowledge of the individual, such as is furnished by a gesture, or a trick of the eyes, when you try to form an estimate of a stranger met for the first time [. . .] In a moment, the twinkling of an eye, you are able to place these [. . .] characters. Pages of description and repetition would not have served you so well.   (1899; *CR* 15)

Later books elicited similar responses. A review of *The Touchstone* emphasised 'her positive genius for finished phrase and telling epigram', and cited for readers' pleasure a series of her 'crisp and brilliant sentences' (*Bookman*, 1900; *CR* 32); another praised the 'scathing exposure' of a social group in *The Custom of the Country*: 'It is wonderful how in a word or two she can call to mind a type or extinguish a pretension or present a complete picture to the eye' (*CR* 211, 214).

Although readers still admire Wharton's social acuity, such stylistic traits can strike the ear now as somewhat forced – Hermione Lee, for example, points to Wharton's epigrams as five-finger exercises for writing, and, in a less than positive echo of the first reviews, as stagy, proto-theatrical, experiments (*Lee* 179–90). Some of Wharton's contemporaries, likewise, were less than warm in their reception. For these, her wit created the tone of the dismissive *bon mot*, or conversational put-down, shared between a small exclusive group. As one American professor wrote in 1924: 'Her cleverness is of the rather disconcerting sort that belongs to the social dictator who has a highly developed sense of form, a keen eye, and a keener tongue. Everything offers the chance for a *mot*.'[1] At its most critical, this kind of judgement hardened into the image of Wharton as a chilly snob, mistress of the grand manner and comfortable only when writing about her own privileged set. Such views focused less on Wharton's analyses of a narrow social circle, than on the limitations of her own class perspectives. So, a younger New England writer, Elizabeth Shepley Sergeant, author of 'Toilers of the Tenements' (*McClure's*, 1910) posited that the cosmopolitan Mrs Wharton approached the social world of *Ethan Frome*, in 'the unconsciously contemptuous key of the person who has a box at the opera' (*New Republic*, May 1915). This image of Wharton as aloof and out-of-touch intensified in the 1930s, with the rise of new forms of social realism, in the exigencies of the Depression. But Wharton herself always dismissed such criticisms. She lamented in a letter in 1904 the trial of hearing that her characters were 'not "real" because they are not navvies & char-women' (*Letters* 91); in her prefaces to *Ethan Frome*, later, she emphasised that she had drawn on her knowledge of the New England countryside, and that she was familiar with other lives outside the hothouse of old money; in her essay 'Tendencies in Modern Fiction' (1934) she continued to challenge narrow definitions of art, and poured scorn on the notion that 'the "real America"' was to be found only in novels about poor whites (*UCW* 173).

Many readers shared Wharton's perspective. From the earliest reviews, critics had remarked qualities even more impressive than her command of the witty phrase. While praising her epigrams, the *Book Buyer*'s review noted deeper explorations of temperament: 'Souls Belated' alone would stamp Wharton 'as somebody to be reckoned with' (*CR* 15). Describing the works as revelations of the inner folds of minds, hearts and souls, critics identified a social vision and psychological insight, which became the subject of another main strand of analysis. This discussion, which has continued in variant forms into this century, was rooted in arguments over the nature of realism; and many early readers asserted Wharton's eminence: 'So much keenness of insight, so much cleverness of phrase were not born, one is inclined to believe, of a day. It is realism carried to the *n*th power' (*Critic*, 1899; *CR* 24). Some centred on Wharton's affinities. Comments that she was 'of the school of Mr Henry James' (*CR* 21), in manner and material, appeared as a refrain throughout her reviews and into her posthumous reputation. But, while she counted James as one of her most intimate friends (*A Backward Glance* devotes him his own chapter), Wharton soon became exasperated with comparisons: 'the continued cry that I am an echo of Mr James (whose books of the last ten years I can't read, much as I delight in the man) [. . .] makes me feel rather hopeless' (1904; *Letters* 91). However, even with *The Greater Inclination*, some found her writings 'superior in many ways' to those of Mr James (*CR* 19); and the *Bookman*'s reviewer of 1899 asserted, 'therefore, she deserves a wholly independent criticism' (*CR* 19). Grant Overton, contemplating her reputation in 1923, was still more assertive:

the intellectual relation between her and the man who was once called her 'Master' is now seen in the light which considerably enhances the dignity of the woman who was once called 'Pupil'. For who, after reading the correspondence of Henry James, published since his death, believes any longer that Mrs Wharton ever owed anything to that man's patronage so nicely tinctured with snobbery?[2]

Another long-running debate worried over the novel: for some, it risked becoming too detached from modern life; for others, it was sinking into the sewer. The former believed the magazine publishing system, with its sensitivity to the family audience, too limiting – a view that, at its extreme, led to artists' expatriate flight to Europe. Editorial demands for wholesome books were reinforced by the dominant image of the hypothetical reader as the pure-minded 'young American girl': 'She is the Iron Madonna who strangles in her fond embrace the American novelist', as Hjalmar Hjorth Boyesen, a forthright Norwegian-born writer, expressed it.[3] For many reviewers, Wharton's work extended artistic possibility – subtle and searching, attentive to the minutiae of experience and hinting at 'suggestive shadows' (*CR* 31), while maintaining the bounds of good taste. Her stories revealed 'a clever analyst of human nature', who resisted the temptation 'to dabble wholly in the mire' (*CR* 23); and her first novel, *The Valley of Decision*, gained her congratulations (and a commission for *Italian Villas and their Gardens*) from the influential editor of the *Century*, Richard Watson Gilder – one of the foremost proponents of the ideal and the decent in literature. This novel's historical mode struck another reader as a felicitous artistic medium whereby 'every sort of immorality, turpitude, suffering, comes to us [. . .] without shocking or moving' (*CR* 54). For some, however, Wharton's realism was too strong; as the *Catholic World* exclaimed, this was a 'repulsive novel', full of 'moral squalor': 'there is not from the first cover of the first volume to the last of the second one honest virtuous woman' (*CR* 61).

Such remarks were echoed later, as reviewers described the 'sordid society' of *The Custom of the Country*, with its assembly of 'as many detestable people as it is possible to pack between the covers of a six-hundred page novel' (*CR* 210); or the action of *Summer* that hovered 'between the neighbouring verges of tragedy and squalor' (*CR* 263). However, most admired Wharton's restraint, and found even her grimmest tales brilliant. Reviewers continued to praise her social realism – particularly her analyses of the various ranks of the American monied classes – and her sensitivity to the inward life, 'the subjective reality' that, for some, constituted the truly modern 'realistic method' (*CR* 22, 23). From the first, too, she was regarded as bringing something new, a female perspective, to bear on women's lives. Gilder had remarked that as writers complained about 'the young American girl', they also underestimated her, and that this was why none had yet 'done her justice in fiction'.[4] A review of *The Touchstone*, by Aline Gorren a *Scribner's* writer interested in 'the Woman Question', anticipated, in its own terms, some of the interests of later twentieth-century criticism. Gorren singled out Wharton's stories for their genius in 'bring[ing] to the surface the underground movements of women's minds', with insights founded in knowledge, not in vapour about 'the soul of Woman' (*CR* 33).

During the 1920s, however, such impressions of innovation, or any risky edge to her writing, began to give place to a more tempered respect, as she became shelved as a 'distinguished representative of the old school'.[5] The Pulitzer Prize for *The Age of Innocence* in 1921, though an honour, compounded the conservative label, awarded as it was for the novel best presenting 'the highest standard of American manners and manhood' (see *Lee* 586–7). So, Vernon Parrington remarked, in an image evoking both fairy tale and society drama: 'She is unconsciously shut in behind plate glass, where butlers serve formal dinners, and white shoulders go up at the mere suggestion of everyday gingham' ('Our Literary Aristocrat', in *The Pacific Review*, June 1921). Writing to the younger Sinclair Lewis, Wharton confessed her despair at being rewarded for 'uplifting American morals' (*Letters* 445); and claimed disgust at the discovery that her novel had been the safe choice, over Lewis's more contentious *Main Street*. Lewis returned the compliment, dedicating to Wharton his next novel, *Babbitt* (1922). While Wharton joined in descriptions of herself as a fusty relic, more seriously she dissociated herself from the incoming generation of modernist writers, whose works were redefining nineteenth-century realism as an outmoded and limited genre. Attacks on Edwardian writers, such as Virginia Woolf's 'Modern Novels' (1919) (reprinted as 'Modern Fiction' in *The Common Reader*, 1925) and 'Mr Bennett and Mrs Brown', presented a new, experimental aesthetic. Woolf scorned, as 'materialist' and old-fashioned, realist writers' interest in the accumulation of detail, or care for plot and characterisation.

In the articles collected as *The Writing of Fiction* (1925), Wharton inveighed, in turn, against what she viewed as the lack of selectivity, and the formlessness, of impressionistic novels which attempted to chart the stream of consciousness: 'the art of rendering life in fiction can never be anything [. . .] but the disengaging of crucial moments against the welter of existence' (*WF* 14). Further essays, 'Tendencies in Modern Fiction' and 'Permanent Values in Fiction' (both 1934) took younger novelists to task for abandoning story and character (Lewis was her exception). Although readers had, she said, been rendered 'insensible to allusiveness and irony' by a 'long course of cinema obviousnesses and of tabloid culture' (*UCW* 179), they could still recognise well-drawn, ordinary people in fiction. Wharton's own adherence to depicting characters, and delicate moral complications, continued to attract appreciative reviews. Some admirers regarded her as above the need to prove herself through cheap experiment. As one wrote in 1923: 'There is no flabbiness about her [...] She does not need to practise the conventional literary dishonesties which close like traps upon novelists whose fame is on the make and who still have much to lose.'[6] Even a major document of the New Deal, Charles and Mary Beard's *The Rise of American Civilization* (1927; reprinted 1933), paid tribute, commemorating *Ethan Frome* as 'chiseled out of cold, gray granite by a hand as remorseless as that which shaped the end of Agamemnon'. But, increasingly lukewarm comments diluted the praise. Although *A Backward Glance* was received as an accomplished self-portrait, by 'our most distinguished contemporary writer of fiction' (*CR* 529), E. M. Forster, for one, felt that though her 'constant prosperity does not spoil her work, [...] it does make for autobiographical monotony' (*CR* 524); and a reviewer of the stories *Certain People* (1930) observed, in places, 'that well bred lifeless quality which has marked certain of her books these latter years' (*CR* 479).

Critical reputation

At her death, her reputation was secure. In London, *The Times* called her 'one of the greatest novelists America had produced' (14 August 1937); but homage was tinctured with notes that she had dated. With their tone of special pleading, some of the most admiring retrospectives contributed to her relegation: notably, fellow American novelist Edmund Wilson's 'Justice to Edith Wharton' (1938; reprinted in *The Wound and the Bow*, 1947); and the British critic Q. D. Leavis's 'Henry James's Heiress: The Importance of Edith Wharton' (*Scrutiny* 8.3, December 1938). Wilson presented a narrative of a decline into 'women's magazine' fiction, and 'feebler second boiling from the tea-leaves' from *The Age of Innocence* onwards; and boasted that he had read only one of Wharton's novels beyond *Old New York*. (It took several decades for critics to challenge his certainties.) Like him, Q. D. Leavis reinforced the image of Wharton's overshadowing by James, and took as her premise the view that the English public, at least, recalled Wharton only 'vaguely as the kind of fiction which was published serially in *Good*

Housekeeping'. Wharton's one-time protégé, Percy Lubbock, damned her further, with his *Portrait of Edith Wharton* (1947), as a frigid autocrat, scarcely in control of her material. Her admirers came to regard themselves as an isolated species; and in 1962, Irving Howe could introduce a short anthology, *Edith Wharton: A Collection of Critical Essays*, with the remark that he had omitted little of substance. (The essays by Parrington, Wilson and Leavis were reprinted here.) While Millicent Bell's *Edith Wharton and Henry James: The Story of their Friendship* (1965) presented a sympathetic and more varied account, the novelist Louis Auchincloss's extensively illustrated *Edith Wharton: A Woman in her Time* (1971) preserved her as a phenomenon of a bygone leisured era. A review of the latter, by Vivian Mercier in *The Nation* (January 1972), asked, in its title, 'Whose Edith?' – a prescient question for the criticism which has followed. Mercier expressed impatience with Auchincloss's perspectives on Wharton as one of 'us', a genteel member of the Social Register; and suggested that other groups might have equally strong claims. Marx would perhaps 'have thought her a better Marxist in her social analysis' than the radical critics who had dismissed her as upper class; and the new feminist movement ('Women's Liberation') might find in her work a deep interest in women's concerns (21). Mercier believed, further, that Wharton must have known passion, and that, though reined in as her times demanded, the evidence was there in her work (22).

With the opening of Wharton's private papers, held at Yale, critical interest exploded. R. W. B. Lewis's pioneering *Edith Wharton: A Biography* (1975) replaced hints and guesses with testimony. Lewis unveiled a more turbulent Wharton, troubled in adolescence and marriage, and transported, in middle age, by the love affair with Fullerton. An appendix dismissed a rumour attributing Wharton's paternity to a putative lover of Lucretia, the Jones brothers' tutor, an Englishman – a refutation which itself stirred up more questions; and Lewis topped this with his detailed account of the Fullerton papers (he printed the poem 'Terminus', in full, in his story of the affair). Capping it all, he ended with an appendix presenting Wharton's 'Beatrice Palmato' outline, and a fragment of the text: a pulsating, and explicit, erotic writing of father/daughter relations ('An instant more, and his tongue had left her fainting mouth, and was twisting like a soft pink snake about each breast in turn', as an early moment in the encounter expressed it). These revelations overturned for ever the image of the aloof and frosty lady, imprisoned in her drawing room; but beyond these, Lewis's book drew attention to the interest of the whole range of Wharton's writing, from her mock reviews for 'Fast and Loose' to her letters. His biography was followed by another founding critical work, Cynthia Griffin Wolff's subtle literary-psychological treatment, *A Feast of Words: The Triumph of Edith Wharton* (1977), which investigated Wharton's writing and creative impulses as acts of emotional and imaginative growth. Wolff took seriously, too, the novels of Wharton's late career, locating their possible beginnings in earlier unfinished manuscripts; and she placed Wharton's work within wider cultural landscapes: with Art Nouveau, for example, illuminating Lily's representation in *The House of Mirth*, or Stravinsky's *Le Sacre du Printemps* (which Wharton saw in May 1913) colouring her visions of 'the primitive' (as in *Summer* and *In Morocco*).

Coinciding with the 'rediscovery' of women writers in the wave of seventies and eighties feminist activism, many of the most influential new readings that followed brought to the fore Wharton's representations of women and of women's experience. Running through many was a general question that had struck some contemporary reviewers. Given the unpleasantness and economic ruthlessness of many of Wharton's female characters, her own identification with a male literary gold standard, and many of her declared reservations about women's capabilities and ambitions, did she even like women? And, further, from the viewpoint of the later twentieth century, could she be in any way described as a radical early feminist writer? Margaret McDowell's earlier *Edith Wharton* (1976) had advanced a sympathetic reading, linking Wharton to other turn-of-the-century women writers. Taking up this theme, and engaging with a range of discourses from fairy tale to New Woman writing, Elizabeth Ammons, in *Edith Wharton's Argument with America* (1980), discussed Wharton's negotiations with the earlier wave of feminism ('the Woman Question'). Ammons traced a change of attitude throughout Wharton's career: from initial uncertainty into a strong critique of women's restricted opportunities, followed, in the 1920s, by a drift into conservatism, and then into a kind of mystical evocation of primal matriarchal powers ('The Mothers') in her late epic diptych. Carol Wershoven, *The Female Intruder in the Novels of Edith Wharton* (1982), traced a different kind of female energy; diverting attention from the conventional centre of consciousness in much of the fiction (the conservative Newland Archer types), she suggested a key narrative pattern of critique and change, generated by the repeated figure of a transgressive female outsider (a woman possibly somewhat resembling Wharton herself). This trend, unwelcome to some of Wharton's admirers, was characterised by James W. Tuttleton as 'The Feminist Takeover of Edith Wharton' (*The New Criterion*, March 1989). However, further studies, into the 1990s, took such interests onwards. Susan Goodman's *Edith Wharton's Women: Friends and*

Rivals (1990), for example, extended discussion into Wharton's own friendships with other women; David Holbrook's *Edith Wharton and the Unsatisfactory Man* (1991) turned the gender focus to Wharton's enfeebled male figures; and Gloria C. Erlich's *The Sexual Education of Edith Wharton* (1992) linked the presentation of female characters to Wharton's own psycho-sexual development.

Wharton's relation to other writers was a significant strand of many studies. In a much reprinted essay, 'The Death of the Lady (Novelist): Edith Wharton's *The House of Mirth*' (*Representations* 9, Spring 1985), Elaine Showalter examined the novel as part of a larger investigation into a nineteenth-century tradition of women's writing. In an argument which aligned Wharton's remaking of earlier women's plots and her own remaking as a professional artist, Showalter contributed to new kinds of literary dialogue which were questioning and revising the (then) dominant canonical male line, from Huck Finn to Hemingway. Such discussions gave Wharton a key position as a writer who crossed the boundary-line between nineteenth- and twentieth-century genres, and, by placing her in new aesthetic and cultural configurations, opened up fresh aspects of her work. Martha Banta, *Imaging American Women: Idea and Ideals in Cultural History* (1987), looked at examples of Wharton's work within a wide-ranging survey of turn-of-the-century visual arts, from family photographs to theatrical posters (a book which crossed conventional barriers between high and popular art). Shari Benstock, *Women of the Left Bank: Paris, 1900–1940* (1986), brought out correspondences between Wharton's vision and those of her more openly avant-garde American contemporaries from whom she had, in life, maintained a distance: among them, modernists such as Gertrude Stein, Jessie Fauset, H. D. and Djuna Barnes. However, Benstock placed Wharton, at last, in the nineteenth century, a precursor but not a progressive.

Sandra M. Gilbert and Susan Gubar included a chapter on Wharton ('Angel of Devastation: Edith Wharton on the Arts of the Enslaved') in their three-volume argument about gendered transactions in modernist writing, *No Man's Land: The Place of the Woman Writer in the Twentieth Century*, vol. II, *Sexchanges* (1989); this presented her as a whirlwind of energy, conducting an impassioned assault, lifelong, on America as a hell for women. Katherine Joslin's persuasively argued *Edith Wharton* (1991) brought to the debate a consistently theorised feminist perspective on women's writing and culture. Joslin framed Wharton's writing as a dialectic with society, that corrected the celebratory themes both of nineteenth-century female domestic writing and of the male 'pastoral romance' (the fantasy of lighting out for the territory). Helen Killoran, *Edith Wharton: Art and Allusion* (1996), pursued

Wharton's use of European and American predecessors under various thematic headings, a project also undertaken in the articles on individual borrowings and echoes assembled in Adeline R. Tinter, *Edith Wharton in Context: Essays on Intertextuality* (1999). Such studies as Donna M. Campbell, *Resisting Regionalism: Gender and Naturalism in American Fiction, 1885–1915* (1997); Hildegard Hoeller, *Edith Wharton's Dialogue with Realism and Sentimental Fiction* (2000); Deborah Lindsay Williams, *Not in Sisterhood: Edith Wharton, Willa Cather, Zona Gale, and the Politics of Female Authorship* (2001); or Robin Peel, *Apart from Modernism: Edith Wharton, Politics, and Fiction Before World War I* (2005) again reinvigorated discussions of Wharton's place within broader narrative traditions. Each, again, illuminated Wharton's complex relationships to writers (for example, in Campbell, the 'local color' regional 'authoresses'), often ignored or oversimplified in accounts of a male tradition.

Interest in Wharton's social critique remained important within these debates, often integrated with considerations of form and genre, and increasingly embedded in specific details of cultural history. Appreciations of her skill with nuance, as in James W. Tuttleton's *The Novel of Manners in America* (1972), had begun to extend into wider, ideological examinations of her studies of changing class and social structures: Gary H. Lindberg's *Edith Wharton and the Novel of Manners* (1975), for example, had highlighted the upsurge in her narratives of those with no manners – the invaders in the drawing room. In the 1980s, as in Wharton's early reviews, the nature of realism began to re-emerge as a key area. Dissolving over-rigid taxonomies of 'Realism' and 'Naturalism', critics suggested that genres (and authors) were more dynamically engaged with forms of social power than merely describing or reflecting them. Walter Benn Michaels, *The Gold Standard and the Logic of Naturalism: American Literature at the Turn of the Century* (1987), and Amy Kaplan, *The Social Construction of American Realism* (1988), both analysed Wharton's work within far-reaching arguments about professional writing as a form of production, an attempt to maintain control in a rapidly changing marketplace. Elsa Nettels, in *Language and Gender in American Fiction: Howells, James, Wharton and Cather* (1997), took up the work of four literary realists in terms of connections between power, authority, gender, class and language, within the contexts of American publishing. (*The Cambridge Companion to Realism and Naturalism*, edited by Donald Pizer, 1995, offers a helpful entrance-point to such debates.)

So, too, Wai Chee Dimock, 'Debasing Exchange: Edith Wharton's *The House of Mirth*' (*PMLA* 100, October 1985), generally viewed as a landmark Marxist reading, looked at characters and their exchanges as part of a wholesale commodification of the social fabric. Dale M. Bauer, *Edith Wharton's Brave New Politics* (1994), gave prominence to the second half of Wharton's career in a sustained socio-historical debate, ranging from eugenics and reproductive rights to the 'Reign of Youth' and mass-culture. Wharton's readings in ethnology and anthropology, and her models of a self developed within social structures, were at the centre of Pamela Knights, 'Forms of Disembodiment: The Social Subject of *The Age of Innocence*' and Nancy Bentley, '"Hunting for the Real": Wharton and the Science of Manners' in *The Cambridge Companion to Edith Wharton* (1995); as well as in Bentley's influential *The Ethnography of Manners: Hawthorne, James, Wharton* (1995). The rituals of a leisure-class culture of display were taken up again in Maureen E. Montgomery's *Displaying Women: Spectacles of Leisure in Edith Wharton's New York* (1998) and Claire Preston's *Edith Wharton's Social Register* (2000). Using *Twilight Sleep* as his major Wharton sample, Phillip Barrish, *American Literary Realism, Critical Theory, and Intellectual Prestige, 1880–1995* (2001), took up the force of realist writing in establishing cultural authority, a mode of what Pierre Bordieu terms 'cultural capital'. All these, in various ways, connected realism with other kinds of middle-class professional discourse (from architecture to management-science), to pay attention to its broader cultural projects: its attempts to understand the place of the individual character within the larger social group; to grasp currents of historical change, and register cultural limits.

At the same time, a growing number of critics began to enter landscapes within or beyond social realism. Janet Beer Goodwyn's *Edith Wharton: Traveller in the Land of Letters* (1990) unfolded Wharton's development as an artist, in fiction and non-fiction, within a narrative of her travels, and her use of topography as a creative resource; this book also contributed strongly to the interest in works beyond the canonical Wharton. Beer followed this with a comparative short-story study: *Kate Chopin, Edith Wharton and Charlotte Perkins Gilman: Studies in Short Fiction* (1997). Others brought mythic shadings to Wharton's texts, reading her in relation to other writers, in the light of her repeated motif of the Persephone myth (concentrated in her ghost story 'Pomegranate Seed', 1931): Josephine Donovan, *After the Fall: The Demeter-Persephone Myth in Wharton, Cather and Glasgow* (1989), and Candace Waid, *Edith Wharton's Letters from the Underworld: Fictions of Women and Writing* (1991). In contrast, Lev Raphael, *Edith Wharton's Prisoners of Shame: A New Perspective on Her Neglected Fiction* (1991), suggested fresh readings of *The Touchstone*, *The Reef* and some later works, in the light of psychological studies in shame. In *Edith Wharton: Matters of Mind and Spirit* (1995), Carol J. Singley turned attention to Wharton's engagement with philosophy, and classical and Christian thought – a 'novelist of morals', rather than of manners, as her preface explained. Wharton's affinities with a very different literary tradition, that of the ghostly and Gothic, had been rising to the surface in scattered studies – among them, Allan Gardner Lloyd-Smith's *Uncanny American Fiction: Medusa's Face* (1989); Martha Banta's 'The Ghostly Gothic of Wharton's Everyday World' (in *American Literary Realism 1870–1910* 27.1, 1991); and Lynnette Carpenter and Wendy Kolmar's *Haunting the House of Fiction: Feminist Perspectives on Ghost Stories by American Women* (1991). Kathy Fedorko, in her groundbreaking *Gender and the Gothic in the Fiction of Edith Wharton* (1995), brought these darker places into the forefront of Wharton studies. With an underpinning of Jungian theories of individuation, Fedorko explored Wharton's inner narratives of gender conflict and resolution through the dimensions of a Gothic inheritance – of hauntings, imprisonment, doubles.

From a different angle, Judith Fryer, *Felicitous Space: The Imaginative Structures of Edith Wharton and Willa Cather* (1986), drew together different kinds of text, verbal and visual (including house-plans and photographs), to explore women's culture within the lived environment. Taking her title from the French philosopher Gaston Bachelard's *Poetics of Space* (1958; translated 1964), Fryer made connections between concepts of space and the female imagination. The effects of realism, its illusions of a dense and solid material reality, its significant piling up of detail, here acquired further layers, enriching readings of the surfaces of Wharton's rooms, houses and furnishings. Marilyn Chandler, *Dwelling in the Text: Houses in American Fiction* (1991), with a chapter on *The Age of Innocence*, traced the home as a significant trope in narratives from Thoreau's *Walden* to Toni Morrison's *Beloved*. Images of interiorised space were again the focus of Jill M. Kress, *The Figure of Consciousness in Literary Criticism and Cultural Theory: William James, Henry James, and Edith Wharton* (2002). Explorations of material culture, underpinned by new historicist and interdisciplinary interests, remain a pervasive critical strand. Lily Bart's costumes feature in Clair Hughes's *Dressed in Fiction* (2006); Wharton's designs, in houses, gardens and fictional texts, in Renee Somers, *Edith Wharton as Spatial Activist and Analyst* (2005), and an array of architectural works, paintings, objects and spaces in Annette Benert's *The Architectural Imagination of Edith Wharton: Gender, Class, and Power in the Progressive Era* (2007), Emily J. Orlando's *Edith Wharton and the Visual Arts* (2007) and an essay-collection, *Memorial Boxes and Guarded Interiors: Edith Wharton and Material Culture* (2007), edited by Gary Totten, all published as this *Introduction* neared completion.

Scholarly articles and monographs burgeon annually, opening up fresh perspectives. Increasingly specialised studies seem set to refine and extend views of Wharton's intellectual and cultural frameworks. Readings in the light of literary naturalism, for instance, have kept her scientific interests in view, as in Bert Bender, *The Descent of Love: Darwin and the Theory of Sexual Selection in American Fiction, 1871–1926* (1996), or, more recently, Paul J. Ohler, *Edith Wharton's 'Evolutionary Conception': Darwinian Allegory in Her Major Novels* (2006); or Wharton's engagement with catastrophic world crisis, in Julie Olin-Ammentorp's *Edith Wharton's Writings from the Great War* (2004). With growing attention to the history of the book and the practices of publishing, more notice is being paid to the contexts in which Wharton's work first appeared or was publicised: in magazines, amid jokes, other serials, advertisements, cartoons, illustrations. So, for example, Edith Thornton analyses the *Scribner's* illustrations of *The House of Mirth*, in '*Beyond* the Page: Visual Literacy and the Interpretation of Lily Bart' (in Beer, Knights and Nolan (eds.), *Edith Wharton's* The House of Mirth, see 'Guide to further reading'); and Martha H. Patterson examines *The Custom of the Country* within a wider study of the New Woman trope, *Beyond the Gibson Girl: Reimagining the American New Woman, 1895–1915* (2005). The turn towards contemporary forms of socio-political understanding, pointed out throughout this *Introduction* – of imperialism, colonialism or globalisation; and of identities, race, class, ethnicity or disability – seems likely to produce many more controversies. Debates remain active about the question of Wharton's anti-Semitism, for example, argued in a spate of articles in the early 1990s, among them: Christian Riegel, 'Rosedale and Anti-Semitism in *The House of Mirth*' (*Studies in American Fiction* 20.2, Autumn 1992); Irene C. Goldman, 'The *Perfect* Jew and *The House of Mirth*: A Study in Point of View' (*Modern Language Studies* 23.2, Spring 1993); and '"The Impossible Rosedale": Race and the Reading of Edith Wharton's *The House of Mirth*' (*Studies in Jewish Literature* 13, 1994). Anne McMaster, 'Wharton, Race, and *The Age of Innocence*: Three Historical Contexts' (in Colquitt, Goodman and Waid (eds.), *A Forward Glance: New Essays on Edith Wharton*, see 'Guide to further reading'), turned to the Africanist presence in the texts. These topics, along with broader racial and ethnic arguments, have been addressed, more recently, by Jennie A. Kassanoff's *Edith Wharton and the Politics of Race* (2004). This book returns to Wharton's class pedigree, to read her work as a sustained apologia of conservatism, a 'racial aesthetic' through which Wharton fended off the welter of democratic pluralism in America. Kassanoff urges that Wharton be read without patronising or protecting her – a view which new biography supports.

Biographical material has continued to galvanise interest, each book bringing new visions of the woman and the writer. The Lewises' selective edition, *The Letters of Edith Wharton* (1988), fanned the flames of her affair with Fullerton; as did the publication of the love diary, in the unlikely setting of an academic journal, edited and introduced by Kenneth M. Price and Phyllis McBride: '"The Life Apart": Text and Contexts of Edith Wharton's Love Diary', *American Literature* 66.4 (December 1994). Shari Benstock, *No Gifts from Chance: A Biography of Edith Wharton* (1994), illuminated more of Wharton's close friendships; Alan Price, *The End of the Age of Innocence: Edith Wharton and the First World War* (1996) and Sarah Bird Wright, *Edith Wharton's Travel Writing: The Making of a Connoisseur* (1997), shed light on her extraordinary range of activities and experiences, as war-worker and traveller. For the next generation, the monumental life by Hermione Lee (2007) will become a new critical landmark. With its strong portrait of 'Mme Warthon', the European writer, Lee's book stirs fresh arguments about literary nationalism; and contributes to wider critical debates which are challenging boundaries through new transnational perspectives.

Although a complete scholarly edition seems far off, new publications are still bringing to light areas of her work so far given comparatively little attention – her revisions, her unfinished novels and plays, her poems and travel-writings. Wharton's own introductions, reviews and literary essays have been collected by Frederick Wegener, in *Edith Wharton: The Uncollected Critical Writings* (1996), a rich resource on which I have drawn throughout this *Introduction*. In recent years, the significant discovery of over 2,600 books surviving from Wharton's library, with her bookplates, markings and inscriptions, has begun to spark other kinds of investigation. Described and catalogued by the bookseller George Ramsden, as *Edith Wharton's Library: A Catalogue* (1999), and acquired by an anonymous benefactor for Edith Wharton's Massachusetts home, The Mount, in 2005, this record will produce new insights into Wharton's interests and influences, her intellectual history and her ways of reading.

Legacies

For critics, now, Wharton can no longer be dismissed as 'Henry James Lite', or as the last of the genteel American realists; but as a writer who draws richly on multiple traditions, and takes readers into new and complex forms of literature, countries without a guide-book. However, as reading neither begins, nor ends, with formal scholarship, I conclude this *Introduction* by taking Wharton's writing onwards, to point to some of the more creative reworkings her books have inspired.

From the beginning, her novels attracted adaptors: the silent film of *The House of Mirth* (1918) is lost, but surviving prints include *The Age of Innocence* (1934) and *The Old Maid* (1939). More recently, screen productions such as Martin Scorsese's *The Age of Innocence*, John Madden's *Ethan Frome*, with Liam Neeson in the title role (both 1993); the sumptuous BBC serialisation of *The Buccaneers* (1995); and Terence Davies's *The House of Mirth* (2000), starring Gillian Anderson (hitherto known for the 'X-Files'), have brought her books new audiences.[7] In the twenty-first century, Wharton again has celebrity status, 'brand recognition', even as a note in a fashion-shoot: 'high-necked Edwardian lace out of Edith Wharton' (American *Vogue*, July 2005: 103). She continues to inspire younger writers. Creative responses range from murder mystery to young adult fiction and chick lit. Lev Raphael's gay, Jewish, campus-murder series deploys a Wharton bibliographer as narrator and reluctant sleuth (see especially *The Edith Wharton Murders*, 1997). In Jennifer Donnelly's *A Gathering Light* (2003), reading Wharton is part of the heroine's coming-of-age. Tama Janowitz's *A Certain Age* (1999) reworks Lily Bart as a cocaine-fuelled Manhattanite. The rapacious 'Victoria's Secret' model, Janey (with her partner, Selden Rose), in Candace Bushnell's, *Four Blondes* (2000) and *Trading Up* (2003), blends Lily and Undine, as she exhausts New York, to conquer Hollywood.

Wharton loathed the idea of 'mechanical' reading (the approach to books as a duty) and, worse, 'mechanical' criticism (summarising plots, to offer ready-made opinions). The reader who trudges through a book as a set task is like 'a tourist who drives from one "sight" to another without looking at anything that is not set down in Baedeker'. Books, she wrote, in characteristic images, should not become dead things: 'fossils ticketed and put away in the drawers of a geologist's cabinet', or 'prisoners condemned to life-long solitary confinement'; they needed to expand 'like growing things that strike root and intertwine branches', to 'talk to each other' in the mind.[8] Asking, 'What is reading, in the last analysis, but an interchange of thought between writer and readers?', with her own works, she invites in her audience to continue these conversations.

Notes

1 Life

1 'Memories of Bourget Overseas' (1936; *UCW* 216).
2 Eric Homberger, *Mrs Astor's New York* (New Haven and London: Yale University Press, 2002), 170. Homberger details the social manoeuvring of the exclusive 'Four Hundred' (the capacity of Mrs Astor's ball-room).
3 *The Condition of Women in the United States: A Traveller's Notes*, trans. Abby Langdon Alger (Boston: Roberts Brothers, 1895), ch. 1, 24.
4 Karl Baedeker (ed.), *The United States, with an Excursion into Mexico: Handbook for Travellers* (Leipsic [Leipzig]: Karl Baedeker; London: Dulan and Co., 1893), 68, 70. Illustrations in Robert Hughes, *American Visions: The Epic History of Art in America* (London: Harvill, 1997), 233–6.
5 *North America*, vol. I (London: Chapman and Hall, 1862), ch. 2, 32, 39.
6 Mrs John Sherwood, *Manners and Social Usages* (rev. New York: Harper's, 1903), 69.
7 Homberger, *Mrs Astor's New York*, 183–4.
8 Maud C. Cooke, *Social Etiquette: or Manners and Customs of Polite Society* (Washington, DC: n.p., 1896), 79.

2 Contexts

1 Hugo Münsterberg, *American Problems: From the Point of View of a Psychologist* (New York: Moffat, 1910), 3–5.
2 See Margaret Münsterberg, *Hugo Münsterberg: His Life and Work* (New York and London: Appleton, 1922).
3 Desley Deacon, *Elsie Clews Parsons: Inventing Modern Life* (University of Chicago Press, 1997), 362.
4 Edith Wharton, Introduction, *The House of Mirth* (Oxford: Oxford World's Classics, 1936), [v]; the Rosetta Stone was found in Egypt in 1799.
5 See Nancy Bentley's excellent analysis, 'Wharton, Travel, and Modernity', in Carol J. Singley, *A Historical Guide to Edith Wharton* (Oxford University Press, 2003), 147–9.

138

6 See Meryle Secrest, *Being Bernard Berenson: A Biography* (Harmondsworth: Penguin, 1980), 139–45.

7 Janet Beer Goodwyn, *Edith Wharton: Traveller in the Land of Letters* (Basingstoke: Macmillan, 1990), 2.

8 James to Alvin Langdon Coburn (1906), *Henry James: Letters*, vol. IV: *1895–1916*, ed. Leon Edel (Cambridge, Mass.: Belknap-Harvard University Press, 1984), 426. Fletcher helped to locate Venetian settings for Coburn's photographs in James's New York edition.

9 Shari Benstock, *Women of the Left Bank: Paris, 1900–1940* (1986; London: Virago, 1994), 13.

10 Henry James, *Hawthorne* (1879; New York: Harper and Brothers, 1880), ch. 2, 42–3.

11 Susan Coolidge, *What Katy Did Next* (Boston: Roberts Brothers, 1886), ch. 9, 228.

12 See Janet Beer, *Edith Wharton* (Tavistock: Northcote House, 2002), 81–5.

3 Works

1 *Lee* (13–15) discusses this phenomenon in detail.

2 Darwin's *The Descent of Man*: 'it occurred to me to investigate some striking or crucial instances, and to rely on the result' (noted in Janet Beer, *Edith Wharton* (Tavistock: Northcote House, 2002), 40).

3 Quoted in Percy H. Boynton, *Some Contemporary Americans: The Personal Equation in Literature* (University of Chicago Press, 1924), 100.

4 Ellen Glasgow, *The Woman Within: An Autobiography* (1954; reprinted New York: Hill and Wang, 1980), 269 (published posthumously); Glasgow owned copies of Freud's work and attempted a major Freudian scene in *Barren Ground* (1925); her novel, *The Sheltered Life* (1932) reprises some of the themes of *The Age of Innocence* in a Southern setting.

5 *Mass and Class: A Survey of Social Divisions* (New York: Macmillan, 1904), 178–9.

6 Jean Frantz Blackall, 'Edith Wharton's Art of Ellipsis', *Journal of Narrative Technique* 17 (Spring 1987): 145.

7 A notorious punishment, administered in the Reign of Terror at Nantes, 1793–4.

8 Review, *Evening Sun*, quoted in advertisement for *Crucial Instances*, *BE* 11 May 1901: 6.

9 Frantz Blackall's suggestion, noted in Sarah Bird Wright, *Edith Wharton A–Z* (New York: Checkmark Books, 1998), 51.

10 'Fiction: *The House of Mirth*', *Times Literary Supplement*, 1 (December 1905): 421. Published anonymously, this generally spiteful review was by Wharton's friend Percy Lubbock.

11 Letter, Lamb House, Rye, England, 17 August 1904: *Henry James and Edith Wharton: Letters: 1900–1915*, ed. Lyall H. Powers (New York: Scribner's, 1990), 36.

12 Edith Wharton, Introduction, *The House of Mirth* (Oxford: Oxford World's Classics, 1936), vi.

13 Jennie A. Kassanoff cites the start of this passage in *Edith Wharton and the Politics of Race* (Cambridge University Press, 2004), 55.

14 Edwin Lawrence Godkin, 'The Expenditure of Rich Men' (*Scribner's Magazine*, 1896), in *Problems of Modern Democracy: Political and Economic Essays* (New York: Scribner's, 1896), 319.

15 Charles Johnston, 'Our National Peculiarities: 1. The American Psychic Atmosphere', *The Arena* (August 1900): 173.

16 Henry George, *The Menace of Privilege: A Study of the Dangers to the Republic from the Existence of a Favored Class* (New York: Macmillan, 1905), 63–71. Godkin, *Problems of Modern Democracy*, 328.

17 See Louise Bolard More, *Wage-Earners' Budgets: A Study of Standards and Cost of Living in New York City* (New York: Holt, 1907).

18 Mrs John Sherwood, *Manners and Social Usages* (rev. New York: Harper's, 1903), 44.

19 Thomas Bender, *The Unfinished City: New York and the Metropolitan Ideal* (New York: The New Press, 2002), 104.

20 Wharton, Introduction, *The House of Mirth*, vii.

21 See essays by Katherine Joslin and Kathy Fedorko in Janet Beer, Pamela Knights and Elizabeth Nolan (eds.), *Edith Wharton's* The House of Mirth (London: Routledge, 2007).

22 Amy M. King's *Bloom: The Botanical Vernacular in the English Novel* (Oxford University Press, 2003) offers an extensive survey.

23 George M. Beard, *American Nervousness: Its Causes and Consequences* (New York: G. P. Putnam's, 1881), 74.

24 Paul Bourget, *Outre-mer: Impressions of America* (New York: Scribner's, 1895), 50.

25 Ibid., 107–9. A reminiscence of John Keats's 'Isabella', echoed later in Nicole Warren's Parisian spree in F. Scott Fitzgerald's *Tender is the Night*.

26 William James Ghent, 'Our Magnates', in *Our Benevolent Feudalism* (New York: Macmillan, 1902), 29.

27 Noted also by Robert McIlvaine, 'Edith Wharton's American Beauty Rose', *American Studies* 7.2 (August 1973): 183–5.

28 George, *Privilege*, 373. Taine, mentioned in the key passage from 'Disintegration' (p. 57 above), was one of Wharton's 'formative influences' (*Letters* 136).

29 Carol J. Singley, *Edith Wharton: Matters of Mind and Spirit* (Cambridge University Press, 1995), 82.

30 Helen Churchill Candee, *How Women May Earn a Living* (New York: Macmillan, 1990), 104.

31 Translated, Mark Ritter and David Frisby, in David Frisby and Mike Featherstone (eds.), *Simmel on Culture: Selected Writings* (London: Sage, 1997): (109–20), 118, 120.

32 In Gary Bridge and Sophie Watson (eds.), *A Companion to the City* (Oxford: Blackwell, 2000), 388–97.

33 For discussion, see Pamela Knights, Introduction, *The House of Mirth* (London: Everyman's Library, 1991), v–xxix.

34 Frances Hodgson Burnett, *The Shuttle* (New York: Frederick A. Stokes, 1907), ch. 38, 379. (The novel was first published as a serial in the *Century*, from November 1906.)

35 See essay by Janet Beer and Elizabeth Nolan, in Beer, Knights and Nolan, *Edith Wharton's* The House of Mirth; and Mary V. Marchand, 'Death to Lady Bountiful: Women and Reform in Edith Wharton's *The Fruit of the Tree*', *Legacy: A Journal of American Women Writers* 18.1 (2001): 65–78.

36 Katherine Joslin, 'Architectonic or Episodic? Gender and *The Fruit of the Tree*', in Clare Colquitt, Susan Goodman and Candace Waid (eds.), *A Forward Glance: New Essays on Edith Wharton* (Newark and London: University of Delaware Press, 1999), 67.

37 W. D. MacCallan, 'The French Draft of Ethan Frome', *Yale University Library Gazette* 27.1 (July 1952): 38–47.

38 All quotations from 'The Life Apart (*L'âme close*)', in *The Heath Anthology of American Literature*, 3rd edn, vol. II, general ed. Paul Lauter (Boston and New York: Houghton Mifflin: 1998), 1047–58.

39 Kenneth M. Price and Phyllis McBride, '"The Life Apart": Text and Contexts of Edith Wharton's Love Diary', *American Literature* 66.4 (December 1994) (663–88): 664.

40 Powers (ed.), *Henry James and Edith Wharton*, 195.

41 For a reading in terms of region, see Pamela Knights, introduction, *Ethan Frome* (new edn, Ware: Wordsworth Classics, 2004), 1–24.

42 Powers (ed.), *Henry James and Edith Wharton*, 239; Helen Killoran, *Edith Wharton: Art and Allusion* (Tuscaloosa and London: University of Alabama Press, 1996), 29–41; *Lee* 379–80.

43 Cynthia Griffin Wolff, *A Feast of Words: The Triumph of Edith Wharton* (1977; rev. edn, Reading, Mass.: Addison-Wesley, 1995), 212.

44 Elizabeth Ammons, *Edith Wharton's Argument with America* (Athens: University of Georgia Press, 1980). Also Ammons, 'Fairy Tale Love and *The Reef*', *American Literature* 47 (1976), 615–28.

45 See especially Kathy Fedorko, *Gender and the Gothic in the Fiction of Edith Wharton* (Tuscaloosa: University of Alabama Press, 1995).

46 See particularly Candace Waid, *Edith Wharton's Letters from the Underworld: Fictions of Women and Writing* (Chapel Hill: University of North Carolina Press, 1991) and Singley, *Matters of Mind and Spirit*.

47 See Killoran, *Art and Allusion*, 37–40.

48 Dale Bauer, 'Wharton's "Others": Addiction and Intimacy', in Carol J. Singley (ed.), *A Historical Guide to Edith Wharton* (Oxford University Press, 2003), 134–8;

for voyeurism in *The Reef*, see Jessica Levine, *Delicate Pursuit: Discretion in Henry James and Edith Wharton* (New York and London: Routledge, 2002).

49 Elaine Showalter, Introduction, *Ethan Frome* (Oxford: Oxford World's Classics, 1996), xxiii.

50 Judith Fryer, *Felicitous Space: The Imaginative Structures of Edith Wharton and Willa Cather* (Chapel Hill: University of North Carolina Press, 1986), 182.

51 For general discussion of masculinities in fiction, see René Girard, *Deceit, Desire and the Novel: Self and Other in Literary Structure* (1966); Eve Kosofsky Sedgwick, *Between Men: English Literature and Male Homosocial Desire* (1985); Peter Middleton, *The Inward Gaze: Masculinity and Subjectivity in Modern Culture* (1992); Ben Knights, *Writing Masculinities: Male Narratives in Twentieth-Century Fiction* (1999).

52 Wolff, *A Feast of Words*, 183.

53 Speaking on Julia Ehrhardt (ed.), *Edith Wharton and Her Novels* (video; BBC Educational, 1995).

54 Karl Baedeker (ed.), *The United States, with an Excursion into Mexico: Handbook for Travellers* (Leipsic [Leipzig]: Karl Baedeker; London: Dulan and Co., 1893), xxx.

55 Stephen Orgel, Introduction, *The Custom of the Country* (Oxford: Oxford World's Classics, 1995); Singley, *Matters of Mind and Spirit*, 56; Cecilia Tichi, 'Emerson, Darwin, and *The Custom of the Country*', in Singley (ed.), *Historical Guide*, 89–114.

56 Willa Cather, *O Pioneers!* (Boston and New York: Houghton Mifflin, 1913), 123.

57 *Benstock* 84; 'Schoolroom Decoration' in *UCW* 57–60; see also 'The Schoolroom and Nurseries', ch. XV, *DH*.

58 See Elizabeth Ammons, Introduction, *Edith Wharton: Summer* (Harmondsworth: Penguin Classics, 1993), xxii–xxv.

59 Godkin, 'The Expenditure of Rich Men', 326.

60 J. A. Hobson, *A Modern Outlook: Studies of English and American Tendencies* (London: Herbert and Daniel, 1910), 179.

61 Ibid., 177.

62 Killoran, *Art and Allusion*, 51 (also *Lee* 431–2). For 'Undine' paintings, see Killoran, *Art and Allusion*, 42–55; and for drowning and mermaids, Maureen Honey, 'Erotic Visual Tropes in the Fiction of Edith Wharton', in Colquitt, Goodman and Waid (eds.), *New Essays*, 82–91.

63 *Lewis* 'Appendix C' 548. Lewis dates the fragment *c.* 1935, but the title features in a notebook (*c.* 1920), with *The Age of Innocence*; discussed in Ammons, *Summer*, xxiv, and *Lee* 581–5.

64 Dale M. Bauer, *Edith Wharton's Brave New Politics* (Madison: University of Wisconsin Press, 1994), 42.

65 Wolff, *A Feast of Words*, 270.

66 Bauer, *Brave New Politics*, 48–50.

67 See Janet Beer, *Kate Chopin, Edith Wharton and Charlotte Perkins Gilman: Studies in Short Fiction* (1997; rev. Basingstoke: Palgrave Macmillan, 2005), 126–30.

68 Ammons, *Summer*, xxiii–xxiv; Bauer, *Brave New Politics*, 28–51.
69 Julie Olin-Ammentorp, *Edith Wharton's Writings from the Great War* (Gainesville: University Press of Florida), 61–5.
70 'Some Eugenic Ideals', in *King Albert's Book: A Tribute to the Belgian King and People from Representative Men and Women throughout the World* (London: Daily Telegraph, *c.* Christmas 1914), 177–8.
71 See *Lee*; Alan Price, *The End of the Age of Innocence: Edith Wharton and the First World War* (London: Robert Hale, 1996); Olin-Ammentorp, *Writings from the Great War*.
72 Sharon Ouditt, *Fighting Forces, Writing Women: Identity and Ideology in the First World War* (London and New York: Routledge, 1994), 34–5.
73 Jay Winter, *Sites of Memory, Sites of Mourning: The Great War in European Cultural History* (Cambridge University Press, 1995), 69.
74 Olin-Ammentorp offers a rich discussion of its diverse elements, *Writings from the Great War*, 115–53.
75 Winter, *Sites of Memory*, 224.
76 Marita Sturken, 'Memorializing Absence', at, 'After September 11', Social Science Research Council www.ssrc.org/sept11/essays/sturken.htm.
77 Loose sheet in 'Subjects and Notes: 1918–1923', Beinecke/22.701. Later in the 1920s, Faulkner would launch his Snopes trilogy (completed 1959), similarly with *Father Abraham* as patriarch.
78 See Richard Godden, *Fictions of Capital: The American Novel from James to Mailer* (Cambridge University Press, 1990), 12–16, which situates Wharton within changing economic narratives of accumulation and consumer affluence.
79 Revd David MacCrae, *The Americans at Home: Pen-and-Ink Sketches of American Men, Manners, and Institutions* (popular edn, rev. Glasgow: John Marr, 1875), 56.
80 See Anne MacMaster, 'Wharton, Race, and *The Age of Innocence*: Three Historical Contexts', in Colquitt, Goodman and Waid (eds.), *New Essays*, 188; also Kassanoff, *Politics of Race*.
81 From 'The Parable of the Old Man and the Young'. See Ben Knights, 'Men from the Boys: Writing on the Male Body', *Literature and History* 13.1 (Spring 2004): 38.
82 Jay Cocks: Ehrhardt (ed.), *Edith Wharton* (video: BBC).
83 See Wolff, *A Feast of Words*, 99–100.
84 Katherine Joslin, *Edith Wharton* (London: Macmillan, 1991), 108–27.
85 12 June 1933: *Yrs Ever Affly: The Correspondence of Edith Wharton and Louis Bromfield*, ed. Daniel Bratton (East Lansing: Michigan State University Press, 2000), 48.

4 Critical reception

1 Percy H. Boynton, *Some Contemporary Americans: The Personal Equation in Literature* (University of Chicago Press, 1924), 103–4.

2 Grant Overton, 'Edith Wharton and the Time-Spirit', in *American Nights Entertainment* (New York: Little and Ives, 1923), 345.

3 Hjalmar Hjorth Boyesen, 'The American Novelist and his Public', in *Literary and Social Silhouettes* (New York: Harper, 1894), 49.

4 Richard Watson Gilder, 'Certain Tendencies in Current Literature', *New Princeton Review* 4 (July 1887): 1–20. Reprinted in Donald Pizer (ed.), *Documents of American Realism and Naturalism* (Carbondale and Edwardsville: Southern Illinois University Press, 1998), 110.

5 Boynton, *Contemporary Americans*, 89.

6 Overton, *American Nights*, 354.

7 See essay by Pamela Knights and Janet Beer on adaptations, and by Knights on spin-offs, in '*The House of Mirth* at the Millennium', in Janet Beer, Pamela Knights and Elizabeth Nolan (eds.), *Edith Wharton's* The House of Mirth (London: Routledge, 2007); and Suzanne Ferriss and Mallory Young (eds.), *Chick Lit: The New Woman's Fiction* (New York and London: Routledge, 2006).

8 Quotations from 'The Vice of Reading' (1903), in *UCW*.

Guide to further reading

There is an immense array of Wharton scholarship. This selection details a few of the critical landmarks mentioned in earlier chapters, and suggests some other starting points. The bibliographical pages of the Edith Wharton Society website; the *Edith Wharton Review;* and the annual survey in *American Literary Scholarship* (Duke University Press) are recommended for keeping track of critical developments; many editions of the major novels (especially by Norton and Broadview) include helpful critical and contextual extracts.

Works

There is no complete standard edition of Wharton's writings. Her major novels are available in many modern editions; and her stories have been extensively anthologised. Useful collections include:

Fiction, autobiography and poetry

The Collected Short Stories of Edith Wharton. Ed. R. W. B. Lewis. 2 volumes. New York: Scribner's, 1968. [Out of print, but in many libraries, it contains eighty-six stories, including Wharton's story-collections, and many uncollected stories.]

The Ghost Stories of Edith Wharton. London: Constable, 1975. [Includes Wharton's preface, an extract from 'Life and I' and eleven stories.]

Edith Wharton: Novels. Ed. R. W. B. Lewis. New York: Library of America, 1985. [*HM, R, CC, AI*: a finely edited collection.]

Edith Wharton: Novellas and Other Writings. Ed. Cynthia Griffin Wolff. New York: Library of America, 1990. [*Madame de Treymes, EF, S, ONY, MR, ABG* and 'Life and I': usefully places *Old New York* alongside autobiographical writings.]

'Fast and Loose' and 'The Buccaneers' by Edith Wharton, ed. Viola Hopkins Winner. Charlottesville and London: University Press of Virginia, 1993. [Wharton's early satirical novella and her last, unfinished, novel.]

Edith Wharton: Collected Stories 1891–1910 and *1911–1937*. Ed. Maureen
        Howard. 2 volumes. New York: Library of America, 2001. [Although
        incomplete, this very useful edition includes novellas *The Touchstone,
        Sanctuary* and *Bunner Sisters*, absent from Lewis's collection.]
Edith Wharton: Selected Poems. Ed. Louis Auchincloss. American Poets Project.
        [USA]: Library of America, 2005. [*Verses, Artemis to Actaeon, Twelve
        Poems*, Uncollected Poems 1879–1938: supplements online sources; a
        timely volume, as critical interest turns to Wharton's poetry.]

Letters, travel and critical writings

The Letters of Edith Wharton. Ed. R. W. B. Lewis and Nancy Lewis. New York:
        Charles Scribner's Sons, 1988. [A selection of about 400 letters, which
        caused some controversy, but which pending a complete edition
        remains indispensable.]
Henry James and Edith Wharton: Letters: 1900–1915. Ed. Lyall H. Powers.
        New York: Scribner's, 1990. [Interesting for evoking the shared
        language of a close friendship.]
Edith Wharton Abroad: Selected Travel Writings, 1888–1920. Ed. Sarah Bird Wright.
        London: Robert Hale, 1995. [An interesting introduction to this field.]
Edith Wharton: The Uncollected Critical Writings. Ed. Frederick Wegener.
        Princeton University Press, 1996. [An invaluable collection of
        Wharton's essays, prefaces and reviews, with illuminating editorial
        commentary.]
The Cruise of the Vanadis. 1992; ed. Claudine Lesage; reprinted, with
        photographs by Jonas Dovydenas: Bloomsbury and Lenox: Edith
        Wharton Restoration/Rizzoli International, 2004. [Makes available
        Wharton's first, unpublished, travelogue.]

Web resources

Websites are subject to change. The following are more established sites,
offering open access to a substantial range of materials:

Cornell University Library: Making of America http://cdl.library.cornell.edu/
        moa/ [Page images of nineteenth-century and early twentieth-century
        magazines and books. Searchable: 'Edith Wharton' leads to first
        printings of early poems, essays and stories, for example, 'Mrs
        Manstey's View', *Scribner's Magazine* 10.1 (July 1891): 699–705.
        Illuminates publishing contexts, literary debates and many writings by
        Wharton's contemporaries mentioned here.]
The Edith Wharton Society www.wsu.edu/~campbelld/wharton/index.html
        [Links to online texts, reviews, bibliographies, news, questions.]

'Edith Wharton's World: Portraits of People and Places' www.npg.si.edu/exh/
   wharton/index.htm
'The Gilded Age: Treasures from the Smithsonian American Art Museum' http://
   americanart.si.edu/collections/exhibits/t2go/1ga
Internet Archive www.archive.org/details/texts [First editions of out-of-
   copyright writings by Wharton and her contemporaries, including
   novels, travel-writings and story collections. Download or use online in
   virtual 'real book' format; searchable.]
Yale University Beinecke Rare Book and Manuscript Library http://beinecke.
   library.yale.edu/dl_crosscollex/SearchExecXC.asp [Images include
   manuscripts of *The Age of Innocence* and *The House of Mirth*, many
   photographs and biographical documents.]

Modern biographies

(ordered chronologically)

Lewis, R. W. B. *Edith Wharton: A Biography.* London: Constable, 1975. [The
   founding modern life.]
Wolff, Cynthia Griffin. *A Feast of Words: The Triumph of Edith Wharton.* 1977;
   rev. edn. Reading, Mass.: Addison-Wesley, 1995. [Approaches the
   writings through Wharton's emotional and psychological
   development.]
Benstock, Shari. *No Gifts from Chance: A Biography of Edith Wharton.* London:
   Hamish Hamilton, 1994. [Updated Lewis; strong on Wharton's
   friendships; draws richly on the letters.]
Dwight, Eleanor. *Edith Wharton: An Extraordinary Life.* New York: Abrams,
   1994. [Particularly wide range of photographs and illustrations.]
   The Gilded Age: Edith Wharton and Her Contemporaries. New York:
   Universe, 1996. [Short introduction to Wharton's social milieu,
   through paintings from the period.]
Price, Alan. *The End of the Age of Innocence: Edith Wharton and the First World
   War.* London: Robert Hale, 1996. [Insights into Wharton's war-work
   and activities.]
Lee, Hermione. *Edith Wharton.* London: Chatto and Windus, 2007. [A
   monumental work, emphasising Wharton's life as a European; pays
   close attention to the poetry; the new authoritative biography.]

Criticism

(ordered alphabetically)

Ammons, Elizabeth. *Edith Wharton's Argument with America.* Athens: University
   of Georgia Press, 1980. [A pioneering exploration in terms of
   women's culture.]

Bauer, Dale M. *Edith Wharton's Brave New Politics*. Madison: University of Wisconsin Press, 1994. [Opens up Wharton's later works within wider cultural and political debates.]

Beer, Janet. *Edith Wharton*. Tavistock: Northcote House, 2002. [A stimulating short introduction, thematically arranged.]

  Kate Chopin, Edith Wharton and Charlotte Perkins Gilman: Studies in Short Fiction, 1997; rev. Basingstoke: Palgrave Macmillan, 2005. [Draws together genre and turn-of-the-century women's culture, in illuminating readings.]

Beer, Janet, Pamela Knights and Elizabeth Nolan, eds. *Edith Wharton's* The House of Mirth. London: Routledge, 2007. [Covers text, contexts, critical history and adaptations; and includes new essays by Joslin (on sexuality), Fedorko (the Gothic), Thornton (illustrations), Beer and Nolan (genre), Knights (literary reworkings).]

Beer Goodwyn, Janet. *Edith Wharton: Traveller in the Land of Letters*. Basingstoke: Macmillan, 1990. [Explores Wharton's imaginative use of place, travel and topography.]

Bell, Millicent, ed. *The Cambridge Companion to Edith Wharton*. Cambridge University Press, 1995. [An influential collection of essays.]

Bendixen, Alfred and Annette Zilversmit, eds. *Edith Wharton: New Critical Essays*. New York: Garland, 1992. [An interesting collection, pioneering many areas later developed in longer studies.]

Bentley, Nancy. *The Ethnography of Manners: Hawthorne, James, Wharton*. Cambridge University Press, 1995. [A landmark examination of Wharton's anthropological approach to her culture.]

Bloom, Harold, ed. *Edith Wharton*. New York and Philadelphia: Chelsea House, 1986. [A snapshot of Wharton criticism in the 1980s.]

  ed. *Edith Wharton's* The Age of Innocence. Philadelphia: Chelsea House, 2005. [A wide-ranging collection of key studies.]

Colquitt, Clare, Susan Goodman and Candace Waid, eds. *A Forward Glance: 'New Essays' on Edith Wharton*. Newark and London: University of Delaware Press, 1999. [Topics range from garden-plans to war; engages with issues of gender, race, genre and politics: an excellent collection of essays.]

Dyman, Jenni. *Lurking Feminism: The Ghost Stories of Edith Wharton*. New York: Peter Lang, 1996. [A specialist study, with interest beyond the ghost stories.]

Ehrhardt, Julia, ed. *Edith Wharton and Her Novels*, London: BBC Educational Developments, 1995 [video-resource] [Extracts from screen adaptations of *AI, EF* and *The Buccaneers*, intercutting directors' and screen-writers' comments with analysis by academic Wharton critics.]

Fedorko, Kathy. *Gender and the Gothic in the Fiction of Edith Wharton*. Tuscaloosa: University of Alabama Press, 1995. [A turning-point in Wharton criticism, fully engaging with the non-realist dimensions of the texts.]

Fryer, Judith. *Felicitous Space: The Imaginative Structures of Edith Wharton and Willa Cather.* Chapel Hill: University of North Carolina Press, 1986. [Illuminating and ahead of its time on domestic and imaginative interiors.]

Joslin, Katherine. *Edith Wharton.* London: Macmillan, 1991. [A lively and persuasive introduction, underpinned by feminist theory.]

Joslin, Katherine and Alan Price, eds. *Wretched Exotic: Essays on Edith Wharton in Europe.* New York: Peter Lang, 1996. [An excellent range of essays, particularly on Wharton as a traveller.]

Kassanoff, Jennie A. *Edith Wharton and the Politics of Race,* Cambridge University Press, 2004. [An extended political argument about Wharton as a conservative within a changing democratic, multicultural nation.]

Killoran, Helen. *The Critical Reception of Edith Wharton.* Rochester, NY: Camden, 2001. [A helpful survey of a century of criticism; overviews of major texts.]

Edith Wharton: Art and Allusion. Tuscaloosa and London: University of Alabama Press, 1996. [Teases out many of Wharton's literary references, and discusses relevant artworks.]

Olin-Ammentorp, Julie. *Edith Wharton's Writings from the Great War.* Gainesville: University Press of Florida, 2004. [Reframes many of the writings in the light of World War II.]

Singley, Carol J. *Edith Wharton: Matters of Mind and Spirit.* Cambridge University Press, 1995. [A view of Wharton as moralist, within a religious and philosophical tradition.]

ed. *Edith Wharton's* The House of Mirth: *A Casebook.* Oxford University Press, 2003. [Valuable collection of key criticism, including Wolff, Kaplan, Showalter and Dimock; reprints Wharton's 1936 introduction.]

ed. *A Historical Guide to Edith Wharton.* Oxford University Press, 2003. [Significant new essays on women, Darwinian elements, addiction, travel and modernity, art and film adaptation. Helpful biographical and bibliographical essays.]

Smith, Christopher, ed. *Readings on Ethan Frome.* San Diego, Calif.: Greenhaven, 2000. [Thematised extracts from a range of studies.]

Vita-Finzi, Penelope. *Edith Wharton and the Art of Fiction.* London: Pinter, 1990. [On Wharton's craft; reproduces interesting selection of drafts of the unpublished novel 'Literature'.]

Waid, Candace. *Edith Wharton's Letters from the Underworld: Fictions of Women and Writing.* Chapel Hill: University of North Carolina Press, 1991. [Readings through myth.]

White, Barbara. *Edith Wharton: A Study of the Short Fiction.* New York: Twayne, 1991. [Interesting specialist study of Wharton's stories.]

Wright, Sarah Bird. *Edith Wharton A to Z.* New York: Checkmark Books, 1998. [A wonderful reference book for all aspects of Wharton's life, work and influences, from 'Académie française' to 'Zola'.]

Index

Cambridge Introductions to Literature

AUTHORS

Jane Austen Janet Todd

Samuel Beckett Ronan McDonald

Walter Benjamin David Ferris

J. M. Coetzee Dominic Head

Joseph Conrad John Peters

Jacques Derrida Leslie Hill

Emily Dickinson Wendy Martin

George Eliot Nancy Henry

T. S. Eliot John Xiros Cooper

William Faulkner Theresa M. Towner

F. Scott Fitzgerald Kirk Curnutt

Michel Foucault Lisa Downing

Robert Frost Robert Faggen

Nathaniel Hawthorne Leland S. Person

Zora Neale Hurston Lovalerie King

James Joyce Eric Bulson

Herman Melville Kevin J. Hayes

Sylvia Plath Jo Gill

Edgar Allan Poe Benjamin F. Fisher

Ezra Pound Ira Nadel

Jean Rhys Elaine Savory

Shakespeare Emma Smith

Harriet Beecher Stowe Sarah Robbins

Mark Twain Peter Messent

Edith Wharton Pamela Knights

Walt Whitman M. Jimmie Killingsworth

Virginia Woolf Jane Goldman

W. B. Yeats David Holdeman

TOPICS

The American Short Story Martin Scofield

Creative Writing David Morley

Early English Theatre Janette Dillon

English Theatre, 1660–1900 Peter Thomson

Francophone Literature Patrick Corcoran

Modern Irish Poetry Justin Quinn

Modernism Pericles Lewis

Narrative (second edition) H. Porter Abbott

The Nineteenth-Century American Novel Gregg Crane

Postcolonial Literatures C. L. Innes

Russian Literature Caryl Emerson

Shakespeare's Comedies Penny Gay

Shakespeare's History Plays Warren Chernaik

Shakespeare's Tragedies Janette Dillon

The Short Story in English Adrian Hunter

Theatre Historiography Thomas Postlewait

Theatre Studies Christopher Balme

Tragedy Jennifer Wallace